Translation and Translating

APPLIED LINGUISTICS AND LANGUAGE STUDY

General Editor
Professor Christopher N. Candlin, Macquarie University

Error Analysis
*Perspectives on second
language acquisition*
JACK C. RICHARDS (ED.)

Stylistics and the Teaching of
Literature
HENRY WIDDOWSON

Language Tests at School
A pragmatic approach
JOHN W. OLLER JNR

Contrastive Analysis
CARL JAMES

Language and Communication
JACK C. RICHARDS AND
RICHARD W. SCHMIDT (EDS)

Learning to Write: First Language/
Second Language
AVIVA FREDMAN, IAN PRINGLE
AND JANIC YALDEN (EDS)

Strategies in Interlanguage
Communication
CLAUS FAERCH AND
GABRIELE KASPER (EDS)

Reading in Foreign Language
J. CHARLES ALDERSON AND
A. H. URQUHART (EDS)

An Introduction to Discourse
Analysis
New Edition
MALCOLM COULTHARD

Computers in English Language
Teaching and Research
GEOFFREY LEECH AND
CHRISTOPHER N. CANDLIN (EDS)

Bilingualism in Education
*Aspects of theory, research and
practice*
JIM CUMMINS AND
MERRILL SWAIN

Rediscovering Interlanguage
LARRY SELINKER

Second Language Grammar:
Learning and Teaching
WILLIAM RUTHERFORD

The Classroom and the
Language Learner
*Ethnography and second-language
classroom research*
LEO VAN LIER

Vocabulary and Language Teaching
RONALD CARTER AND MICHAEL
McCARTHY (EDS)

Observation in the Language
Classroom
DICK ALLWRIGHT

Listening to Spoken English
Second Edition
GILLIAN BROWN

Listening in Language Learning
MICHAEL ROST

An Introduction to Second Language
Acquisition Research
DIANE LARSEN-FREEMAN AND
MICHAEL H. LONG

Language and Discrimination
*A study of communication in
multi-ethnic workplaces*
CELIA ROBERTS, TOM JUPP AND
EVELYN DAVIES

Translation and Translating:
Theory and Practice
ROGER T. BELL

Language Awareness
in the Classroom
CARL JAMES AND
PETER GARRET (EDS)

Rediscovering Interlanguage
LARRY SELINKER

Process and Experience in the
Language Classroom
MICHAEL LEGUTKE AND
HOWARD THOMAS

Translation and Translating: Theory and Practice

ROGER T. BELL

LONGMAN
LONDON AND NEW YORK

Longman Group UK Limited,
Longman House, Burnt Mill, Harlow,
Essex CM20 2JE, England
and Associated Companies throughout the world.

Published in the United States of America by Longman Inc., New York

First published 1991
Third impression 1994

British Library Cataloguing in Publication Data
Bell, Roger T. (Roger Thomas) *1938-*
   Translation and translating: theory and practice. -
  (Applied linguistics and language study).
  1. Languages. Translation
  I. Title II. Series
  418.02

  ISBN 0-582-01648-7

Library of Congress Cataloging-in-Publication Data
Bell, Roger T.
   Translation and translating: theory and practice/Roger T. Bell.
    p. cm. — (Applied linguistics and language study)
   Includes bibliographical referneces and index.
   ISBN 0-582-01648-7 (pbk.)
   1. Translating and interpreting. I. Title. II. Series.
  P306.B39 1991
  418'.02—dc20
                                             90-20545
                                                 CIP

Typeset by Opus Design Company, Oxford in 10 on 12 pt Ehrhardt.
Produced by Longman Singapore Publishers (Pte) Ltd
Printed in Singapore

Contents

Acknowledgements

This book has been growing steadily with pilot versions of parts of it emerging over the period 1984–90 as teaching materials and papers, but the whole was only brought together as a complete first draft by dint of five weeks' steady word-processing in Lancaster during August and early September 1988. The time and place were significant. Lancaster was, in many ways, an ideal place to write; quiet and, in the 'summer' of 1988, wet and cold. It was, as the proverb might have said, an ill blow that winds nobody good; the holiday trade's loss was my gain, since the temptation to go out was not there to be resisted.

I was very conscious of technological support as I wrote. The text was word-processed, the London Weather Centre gave me, via the radio and television, the daily forecasts I wanted to hear – showers and bright intervals, probably with the bright intervals omitted – and Radio Three, as always, provided wonderful 'music while you work'.

I am grateful to several organizations for help during the creation of this book. My particular thanks go to the British Council for providing support which allowed me to try out some of the ideas in this book in Brazil, Greece, Hong Kong and Pakistan during the past six years.

Equally, in the creation of any book, librarians have always played a quiet but crucial role. I would single out for particular thanks the ever-helpful and professional staffs of the library in the School of Languages in the Polytechnic of Central London and of the Senate House Library of the University of London.

I owe a particular debt of gratitude to my colleagues in the School of Languages at the Polytechnic of Central London and to Alan Collins of the Department of Psychology at the University of Lancaster and to the several individuals who were generous enough to comment in detail on early versions of the manuscript; Vera Adamson, Chris Candlin, Mark Hilton, Carl James, Riccardo Steiner. I am particularly grateful to Duncan Bell, Judy Bowles and Susan Grant who also carried out a meticulous proofreading of the text.

Finally, I need to thank Alida Baxter, Stella Bortoni, John and Ann Corsellis, Iain and Jan Rankin, Russ and Jill Russell, Eric Hutchison, Caroline Large and Joel Ryce-Menuhin who, in their own very different ways, made this book possible.

There are many more without whose support this book would not have been written – in particular, my long-suffering students. To all of them, named or not, I offer my thanks, acknowledge their good ideas and exonerate them from the bad parts of this book; those are, of course, down to me alone.

Roger T. Bell
Lancaster and London
1989

The Publishers are grateful to Editions Gallimard for permission to reproduce the poem 'Poésie' by Paul Valery from *Autres Rhumbs* issue of *Tel quel* © Editions Gallimard, and to Cambridge University Press and the author for a figure from Gregory, M. (1967) 'Aspects of Varieties Differentiation' in *Journal of Linguistics* 3.

General Editor's Preface

For someone who is professionally engaged in conceptualising and organising postexperience programmes in Applied Linguistics (and I don't mean by that just language teaching) the discipline of Translating has always posed problems. Very largely, I suspect, because it has presented the twin (and both equally inaccessible to the outsider) qualities of the guild and the mystery. Guilds imply masters of their craft and apprentices in training, learning the ways, moving up the accreditation ladder, in turn becoming *meister*, measured by the excellence of their practice, evaluated by their products. In a way, a commitment to secrecy, exclusivity and to the preservation of hard-won rights. Mystery, because the processes did remain a secret, a property of the guild, where (if this isn't too farfetched in an utilitarian world), at least for some branches of the discipline, words were transmuted into gold by a process of lexical alchemy.

The problems posed were partly of professional access, since although we are all involved in translating all the time, if not between languages, then between dialects, registers and styles, nonetheless Translating was and is a profession, with its own codes of conduct and criteria of performance, not accessible to all. As a linguist, however, there were other difficulties, only partly alleviated by the rather few notable landmarks in the Translating literature devoted to these topics, namely, the lack, apparently, of much concern with theory and, more especially, with the need for a principled connection to be made between the process and product of translating and the intellectual traditions which might be expected to underpin its work, in particular those of linguistics and psychology. Among applied linguistic disciplines, Translation stands in sharp contrast here to language teaching, for example, or, in particular, to speech pathology.

In short, there was much said and written about Translation as a craft to be emulated, much less about Translation as an intellectual enquiry to be researched and explored (though, again, there are honourable exceptions well documented in this book). We should, however, be both careful and realistic. Translation is characteristically purposeful as a profession, it has targets and goals. It is done on behalf of sponsors. It lacks (except in rare cases) the leisure of reflective consideration about the researchable questions of why like this, why here. Nonetheless, Translators as applied linguists do have certain obligations to the furthering of our understanding of language and of our ability to explain the acts of communicating in which we are continually engaged, and that is a primary motivation for this new book in the **Applied Linguistics and Language Study Series**.

Roger Bell addresses these questions in a systematic way, beginning in much the same way as I, though from the perspective of one professionally concerned with Translation. The book has a three part structure, a focus on *model*, a focus on *meaning* and a focus on *memory*, each of which terms is itself, like much Translating, an exercise in the unpacking of metaphors. *Model*, for example, is not simply a theoretical construct, a set of principles for the understanding of natural phenomena, a representation implying an explanation, it is also a model in the sense of an objective, a yardstick against which translators and their translations can be evaluated and assessed. If you like, it is both a model for the process and a model for the competence. Similarly, *meaning* is not a matter of denotation only, of sense, but a much wider concept more in tune with *understanding*, incorporating the interpersonal and the pragmatic into the ideational and the textual. This extension is, of course, vital since only those whose view of translation has been ineluctably reduced to the present capacities of the machine will see meaning in translation as being 'only a matter of reproducing the ideas and the facts' as one recent commentator on Translating described his objectives. *Memory* remains the ultimate test of metaphorical interpretation, even in these days of sophisticated experimentation in psychology and neurobiology. It is as well to recall here Rose's comment that '*studying the biochemistry and anatomy of memory is like studying the chemistry and design of the recording head of a tape recorder and a cassette of magnetic tape. To know how the tape recorder works the thing must be studied. But no amount of information revealed by such a study will enable one to predict the message on the tape. For that, one has to play the machine*'. Memory is not just neural it is also context dependent. Much recall remains to be inferred from action and needs to be linked to task.

In its attempt to characterise the process of translating, Roger Bell's book is very much concerned with seeking to understand this '*playing of the machine.*' To do so, he argues, requires a double awareness, that of linguistic texture in terms of structure and of discourse, and of text processing in terms of construction and interpretation, linking linguistics with psychology in an attempt to understand what it is that translators do when they translate. Such an approach, of course, makes my problem at the outset of this Preface much more tractable. It provides a warrant for translators to engage in the analysis of the texts that they have to translate and the texts they themselves create. That they do, in the context of their professional work, is undeniable, what is significant is the need to have a model in terms of which to describe, justify and explain to others what they have done. Professor Bell's approach offers the techniques of linguistics to translators in an essentially contrastive and comparative endeavour. It becomes easy to motivate its inclusion. There remain questions, naturally enough, about the choice of linguistic model and selection of the unit of analysis upon which such explanatory translation would focus. Like the author, I am of the opinion that systemic linguistics offers such a convenient tool, not only in its focus on the clause but also because of the importance it accords to the social and the psychological. Chapter Four, in particular, sets out in summary the descriptive apparatus of such a model and links it to the preceding Chapter Three with its focus on meaning as sense and Chapter Five with its focus on meaning as use.

However, this is all seen from the perspective of the linguist, and to his or her benefit, not necessarily from that of the translator. What is it that translation can characteristically bring to the linguist's work which should not continue to be ignored? On the one hand, we may argue as linguists, an opportunity of seeking the universal through the particularity of languages, drawing on the comparisons and equivalences sought by the translator in professional work. An opportunity of searching for an elusive *tertium comparationis* against which to negotiate the original and the translated text. Much more than this, however, if only translation research would focus more on it, is the opportunity translation (or more exactly, translating) gives to the linguist in understanding how it is that we do construct texts and how we do go about making meanings. In short, it concentrates our attention on the process in a very tangible and goal-directed way. Not that this lack of research activity is especially or uniquely the responsibility of translators. It is equally significant when one examines the annals of research into applied psychology how little that has directed its attention to translation. Writing from Sydney, it all seems a little familiar – *terra australis incognita* – one might say. It is this lack of much attempt to explore the psycholinguistic which Roger Bell's book begins to repair. Negotiating the meaning of texts is not just a sociolinguistic matter, it is a psycholinguistic one as well, and this is the focus of the third Section of this book. It reminds linguists of the need to take a language processing perspective on their analyses. Fortunately, with current work in artificial intelligence and the use of computers for automatic parsing and analysis such a dimension is of keen interest. There is much room, nonetheless, for the smaller scale experimentation on the factors affecting the text conversion and creation process which is translation. **Translation and Translating** provides just such an emphasis.

Professor Christopher N Candlin
General Editor

Introduction

This book derives from a feeling of considerable unease and puzzlement about the way translation has been treated, over a substantial period, by translation theorists on the one hand and linguists on the other.

The translation theorists, almost without exception,[1] have made little systematic use of the techniques and insights of contemporary linguistics (the linguistics of the last twenty years or so) and the linguists, for their part, have been at best neutral and at worst actually hostile to the notion of a theory of translation.

This state of affairs seems particularly paradoxical when one recognizes the stated goal of translation: the transformation of a text originally in one language into an equivalent text in a different language retaining, as far as is possible, the content of the message and the formal features and functional roles of the original text (an informal definition which will be much modified as we go along). It does seem strange that such a process should, apparently, be of no interest to linguistics, since the explanation of the phenomenon would present an enormous challenge to linguistic theories and provide an ideal testing ground for them.

Equally, it is difficult to see how translation theorists can move beyond the subjective and normative evaluation of texts without drawing heavily on linguistics. The need for access to and familiarity with the accumulated knowledge about the nature and function of language and the methodology of linguistic enquiry must become more and more pressing and less and less deniable if translation theory is to shake off individualist anecdotalism and the tendency to issue arbitrary lists of 'rules' for the creation of 'correct' translations and set about providing systematic and objective descriptions of the process of translation.

The essential argument of this book rests on the following assumptions:

(a) that the paradox we have been describing has arisen as a result of a fundamental misunderstanding, by both translation theorists and linguists, of what is involved in translation;

(b) that this misunderstanding has led, inevitably, to the failure to build a theory of translation which is at all satisfactory in a theoretical or an applied sense;

(c) that the co-occurrence of exciting advances in cognitive science, artificial intelligence and text-linguistics with the emergence of a genuinely socially and semantically based functional theory of linguistics – Systemic linguistics – makes this an ideal moment to attempt to resolve the paradox and develop an adequate theory of translation.

In 1961 Halliday wrote a paper on linguistics and machine translation[2] in which he made the remark:

> It might be of interest to set up a linguistic model of the translation process, starting not from any preconceived notions from outside the field of language study, but on the basis of linguistic concepts such as are relevant to the description of languages as modes of activity in their own right.

It is precisely this task which we have set ourselves; to model the process of translating, setting it particularly within a Systemic model of language.

We have two motivations for wishing to do this; one intrinsic and the other utilitarian. From the point of view of linguistics, we believe the attempt to create such a model to be inherently interesting and valuable as a vehicle for testing theory and for investigating language use. From a practical point of view, we recognize that in a rapidly changing world in which knowledge is expanding at an unprecedented rate, information transfer is coming to depend more and more on efficient and effective translation.

The goal of this book is, then, (1) to outline the kinds of knowledge and skill which we believe must underlie the practical abilities of the translator and (2) to build this outline into a model of the translation process. In the longer term, we intend that this model will make its own contribution to the creation of an intellectually satisfying and practically applicable theory of translation within a broadly defined applied linguistics.

The organization of the book reflects an underlying belief; that the major need – from both the theoretical and the practical points of view – is for descriptions and explanations of the process of translating.

Such a model will be located within the more general domain of human communication and will, necessarily, draw heavily on both psychology and linguistics.

This will entail developing familiarity with and competence in the use of psychological and psycholinguistic models of memory and information processing on the one hand and linguistic models of meaning (in the broadest sense), including meaning 'beyond the sentence' on the other.

It is for this reason that the book is divided into three unequal parts: *model*, *meaning* and *memory* (the terms are inspired by Stevick's influential book on language learning[3]). The dominance of Part 2 (meaning) is intended to emphasize the centrality of meaning in translation, whether approached from a theoretical position or with practical applications in mind.

There is, however, a structural problem which faces the writer. The centrality of 'meaning' is not in doubt nor is the need to present a model of the process and to justify that model by providing insights from linguistics and psychology which underpin it. The problem is simply stated; which should come first, the presentation or the justification?

There are two obvious solutions, if we accept that the model and the justification must come either side of 'meaning': (a) model + justification or (b) justification + model.

We have adopted the first approach; to present the model of the process early on, even though the underpinning from linguistics and psychology on which it depends has yet to be provided. This is, of course, less satisfactory in one sense but it does have the advantage of trying the patience of the reader less than the second does. The reader is still, however, faced by the difficulty of needing to move back and forth between the model and the justification but, given the linear nature of books and of the physical aspects of the process of reading, this seems inevitable and, in any case, this is a book about translation theory not a 'who-done-it'!

It may be helpful, at this point, to list the major concerns of each chapter, recognizing as we do that many issues tend to recur and to cross chapter boundaries.

Part 1 contains two chapters which focus on two rather different issues: (i) a general introductory discussion of the nature of translation and (ii) the presentation of an outline model of translating.

Chapter 1 asks the question: 'What is translation and how may we best describe and explain it?' In answer, we distinguish translation as process from translation as product and propose the building of a model of the process of translating, as a first step towards a multidisciplinary general theory of translation.

Chapter 2 asks the question: 'What would a model of translating look like?' and, before providing a model, raises the related question; 'What knowledge and skills must the translator possess in order to be able to translate?', i.e. how can we specify translator competence?

Specifying translator competence requires that we consider both abstract knowledge systems (linguistic and real world knowledge) and the crucial practical skills of reading and writing. Once the ground has been cleared in this way, we are able to move on to ask the question which underlies the whole of the book: 'What do translators do when they translate?' To answer this, we present an initial and integrated model of the process of translating which raises the key issues which occupy our attention for the remainder of the book; the nature of 'meaning' and the storage and processing of information in memory.

The chapter is brought to a close with a section in which the model is used to show how a short translation (a French poem) might be tackled.

Part 2 focuses on meaning: traditional word- and sentence-meaning, semantic sense (logic and grammar) and communicative value (rhetoric) and sets each of these within a Functional (Systemic) model of language and links them with text and discourse.

Chapter 3 introduces the problem of 'meaning' (limited, at this point, to a rather conservative view of 'semantic sense') by asking 'What does this word/sentence mean?' and provides a response which brings in concepts from traditional semantics. A number of crucial conceptual distinctions are introduced and discussed and some techniques proposed for the study of various aspects of meaning.

The distinctions include, (i) sense and reference, (ii) denotation and connotation, (iii) hyponomy, synonymy and antonymy, (iv) entailment, implicature and presupposition and (v) proposition, sentence and utterance. Among the techniques we discuss are, (i) the use of componential analysis for the specification of word-meaning, (ii) the creation of semantic and lexical fields, and (iii) the measurement of connotative meaning using the technique of the semantic differential.

Chapter 4 takes the notion of 'semantic sense' further by asking 'how are logical relationships organized and mapped onto the syntactic systems of a language and realized as text?'. Specifically, in this chapter, we investigate the nature of (i) cognitive meaning and its expression through the systems of TRANSITIVITY, (ii) interactional meaning and its expression through the MOOD systems and (iii) discoursal meaning and its expression through the THEME systems.

In other words, 'semantic sense' is extended to include the ideational, interpersonal and textual macrofunctions of language and the logical, grammatical and rhetorical systems which realize them.

Chapter 5 rounds off the investigation of 'meaning' by shifting the focus away from the semantic sense of the clause and onto the communicative value of the utterance (or text) asking: (1) 'How can text be distinguished from non-text?'; (2) 'How are sentences given a particular communicative value?' or 'How is it that a particular syntactic structure comes to count as a speech act of a certain kind?'; and (3) 'What relationship between the addresser (the speaker/writer) and the addressee (the hearer/reader) is signalled by the structure of this text?; what medium is used to realize it?; what function does it have?'

This leads first to an expansion of the outline model of discourse variation (introduced first in Chapter 1, Section 1.1) which involves indicators of dialect and markers of style (tenor, mode and domain) and, in the next chapter, to a discussion of text-types.

Part 3 has 'memory' as its general topic and focuses on two fundamental aspects of information, memory and knowledge which are crucial to any understanding of the translating process: (1) the specific issue of text-processing and (2) the more general but related issue of the storage and retrieval of information.

Chapter 6 asks a number of questions which centre on the topic of text-processing: (1) 'How are text-types recognized?' this leads to the presentation of a three-level text-typology; (2) 'What knowledge and skills do text-processors possess which allow them to negotiate meaning through texts?'; and (3) 'How do communicators activate the knowledge and skills they have to synthesize (write) and analyse (read) texts?'

Chapter 7 is concerned with the psycholinguistic processes involved in memory and in information processing within the context of human communication asking the question: 'How is information received and how is it organized and stored in memory?' This involves us in a discussion of the relationship between sensation and perception, the processes of encoding and decoding, the nature of the memory systems and of the types of entry stored there.

The model which is proposed for these processes is of particular importance for our own goal; the building of a model of the process of translating. Gaining new information, integrating it into long-term memory and recalling it when required are all essential parts of the translator's knowledge and skills and, therefore, elements in the model being developed in this book (and, indeed, in any model of the process).

We are convinced that it is now a matter of extreme urgency for the attempt to be made to understand what translation is and how it happens, i.e. for work to be pressed ahead on the building of an intellectually and practically satisfying theory. We further believe that there are good reasons (both practical and theoretical) for undertaking the task we have set ourselves. We can only hope that this book will make a small contribution to that understanding.

1. Nida 1964, 1966, 1974; Catford 1965; and a number of Continental and Canadian scholars such as Wilss 1980, 1982, 1983; Lefevre 1975 stand out in contrast.
2. Halliday and McIntosh 1961. 137.
3. Stevick 1976. The full title is *Memory, meaning and method*.

This book
is dedicated with gratitude to
the memory of
Vera Adamson
who taught me how to do
research in Linguistics

Part 1: MODEL

This book is, as we pointed out in the introduction, divided into three almost equal parts; model, meaning and memory. The first sets translation in the context of applied linguistics – arguing that the study of translation is best served by the construction of models of the process of translating – and provides an outline model of that process.

In Chapter 1, we investigate the nature of translation and the characteristics of the translator, suggest some approaches to the description and explanation of translation as both process and product and make some general comments on scientific method and the use of models and analogies as heuristic devices in the evolution of a theory. Finally, in the first chapter, we present a number of criteria for an adequate theory of translation; requirements which the rest of the book will be involved in explicating and testing.

Chapter 2 represents an initial attempt at building a simple model of the translating process. We approach this task by providing a model which draws on insights which will be presented in a more substantial manner in the chapters which follow; meaning, language as a system of options for the expression of meaning, textuality and discourse, speech acts, parameters of stylistic variation in discourse, text-processing and human information processing.

The integrated model we present combines the knowledge and skills of the translator – the specification of these forming an introduction to the process – in a multi-stage, multi-directional system which is explained and, finally, shown in operation carrying out a short translation from French to English.

As a whole, Part 1 can be seen as addressing two sets of issues both of which set the scene for what is to follow in Part 2 and Part 3: the placing of 'translation theory' within a broadly defined applied linguistics and the modelling of the process which, we argue, must form the basis of an applied linguistic theory of translation.

1 Perspectives on translation

This book is concerned with translation and, in particular, with proposing a new orientation to the study of translation. In this first chapter, we intend to set the scene for what is to follow by asking three questions which, we believe, lie at the root of any attempt to understand the phenomenon of translation and, if such is our goal, improve our own work as translators or as trainers of others in the task.

The three questions, which constitute the three sections of this chapter and recur in different guises throughout the book, are:

(1) What is translation?
(2) What is a translator?
(3) What is translation theory?

We shall soon discover that these questions are fraught with ambiguity and the answers to them, not surprisingly, are far from satisfactory.

Since documentary evidence of translation can be traced back for at least two millennia and present-day international communication depends heavily on it, it is surely paradoxical that a phenomenon as widespread in time and in space as translation is should be so ill-understood. Attempts at explaining it appear stuck at the pre-scientific stage of anecdote that the life sciences had reached in the late eighteenth century; the study of 'natural history'.[1]

The development of the study of translation, from that point, stands in the strongest contrast with that of the life sciences. In their case, careful – not to say, meticulous – description of what was observed led rapidly to the development of botany, biology, zoology; sciences dedicated to the creation (or discovery) of theories which made sense of the flora and fauna. The theory of evolution is, of course, the classic nineteenth-century example.

Translation theory, on the other hand, appears still not to have taken this second step and remains, as it were, in the hands of the 'naturalists'. We therefore wish now (a) to assert that we believe that the time is ripe (perhaps overripe) for a theory of translation to emerge – a theory of translation which would explain what translation is, how it works and how it fits into human communication and human society – and (b) to make clear our desire to contribute to the development of such a theory.

Why is it that, in spite of having been a hotly debated topic over such a long period of time,[2] translation still seems to be a mysterious phenomenon which defies understanding and still lacks a comprehensive theory which can explain what it is and how it happens?

There are a good number of reasons for this but chief among them, we would suggest, is the fact that the word 'translation' is itself ambiguous and this, when linked with an emphasis on only one of the possible meanings of the term, can be seen as the major cause of the stagnation in which the study of translation has found itself for such a long period.

We shall argue, in this book, that the answers which have been suggested are so unsatisfactory essentially because they are answers to the wrong questions. We further argue that an adequate description and explanation of the phenomenon of translation requires us to address a quite different set of problems and ask quite different questions.

This chapter marks the beginnings of our attempt to address these problems and to start to 'make sense' of translation; to begin, that is, the creation (or discovery; it depends on your attitude to theory which you say; see Section 1.3.3) of a theory of translation.

1.1 What is translation?

The study of translation has been dominated, and to a degree still is, by the debate about its status as an **art** or a **science**, so we shall begin with this issue.

The linguist inevitably approaches translation from a 'scientific' point of view, seeking to create some kind of 'objective' description of the phenomenon and this will be the fundamental orientation of this book. It could, however, be argued that translation is an 'art' or a 'craft' and therefore not amenable to objective, 'scientific' description and explanation and so, *a fortiori*, the search for a theory of translation is doomed from the start.

It is easy to see how such a view could have held sway in the last century, when scholars – for the most part, dilettante translators engaging in translation as a pastime – were preoccupied with the translation of literary texts and, in particular, Classical authors; Latin and Greek. Not untypical is the description, by a contemporary, of the Scottish peer, Lord Woodhouselee (1747–1814) as:

> a delightful host, with whom it was a memorable experience to spend an evening discussing the Don Quixote of Motteux and of Smollett, or how to capture the aroma of Virgil in an English medium, in the era before the Scottish prose Homer had changed the literary perspective north of the Tweed.[3]

It is also understandable that the attitude should have continued into the present century, during which both translation and translation theory have been dominated, at least until very recently, by Bible translators (especially Nida[4]).

What is less comprehensible is that the view should still persist in the closing decade of the twentieth century, when the vast proportion of translations are not literary texts but technical, medical, legal, administrative (the issue of text-types is taken up in Chapter 6, Section 6.1) and the vast majority of translators are professionals engaged in making a living rather than whiling away the time in an agreeable manner by translating the odd ode or two on winter evenings.

Nevertheless, the supposed dichotomy between 'art' and 'science' is still current enough to form the title of a book on translation theory published in 1988: *The science of linguistics in the art of translation*,[5] where (even though care is taken to distinguish 'pure' linguistics from applied linguistics) the main emphasis is still on literary translation since, we are told: 'The quintessence of translation as art is, if anything, even more patent in literary texts.'[6]

'Translation' has been variously defined and, not infrequently, in dictionaries of linguistics, omitted entirely[7] and the following definitions have been selected (and edited) partly because they are, in some sense, typical and partly because they raise issues which we will be pursuing in detail later.

> Traduire c'est énoncer dans une autre langage (ou langue cible) ce qui a été énoncé dans une autre langue source, en conservant les équivalences sémantiques et stylistiques.[8]

> Translation is the expression in another language (or target language) of what has been expressed in another, source language, preserving semantic and stylistic equivalences. [my translation]

There are, in spite of the differences, common features shared by the two definitions we have given so far; the notion of movement of some sort between languages, content of some kind and the obligation to find 'equivalents' which 'preserve' features of the original. It is this notion of 'equivalence' which we are about to take up.

1.1.1 Equivalence: semantic and stylistic

Let us add to the definitions we have given so far a third which, in its extended form, takes us directly into the problem we must address; the nature of equivalence.

> Translation is the replacement of a representation of a text in one language by a representation of an equivalent text in a second language.[9]

The authors continue and make the problem of *equivalence* very plain:

> Texts in different languages can be equivalent in different degrees (fully or partially equivalent), in respect of different levels of presentation (equivalent in respect of context, of semantics, of grammar, of lexis, etc.) and at different ranks (word-for-word, phrase-for-phrase, sentence-for-sentence).[10]

It is apparent, and has been for a very long time indeed, that the ideal of total equivalence is a chimera. Languages are different from each other; they are different in form having distinct codes and rules regulating the construction of grammatical stretches of language and these forms have different meanings.

To shift from one language to another is, by definition, to alter the forms. Further, the contrasting forms convey meanings which cannot but fail to coincide totally; there is no absolute synonymy between words in the same language, so why should anyone be surprised to discover a lack of synonymy between languages?

Something is always 'lost' (or, might one suggest, 'gained'?) in the process and translators can find themselves being accused of reproducing only part of the original and so 'betraying' the author's intentions. Hence the traitorous nature ascribed to the translator by the notorious Italian proverb; *traduttore traditore*.

If equivalence is to be 'preserved' at a particular level at all costs, which level is it to be? What are the alternatives? The answer, it turns out, hinges on the dual nature of language itself. Language is a formal structure – a code – which consists of elements which can combine to signal semantic 'sense' and, at the same time, a communication system which uses the forms of the code to refer to entities (in the world of the senses and the world of the mind) and create signals which possess communicative 'value'.

The translator has the option, then, of focusing on finding *formal* equivalents which 'preserve' the context-free semantic sense of the text at the expense of its context-sensitive communicative value or finding *functional* equivalents which 'preserve' the context-sensitive communicative value of the text at the expense of its context-free semantic sense.

The choice (and it goes back to Classical times; Cicero 46 BC) is between translating word-for-word (literal translation) or meaning-for-meaning (free translation).

Pick the first and the translator is criticized for the 'ugliness' of a 'faithful' translation ; pick the second and there is criticism of the 'inaccuracy' of a 'beautiful' translation. Either way it seems, the translator cannot win, even though we recognize that the crucial variable is the *purpose* for which the translation is being made, not some inherent characteristic of the text itself.

Perhaps there is less need today than there used to be in the 60s and 70s to assert that variation is in no sense an inconvenient characteristic of language in use but its very nature without which it would be unable to function as a communication system. That said, we need to specify the choices which are available to the communicator and the functions such choices may be called upon to play.

Faced by a text – written or spoken – in a language which we know, we are able to work out not only (1) the semantic sense of each word and sentence (as we shall do in Chapter 3) but also (2) its communicative value, (3) its place in time and space and (4) information about the participants involved in its production and reception. We might take, as a light-hearted model of the questions we can ask of a text, the first verse of a short poem by Kipling;

> I keep six honest servingmen;
> (They taught me all I knew);
> Their names were What? and Why? and When?
> And How? and Where? and Who?[11]

Each of these questions defines one (or more) parameters of variation:

What? is the *message contained in the text*; the content of the signal; the propositional content of the speech acts.

Why? orients us towards the *intention of the sender*; the purpose for which the text was issued, the illocutionary forces of the speech acts which constitute the underlying structure of the text; the discourse. These run the whole gamut from *informing* through *persuading* to *flattering*. . . and, as we shall see, it is rare for a text to possess a single function. Multiple functions are the norm rather than the exception for adult language, so our task as receivers of texts, is to tease out the primary function from those which are secondary; a fundamental difficulty which we shall address in Chapter 6, Section 6.1 in the attempt to devise a text-typology.

When? is concerned with the *time of the communication* realized in the text and setting it in its historical context; contemporary or set in the recent or remote past or future.

How? is ambiguous, since it can refer to:

(a) *manner of delivery*: the tenor of the discourse; serious or flippant or ironic. . .
(b) *medium of communication*: the mode of the discourse; the channel(s) – verbal/non-verbal, speech/writing – selected to carry the signal.

Where? is concerned with the *place of the communication*; the physical location of the speech event realized in the text.

Who? refers to the *participants involved in the communication*; the sender and receiver(s). Both spoken and written texts will reveal, to a greater or lesser extent, characteristics of the speaker or writer as an individual and also, by inference, the attitude the sender adopts in relation to the receiver(s) and to the message being transmitted.

We take it as axiomatic that language is a *code* which possesses *features* – phonological (and, in the case of written languages, graphological), syntactic, lexical and semantic – and that language use is made possible by making selections from among these sets of code features in order to create *texts* which act as adequate vehicles for the communication of meaning.

We would further expect to find, in any stretch of language, *choices* which function as *indicators* of the temporal, physical and social provenance of the *user* and these we would term *dialect* features. Equally expected would be *markers* of the *use* to which the language was being put and these we would term *register* features.

For the translator, both dialect and register features are important but, of the two, it is the parameters of register which are probably the more significant. We shall therefore concentrate on them.

The task which faces the analyst attempting to describe register variation is easier to state than to resolve. What has to be discovered in the text are the *markers* of the relationship between sender and receiver(s) (addressee relationship), the channel(s) selected for the transmission of the message (medium) and the function of the discourse (domain).

In essence, as we see, the problem is to relate (a) sociological variables present in (i) the participants (their role relationships), (ii) the purposes they bring to the event (the 'symbolic or rhetorical channel'[12]) and (iii) the setting of the event (the 'ongoing social activity'[13] with (b) the linguistic features which combine to create the text which is realized in and as interaction (discourse).

It is precisely in order to act as a link between the sociological and the linguistic that the notion of discourse is required (as shown in Figure 1.1).

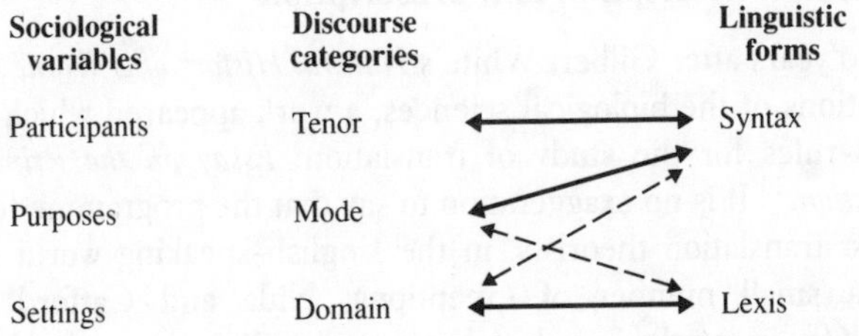

Sociological variables	Discourse categories	Linguistic forms
Participants	Tenor	Syntax
Purposes	Mode	
Settings	Domain	Lexis

FIGURE I.I Discourse parameters

The arrows between the discourse categories and the linguistic forms[14] are intended to be suggestive of the extent to which discourse categories draw on particular parts of the linguistic code; the solid arrow indicates 'more commonly', the dotted arrow 'less commonly'.

We shall examine each of the three register categories – tenor, mode and domain of discourse – in detail later (in Chapter 5, Section 5.3) but have introduced them here in order to ensure that the issue of stylistic variation has been raised as early as possible and the terminology for discussing it is available for use when we begin building the model of the translation process in the next chapter (in Chapter 2, Section 2.2).

It is, no doubt, the seeming chaos of variation faced in texts by translators and the inevitable inability of a theory of translation to be strongly predictive which has led some to go so far as to deny the very possibility of creating a 'single valid comprehensive theory of translation'[15] and fall back on stressing the 'subjective', 'craft' nature of the activity.[16]

Others, sharing the same sentiment, give way, on occasion, to outbursts of despairing hyperbole;

> No simple theory or set of rules can ever suffice to provide meaningful answers to what has [been] described as 'probably the most complex type of event yet produced in the evolution of the cosmos'.[17]

The reliance on personal experience and the promulgation of 'general principles', on the basis of mere anecdotalism is still common and, in spite of the fact that most would probably now admit that 'it would almost be true to say that there are no universally accepted principles of translation',[18] lists of approved techniques and rules for translation continue to appear.[19] It is to this issue of 'rules' which we now move.

1.1.2 Rules: description and prescription

Just two years after Gilbert White's *Natural History of Selborne* laid the foundations of the biological sciences, a work appeared which set the ground-rules for the study of translation: *Essay on the Principles of Translation*.[20] It is no exaggeration to say that the programme followed by most translation theorists, in the English-speaking world at least (with a small number of exceptions; Nida and Catford in the mid-1960s in particular), has been, and still is, dominated by the thinking put forward in an essay written two centuries ago in 1791.

The first chapter of the essay has an extremely significant title: 'Description of a good translation: general rules flowing from that description.'[21]

Translation theory finds itself today seriously out of step with the mainstream of intellectual endeavour in the human sciences and in particular in the study of human communication; to our mutual impoverishment. The fundamental cause of this state of affairs is, we firmly believe, the normative approach – the setting up of a series of maxims consisting of do's and don'ts – which can be traced back to the orientation quoted above.

Let us, therefore, reproduce the writer's definition of a 'good translation', some of the argument he adduces in support of it and the three 'general laws of translation' which he deduces from the definition.[22]

Tytler (i.e. Lord Woodhouselee) argues that, the 'Rules of the Art' would flow naturally from an accurate definition, or description, of a 'good translation' but concedes that 'there is no subject of criticism where there has been so much difference of opinion', explaining this by reference to the substantial differences 'in genius and character' between languages and the two extreme positions adopted in relation to translation; 'to attend only to the sense and spirit of the original' or, additionally, to convey the 'style and manner of writing' of the original author. He continues:

> According to the former idea of translation, it is allowable to improve and embellish; according to the latter, it is necessary to preserve even blemishes and defects...

and then makes an appeal to a compromise position between them saying:

> As these two opinions form opposite extremes, it is not improbable that the point of perfection should be found between the two.

This leads him to a considered definition:

> I would therefore describe a good translation to be, *That in which the merit of the original work is so completely transfused into another language, as to be as distinctly apprehended, and as strongly felt, by a native of the country to which that language belongs, as it is by those who speak the language of the original work.*[23]

From this, he tells us, three 'laws' follow:

I.   That the Translation should give a complete transcript of the ideas of the original work.
II. That the style and manner of writing should be of the same character with that of the original.
III. That the Translation should have all the ease of original composition.

Tytler then notes that 'under each of these general laws of translation, are comprehended a variety of subordinate precepts' and the rest of the essay (over 200 pages) consists of an exposition of the 'laws' and 'precepts' in action.

Let us consider the nature of Tytler's rules. They are all, it will be recognized, *normative prescriptions* deriving directly from the subjective and evaluative description of the 'good translation'. The terms used – 'law', 'precept' – are indicative of this. They are like the rules of etiquette; what people are told they *ought* and *ought not* to do in particular circumstances, by reference to essentially arbitrary norms of behaviour.

Grammatical examples of such rules are such classics as 'do not end a sentence with a preposition', 'do not split infinitives' and so forth. The fact of the matter is that a preposition is often a useful form to complete a clause or sentence with and even the most cautious of writers (and, even more frequently, speakers) find that they have to sometimes split an infinitive.

There are, however, two very different kinds of rule which control behaviour (see a more extended discussion in Chapter 5, Section 5.2); those which *regulate* an already existing activity (the kind of rule we have been discussing) and those which *define* an activity which neither pre-exists the formulation of the rules nor can be thought to have any existence without them.

The 'rules' and 'principles' promulgated for translation have, for centuries, been of this first, normative, regulatory type. Translators have been told what to do (prescriptive rules) and what not to do (proscriptive rules) but, very rarely, why they are to conform to these dictates (we give a list in the next chapter; Section 2.3.2).

The 'rules' discussed in linguistics, on the other hand, seek to be of the second, descriptive, constitutive type. The rules of the code – what elements are available and how they may legitimately combine – are straightforward examples; rules which determine relationships and are all-or-none in application. A particular string of sounds or letters, for example, either does or does not constitute a word in a particular language: *the* in English does while, *teh, hte, eht* and *eth* do not (though we might want to argue for the last being an abbreviated form of 'Ethel').

The contrast between what people ordinarily assume 'grammar' to mean and this, descriptive, orientation of the linguist is clearly paralleled in translation theory; the frequent assumption that the purpose of a theory of translation is to devise and impose prescriptive rules as a means of both regulating the process and evaluating the product. Our position is (when playing the role of a descriptive linguist), necessarily, the converse; we are in search of descriptive rules which help us to understand the process, not normative rules which we use to monitor and judge the work of others.

1.1.3 Translation; process and product

At the beginning of this chapter, we provided a definition of translation which focussed on the requirement that the content and style of the original text (SLT) should be preserved as far as is possible in the translated text (TLT) and we spent the first sub-section (1.1.1) considering the nature of 'equivalence'.

An alternative definition, given below, makes a second crucial point by distinguishing 'process' from 'result':

> The process or result of converting information from one language or language variety into another... The aim is to reproduce as accurately as possible all grammatical and lexical features of the 'source language' original by finding equivalents in the 'target language'. At the same time all factual information contained in the original text... must be retained in the translation.[24]

It is this distinction which we wish to take up now. In the definition we have just seen, the term 'translation' is given two meanings. We would suggest that there are, in fact, three distinguishable meanings for the word. It can refer to:

(1) *translating*: the process (to translate; the activity rather than the tangible object);
(2) *a translation*: the product of the process of translating (i.e. the translated text);
(3) *translation*: the abstract concept which encompasses both the process of translating and the product of that process.

Clearly, a theory of translation, to be comprehensive and useful, must attempt to describe and explain both the process and the product. Our present situation, however, is one in which translation theory has, for the most part, concentrated on the product to the exclusion of the process and has adopted a normative attitude to it by making inferences back to it through the description and evaluation of the product (see the previous section on this).

If we accept that we have a responsibility to attempt to describe and explain the process and that the process itself is, essentially, mental rather than physical, we are committed to undertaking the investigation within the discipline of psychology and, more specifically, within the framework of psychological studies of perception, information processing and memory; cognitive science.[25]

Equally, given that the process crucially involves language, we shall need to draw on the resources of linguistics and, more precisely, those branches of linguistics which are concerned with the psychological and social aspects of language use: psycholinguistics and sociolinguistics. The first of these examines the process in the mind of the translator, the second places the source language text (SLT) and target language text (TLT) in their cultural contexts.

1.1.4 Summary

We have introduced the notion of 'translation' in this section and have raised three key issues:

(1) the problem of 'equivalence' between texts and the extent to which it is desirable or even possible to 'preserve' the semantic and/or stylistic characteristics of the SLT in the course of translating it into the TLT;

(2) the notion of 'rule'; the distinction between the constitutive rule which defines an activity and the regulative rule which seeks to constrain the activity by reference to predefined norms of behaviour which are often assumed rather than explicitly stated;

(3) the need to recognize and act upon the distinction between translation as (a) *process* (translating), as (b) *product* (translated text) and as (c) *concept* (the overall notion which subsumes both the activity and the entity).

We are about to move on to the translator but, before we do, we should perhaps make clear that, although we intend to describe in a rather informal way what the translator does (to be, that is, descriptive about the process) our rejection of the notion of the 'good translation' is not matched by a similar rejection of the 'good translator'. We believe (as translator trainers surely must) that translator competence is variable from individual to individual and is, in principle at least, measurable against agreed objective criteria (a point which is taken up in some detail in the next Chapter, Section 2.1).

1.2   What is a translator?

One seemingly quirky answer to this question would be to say that all communicators are translators. All communicators, as receivers – whether listeners or readers, monolinguals or bilinguals – face essentially the same problem; they receive signals (in speech and in writing) containing messages encoded in a communication system which is not, by definition, identical with their own.

This realization underlies particular views of reading which insist that 'making sense' of a text is, in fact, to deconstruct it and then to reconstruct it.[26] Writers on translation, too, have been particularly aware of the same phenomenon;

> Any model of communication is at the same time a model of translation, of a vertical or horizontal transfer of significance.

No two historical epochs, no two social classes, no two localities use words and syntax to signify exactly the same things, to send identical signals of valuation and inference. Neither do two human beings.[27]

In what way, then, is the role of the translator (and the interpreter) different from that of the 'normal' communicator? The translator has been defined as a 'bilingual mediating agent between monolingual communication participants in two different language communities',[28] i.e. the translator decodes messages transmitted in one language and re-encodes them in another.

It is this re-encoding process which marks the bilingual translator off from the monolingual communicator. As receivers, both have the same involvement in decoding – the difference is one of degree rather than of kind – but their encoding behaviour is in strong contrast.

When taking a turn as a sender, the monolingual is obliged (a) to encode into the language used by the sender, (b) to encode messages which are different from those received and (c) to transmit them to the previous sender. The translator's acts contrast on all three scores. For the translator, the encoding (a) consists of re-encoding into a different language, (b) concerns the same message as was received and (c) is aimed at a group of receivers who are not the same as the original sender.

Even so, it is clear that translation is, as we have been arguing, a particular instance of a more general phenomenon (the exchange of information by means of language) and, hence, as a preliminary to a discussion of multilingual information exchange (of which translation is an example), we shall propose a model of the process of the exchange of information (see Figure 1.3). This initial and rather simplified model will serve two purposes: (a) to set the whole discussion of translation in the wider context of human communication and (b) to provide a basis on which to build general and more specific models of particular parts of the translation process later (beginning with simple general models in Figures 1.4 and 1.5, moving to a more sophisticated model in Chapter 2 and expanding aspects of the model in Chapters 3–7 inclusive).

1.2.1 Memory, meaning and language

The translator, like any other communicator, lives in the world of the senses through which perceptions are integrated as concepts, experiences can be 'recalled' and even 'relived' through the systems of memory.

As we shall see in Chapter 7 (when we consider memory systems), it is essential to distinguish between **sensation** – receiving stimuli from the outside world through the senses – and **perception**; the organization of these impressions into an endlessly varied but stable and consistent world with agreed dimensions of space and time.

Central to the processes of sensation and perception are the three terms **aggregate**, **whole** and **system**, related in the manner shown in Figure 1.2.

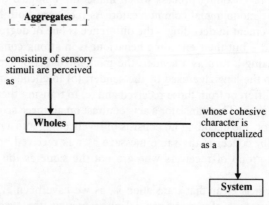

FIGURE 1.2 Sense and perception

This figure can be read in the following way: the chaotic aggregates which are fed into the mind through the senses have 'boundaries' put around them by the processes of perception and are thus converted into information-bearing 'wholes'. What converts the formless aggregate into the structured whole is the perception of 'system' or 'pattern'. Note, too, that *aggregates* and *wholes* are substantial 'things' in the 'real world', in contrast with *system* which is abstract and exists (if at all) in the mind.

But there is more to it than this. Just like any other individual, the translator 'understands' new experiences in terms of ones which have gone before and deals with them as though they were recurrences of the same event. Memory, clearly, contains more than 'records' of past experiences; it also has plans for action on the basis of what we know and what we have done. It is also clear that much of our experience of the external world of the senses and of the inner world of the mind is mediated by language; the concepts stored in our memories refer to entities via the conventions of language and do so variably depending on the language used.

What do communicators know about language? The answer to this would constitute the whole of linguistic scholarship to date but, suffice it to say: knowledge of the options available for (1) converting amorphous 'ideas' into concepts which are organized into propositions (semantic knowledge), (2) mapping propositions, which are universal and not tied to any language, onto the clause-creating systems of a particular language (syntactic knowledge) and (3) realizing clauses as utterances and texts in actual communicative situations (rhetorical knowledge).

We shall be considering each of these throughout the rest of this book and would pause here to make what is, perhaps, an obvious point. While all this applies to human beings in a general sense, it applies to translators in a very particular sense; for the translator there are, at the very least, two languages and two cultures involved rather than one.

In addition, it is almost certainly the case that translators are more consciously aware of language and the resources it contains than monolingual communicators are. Both possess *procedural* knowledge about language (they know how to operate the system) but to possess *factual* knowledge (knowing that the system has such and such characteristics) is an altogether different story, as students of linguistics quickly discover during their initial attempts to explain just what it is that they are doing when they speak or write. We shall take up the distinction between procedural and factual knowledge later (in Chapter 7, Section 7.2) but mention it here because it makes clear the magnitude of the task which faces us; we are embarking on the attempt to turn the procedural knowledge which translators possess into factual knowledge which can be probed, shared, discussed.

The question that we would wish to ask, then, is 'How does the translator move from one language to the other in the course of translation?' and the answer we shall give will be in the form of a very simple model of the process.

1.2.2 The communication process

The translator, as we have been saying, is by definition a communicator who is involved in written communication. We might, therefore, begin by providing a rough, general model of the process of written communication before moving on to the specific and particularly problematic process in which translators are involved.

The model, presented in Figure 1.3 derives ultimately from work in information theory,[29] and contains nine steps which take us from encoding the message through its transmission and reception to the decoding of the message by the receiver. It provides us with a starting point for the explanation of the process of communication, albeit limited to the monolingual and, by implication, to dyadic interaction; one sender and one receiver.

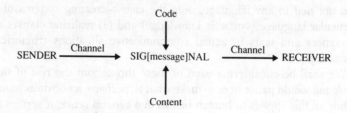

FIGURE 1.3 Monolingual communication

Even with these limitations, however, it contains within it the elements and processes which need to be explained and raises a large number of questions which require an answer if we are to succeed at all in our attempt to make sense of the phenomenon of translation. We could describe this process in terms of nine steps:

(1) the sender selects message and code
(2) encodes message
(3) selects channel
(4) transmits signal containing message
(5) receiver receives signal containing message
(6) recognizes code
(7) decodes signal
(8) retrieves message and
(9) comprehends message.

We ought not, however, to assume that this is a simple, unidirectional and linear process nor that each step must be completed before the next can be started. Processing is by its very nature both cyclic (the sender sends more messages or the receiver takes over the sender's role) and cooperative (the sender may well begin again at step 1 while the receiver is no further advanced than step 5 or 6).

A second model (Figure 1.4) is now needed to provide a clear contrast between the processes of monolingual communication and translation. It can be read as a continuation of the model above by equating step 5 in the monolingual process presented above with step 1 in the bilingual process given below, i.e. 'receiver receives signal containing message' is equated with 'translator receives signal 1 containing message'. This model is, it must be admitted, rather crude and vague at this stage but none the less serves to focus our attention on the points of similarity and difference between translation and 'normal' communication.

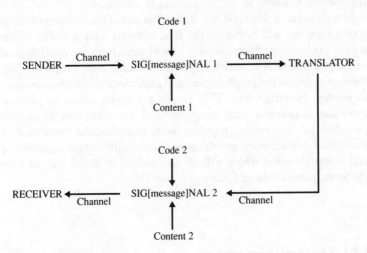

FIGURE 1.4 Translating

(1) translator receives signal 1 containing message
(2) recognizes code 1
(3) decodes signal 1
(4) retrieves message
(5) comprehends message
(6) translator selects code 2
(7) encodes message by means of code 2
(8) selects channel
(9) transmits signal 2 containing message.

We might comment here. There are several crucial points of difference between monolingual communication and bilingual communication involving translation (we are sticking to written communication in both cases): there are two codes, two signals (or utterances or texts) and, given what we have been saying about the impossibility of 100 per cent equivalence, two sets of content (i.e. more than one message).

It follows, then, that in our modelling of translating, we shall need two kinds of explanation: (1) a *psycholinguistic* explanation which focuses mainly on steps 7 and 3 in Figure 1.3 – decoding and encoding – and, (2) a more *text-linguistic* or *sociolinguistic* explanation which focuses more on the participants, on the nature of the message and on the ways in which the resources of the code are drawn upon by users to create meaning-carrying signals and the fact that a sociocultural approach is required to set the process in context.

In the course of this book, we shall adopt any of these orientations as appropriate but will begin (in the next chapter) with a model of the translating process which assumes a movement from the physiological to the psychological activities involved in reading and comprehending the source text to the psychological and physiological activities involved in writing the target text. This entails a complex series of physical processes concerned with sensation and the reception of stimuli provided by the senses together with psychological processes of perception and memory; problems associated with reception, decoding and comprehension which will be approached in detail only in later chapters (particularly in Chapters 6 and 7).

1.2.3 The translation process

There are probably as many definitions of 'translation' as there are of 'sentence' (and probably no more revealing). One which is not totally unattractive (and which we have already used) is: 'the replacement of a representation of a text in one language by a representation of an equivalent text in a second language.'[30]

The question which immediately arises is: 'How does this happen?' A partial answer, which serves to draw together the discussion in this section, is provided by Figure 1.5: a much simplified outline of a more comprehensive model of the translation process which will be presented in Chapter 2 (in Section 2.2).

The model shows, in extremely simplified form, the transformation of a source language text into a target language text by means of processes which take place within memory: (1) the **analysis** of one language-specific text (the source language text, the SLT) into a universal (non-language-specific) semantic representation and (2) the **synthesis** of that semantic representation into a second language-specific text (the target language text, the TLT).

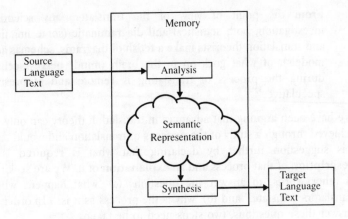

FIGURE 1.5 Translation process

1.2.4 Summary

In this section we have moved from discussing the abstract notion 'translation' and the problems entailed in its description and explanation, to the locus of the activity: the translator. We have, very briefly, outlined the knowledge the translator has to have in order to translate, set the process of translation in the context of human communication and, finally, provided the simplest possible model of the process of translation. All of these issues will reappear later and will be dealt with in a much less summary fashion.

We need next to decide how we are going to tackle the description and explanation of translation. This will require us to decide on (1) the kind of **theory** which will be most revealing for our purposes (and this will involve distinguishing models from theories and specifying the characteristics which theories in general and a theory of translation in particular should possess) and, (2) the type of **methodology** which will be most appropriate.

1.3 What is translation theory?

The study of translation seems to be permeated by misunderstanding on both sides, linguists tending to misconstrue the objectives and methods of translation theory and translation theorists to demonstrate a far from adequate grasp of the principles of linguistics and its methods of investigation. One recent quotation will make this point:

From the point of view of the translator, any scientific investigation, both statistical and diagrammatic (some linguists and translation theorists make a fetish of diagrams, schemas and models), of what goes on in the brain (mind? nerves? cells?) during the process of translating is remote and at present speculative.[31]

We have been arguing that advances in translation theory can only be achieved through a study of the **process** of translation and would take this suggestion further by declaring that what is required is a **description** of that process and an **explanation** of it. We are seeking, in other words, to answer the questions (a) 'what happens when translators translate?' and (b) 'why is the process as it is?'. In order to answer these questions, two steps need to be taken.

First of all, given the emphasis which has been placed on the evaluation of the product, it seems essential that the balance be redressed through the systematic study of the *process*. It is the process which creates the product and it is only by understanding the process that we can hope (if we see ourselves in such a role) to help ourselves or others to improve their skills as translators. The need for such a shift of attention has, indeed, already been argued for and we strongly endorse the sentiment expressed:

> part of a theory of. . . translation would account for the process
> of moving from original text to mental representation and how it
> differs from the original text.[32]

Secondly, we must – following the proposal made by Bassnett-McGuire[33] – adopt a **descriptive** rather than a **prescriptive** approach to our investigation of the process, recognizing that the purpose of translation theory is:

> to reach an understanding of the processes undertaken in the act
> of translation and, not, as is so commonly misunderstood, to
> provide a set of norms for effecting the perfect translation.[34]

In short, instead of making subjective and arbitrary judgements on the extent to which one translation is 'better' than another and insisting that 'goodness' resides in the faithful adherence to an imposed set of commandments, our orientation has to be towards the objective specification of the steps and stages through which the translator works as the source text in the original language is transformed into the target text; a focus on the process which creates the translation rather than on the translation itself.

We must not, however, make exaggerated claims for our theories and models. As de Beaugrande warns:

> it is inappropriate to expect that a theoretical model of translation should solve all the problems a translator encounters. Instead, it should formulate a set of strategies for approaching problems and for coordinating the different aspects entailed.[35]

It is clear from comments like these that there is a growing acceptance that translation studies must (1) be re-oriented towards description, whether of process or product, and away from prescription and, increasingly, that (2) the most revealing way of dealing with the product is within the conventions of text-linguistics (see the conclusion of this chapter and Section 1.3.2 for a parallel statement in relation to translation theory).

The terms 'theory' and 'model' have just been used. We need to be clear what these mean and how they fit into the investigative process in which we are engaged.

1.3.1 Theories, models and analogies

We have already argued that (1) it is essential to distinguish between sensation – receiving stimuli from the outside world through the senses – and perception, the organization of these impressions into a systematic world with finite dimensions of time and space and that (2) the processes of sensation and perception are best explained by demonstrating the relationship between the three terms *aggregate*, *whole* and *system* shown in Figure 1.2.

We can draw on this and convert the representation we have given of sensation and perception into a model of scientific enquiry by replacing some of the terms (though not changing the process itself) with others which are more commonly used in science.

In other words, the chaotic aggregates of normal sensation are the phenomena studied by the scientist. They are fed into the mind through the senses, have 'boundaries' put around them by the processes of perception and are thus converted into information-bearing data. The **explanation** of the **system** is the **theory** of the scientist which, when passed on to others, is realized as a **model**.

Just as before, we should note the substantial, 'real world' quality of the phenomena, the data and the model on the one hand and the contrasting abstraction of the theory which we 'discover' (if we believe

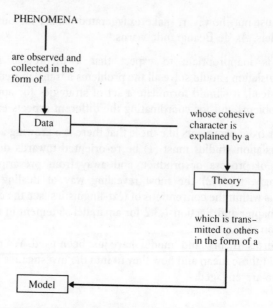

PHENOMENA

are observed and
collected in the
form of

Data

whose cohesive
character is
explained by a

Theory

which is trans-
mitted to others
in the form of a

Model

FIGURE 1.6 Perception and enquiry

that ideas pre-exist their discovery) or 'create' (if we believe they do not) on the other.

Before continuing, however, two notes of caution should perhaps be struck, firstly about the extent of our knowledge of the way human communication works and, secondly, about the status of 'theories' and 'models'.

It is true that a certain amount is known about the mechanisms of human communication – but only a little – and all we can hope to do, at the moment, is report what is known and model it in a way which makes that knowledge accessible and available for further thought and investigation. We shall make considerable use of **models** and **analogies** hoping, thereby, to provide clues to the way in which we imagine that the system may work. But, as Wilss warns us:

> Neither psycholinguistics nor neurology can as yet provide reliable information on how linguistic data are stored in the brain, how linguistic matching procedures take place and what mental structures are active in recalling linguistic information.[36]

Given that, we must be clear about what theories and models are and how they relate to each other.

A **theory** is an explanation of a phenomenon, the perception of system and order in something observed. It exists (if at all; philosophical debate has raged for two millennia over the existence of abstract entities) in the mind. It has no tangible manifestation. It is an idea (which might well be unique to the individual who 'has' it) which constitutes the internal representation of a phenomenon, e.g. my own idea of the layout of the actual London Underground system.

A **model** is, in contrast, an external rather than an internal representation of the explanation; a realization of the theory. It exists as a tangible object (a diagram, a formula, a text) which 'stands for' the idea embodied in the theory. The London Underground system, for example, is represented by two very different kinds of map: (1) the schematic plan in which stations are shown as equidistant, lines are not curved, etc., and (2) a map in which the lines are drawn in relation to the roads under which they run or which they cross.

A model must, therefore, possess a number of characteristics if it is to be useful.

1. It must faithfully *represent* the theory that it 'stands for', i.e. indicate what the phenomenon 'really' is rather than what it appears to be.

2. It must do this by revealing *significant characteristics* of the phenomenon explained by the theory. Clearly, given that a model 'stands for' something far more complex than itself, no model can present us with the full complexity of the original but no model is required to do that. The essential constraint on a model is not that it should be a 'copy' of the original phenomenon but that it should focus attention on those parts of the phenomenon which are considered to be most essential by the theory.

3. It must have a *heuristic* function; making it easier to grasp the explanation (i.e. the theory) and doing that in a way which makes further study easier and leads to deeper understanding. This is achieved by means of analogy. A model proposes that we view a phenomenon *as if* it were other than it appears. For this reason, a model may be extremely fanciful (for example, the one we use in Chapter 7 to explain information-processing involves a number of 'demons' in charge of the several stages) but the essential constraint on a model is not that it should be 'real' (in the sense of being a copy of the phenomenon) but that it should be revealing of known facts about the original; there is no need to claim that the model does any more than *specify* the components involved and the relationships they have with each other.

The models we shall be proposing will be analogies with these kinds of characteristics. They ask us to imagine the phenomena we are studying *as if* they were something else, in order to help us to understand them more fully.[37] We do this with the translation process itself (Chapter 2), relating logical propositions to syntactic structures and realizations of both in utterances and texts (Chapters 4 and 5), text-processing (Chapter 6) and information-processing and memory (Chapter 7).

What, then, of the theory we are searching for? What characteristics should we expect it to have and what criteria should there be for evaluating alternative theories? It is this issue, the specification of the requirements for a theory of translation, to which we now turn.

1.3.2 Requirements for a theory of translation

A model, like all models, is an attempt at a *description* rather than an *explanation*. An explanation is a *theory*. A theory may be defined as 'a statement of a general principle, based upon reasoned argument and supported by evidence, that is intended to explain a particular fact, event, or phenomenon',[38] i.e. while a model answers the question 'what?', the theory answers the question 'why?'.

Given the ambiguity of the word 'translation', we can envisage three possible theories depending on the focus of the investigation; the process or the product. These would be:

1. A theory of translation as *process* (i.e. a theory of translating). This would require a study of information processing and, within that, such topics as (a) perception, (b) memory and (c) the encoding and decoding of messages, and would draw heavily on psychology and on psycholinguistics.

2. A theory of translation as *product* (i.e. a theory of translated texts). This would require a study of texts not merely by means of the traditional levels of linguistic analysis (syntax and semantics) but also making use of stylistics and recent advances in text-linguistics and discourse analysis.

3. A theory of translation as both process *and* product (i.e. a theory of translating and translation). This would require the integrated study of both and such a general theory is, presumably, the long-term goal for translation studies.

For the moment at least, we are after a theory of translating and, given that there is considerable agreement on the characteristics which a theory should possess, we can state what our ideal theory should look like.

Essentially, a theory is judged on the extent to which it is externally and internally adequate. It must correspond with the data (which is external to itself) and also conform to particular (internal) design features.

Ideally, a theory must reflect four particular characteristics:

(1) *empiricism*;   it must be testable
(2) *determinism*;   it must be able to predict
(3) *parsimony*;   it must be simple
(4) *generality*;   it must be comprehensive.

Clearly, a theory of translation would be required to conform, as far as possible, to these criteria and the greater the conformity the more powerful the theory. However, the relationship between external and internal adequacy resolves itself into the long-running issue of idealization and abstraction. The more idealized the data, the more abstract and the further from the 'fuzziness' of the 'real world' does the theory become.[39]

It may be that, once again, we are now asking too much of translation theory – at least for the moment – in contrast with the rather minimal (or, even, impossible) demands which have been made on it in the past.

From the applied linguistic point of view, translation theory can be criticized for having limited its activities to the level of **technique** (the language teaching equivalent of classroom activities) or, at best, to that of **method** (in language teaching terms, the equivalent of global collections of techniques; audio-visual method, direct method, etc.), when what is needed is a principled **approach** from which the rest would flow.[40]

Equally, in descriptive rather than applied terms, it might perhaps be more feasible to think of developing an *approach* rather than a theory, i.e. an orientation to the problem of describing and explaining the translation process which derives from an amalgam of insights from psychology and linguistics into the nature of the activity of translating. If we adopt this plan of action, we can draw upon considerable expertise in applied linguistics, from which the approach, method, technique series comes, and produce a tentative initial list of what we might expect from a theory of translation:

(1) statements of the conventions which constrain the activity of translation rather than definitions of rules which determine it;

(2) models which offer probabilistic *post facto* explanations of what has been done, rather than deterministic *a priori* models which claim to predict what will be done;

(3) models of the dynamics of the process itself rather than static descriptions of the structure of the product;

(4) indications of the relationships which exist between translation on one side and broader notions such as communicative competence, discoursal coherence and appropriateness in the use of the code, rather than the more narrowly defined concerns of 'core' linguistics, i.e. linguistic competence, textual cohesion and grammaticality in the usage of the code on the other.

We are, to summarize, in search of 'an integrated, interdisciplinary, multimethod, and multilevel approach' to the explanation of the phenomenon of translation[41] and we would locate the approach within a broadly defined **applied linguistics** which would embrace, in addition to the teaching and learning of foreign languages, lexicology and lexicography, speech pathology, stylistics, language planning.[42]

We firmly believe that such an approach will facilitate the creation of a more relevant and up-to-date theory of translation which will take its rightful place as a key area in the human sciences (particularly linguistics – broadly defined – and psychology) and are encouraged by a striking assertion from a major figure in translation theory:

> In short: *inside or between languages, human communication equals translation*. A study of translation is a study of language.[43]

How, though, are we to set about creating such an approach? This question brings us to the final part of this section: methodology.

1.3.3 Methodology; investigating translation

An initial and seemingly significant objection to the notion of describing and explaining the phenomenon of translation might well be that the whole of the process (with the obvious exception of the physical aspects of reading and writing) takes place in the mind of the translator and, given that we have, therefore, no direct access to it, we shall be forced back into precisely the unsatisfactory kind of description of the product which we have been saying that we wish to avoid.

We would counter this by pointing out that it is perfectly legitimate to build up a model on the basis of inferences drawn from an objective study of the product. Indeed, such an approach would constitute no more than a special instance of the classic engineering problem of the 'black box' which contains a mechanism which converts input into output but is otherwise totally inaccessible. How is it possible, in such a case, to specify the nature of the mechanism? The solution is to 'work back' from the output of the mechanism (the product) and make a set of statements about the necessary characteristics of the system itself (the process), i.e. to make use of the logical process of **induction**.

This analogy, however, does not fit the process of translation exactly, since we *do* have a degree of access to it through the substantial insights we have into the workings of our own minds. This being the case, it should be possible by introspection (i.e by adopting a **deductive** approach to the problem), to build a model of what we ourselves are doing when we translate.

Ultimately – as the development of psychology has shown – a multiple approach, involving both induction and deduction in a cyclic investigation, is more likely to be revealing than the strict adherence to either induction or deduction alone (see Figure 1.7).

We might illustrate this by taking up another issue which has exercised translation theorists over a very long period indeed; the problem of the size of the *unit of translation*. The question 'What is the unit of translation?' resolves itself all too readily into a search for the answer to the question 'What ought the unit of translation to be?' The notion 'unit of translation' – sometimes written 'UT' – has been defined in these terms:

> The smallest segment of an SL [source language] text which can be translated, as a whole, in isolation from other segments. It normally ranges from the word through the collocation to the clause. It could be described as 'as small as is possible and as large as is necessary' (this is my view), though some translators would say that it is a misleading concept, since the only UT is the whole text.[44]

It is difficult to imagine a better example of an issue which cries out for empirical investigation. If we ask what the unit is that the translator actually processes in the course of translating, we discover that there is good psychological and linguistic evidence to suggest that the unit tends to be the clause (see Chapter 6, Section 6.3.3 for discussion on text-processing). There is also experimental evidence[45] which supports the notion of co-occurrence between cognitive 'chunk' boundaries and syntactic boundaries within the clause; boundaries between

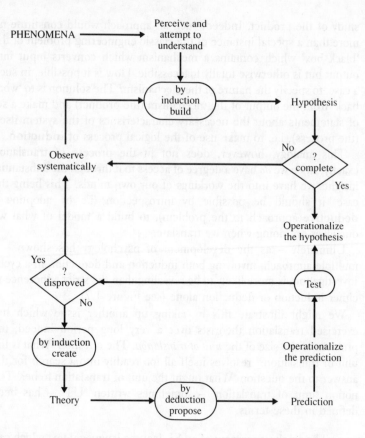

FIGURE 1.7 The cycle of enquiry

major structural units (Subject, Predicator, Complement, etc.) and the forms which realize them (phrases for the most part). For example,

the United Nations Secretary General reported substantial progress in the peace negotiations in Geneva today

would be likely to be segmented during reading into five or six units:

[the United Nations Secretary General]
[reported]
[substantial progress in the peace negotiations]
[in Geneva]
[today]

or

> [the United Nations Secretary General]
> [reported]
> [substantial progress]
> [in the peace negotiations]
> [in Geneva]
> [today]

and not

> [the United]
> [Nations Secretary]
> [General reported substantial]
> [progress in the]
> [peace negotiations in]
> [Geneva today]

nor even

> [the United]
> [Nations]
> [Secretary]
> [General re]
> [ported sub]
> [stantial]
> [progress in the]
> [peace negoti]
> [ations in Ge]
> [neva to]
> [day]

as it would be in speech with the rhythmic boundaries (of the feet) cutting through lexical and syntactic units.

We intend to approach translation issues in this way throughout the book, i.e. by providing text which illustrates the problem and working from that towards descriptive rules rather than prescribing or proscribing, *a priori*, what *should* be done.

1.3.4 Summary

In this final section, we have been addressing the issue of 'theory' in relation to translation by distinguishing models from theories, specifying what a theory of translation ought to contain and giving some indication of the methodology we shall employ in our search for a theory.

1.4   Conclusion

In this chapter we have cleared the ground for what is to follow. The three-way ambiguity of the term 'translation' has been used to distinguish process from product and from the concept which combines them both.

We have considered, briefly, the nature of translation, placed translation in the wider context of human communication and outlined a programme for the creation of a theory of translation, concentrating (initially at least) on the process and probing, at least implicitly, the question 'What do translators actually do?'

The answer to this question, central though it is to our own interests, seems enormously elusive. As a contemporary literary translator puts it;

> If someone asks me how I translate, I am hard put to find an answer. I can describe the physical process: I make a very rapid first draft, put it aside for a while, then go over it at a painfully slow pace, pencil – and eraser – in hand. But that is all outside. Inside the job is infinitely complex. . .[46]

Our position is simply stated: we intend to take on the task of describing this 'infinitely complex' internal process and are convinced that this can only be achieved through the reintegration of the study of translation within the human sciences – particularly psychology and linguistics – as a highly significant branch of applied linguistics.

What is involved is spelled out (by de Beaugrande) in relation to text-linguistics and applies, of necessity, to translation and we would go along with a programme of work based on the following assumptions and approaches:

> *Probabilistic* models are more adequate and realistic than *deterministic* ones. Dynamic accounts of *structure-building operations* will be more productive than static descriptions of the structures themselves. We should work to discover *regularities, strategies, motivations, preferences* and *defaults* rather than *rules* and *laws*. *Dominances* can offer more realistic classifications than can *strict categories. Acceptability* and *appropriateness* are more crucial standards for texts than *grammaticality* and *well-formedness. Human reasoning processes* are more essential to using and

conveying knowledge in texts than are *logical proofs*. It is the task of science to systematize the *fuzziness* of its objects of inquiry, not to ignore it or argue it away.[47]

In the next chapter, we shall begin the study of the process and offer an outline model which will be expanded, in the course of the book, to include the physiological mechanisms of sensation and the psychological mechanisms of perception and a model of the activities of the mind as it organizes, comprehends and stores information in memory. As we do this we realize that we shall be forced to abandon

the traditional contention of linguists that language is an isolated faculty ... [and] define language processes as *specializations* of more general process types. Syntax would then be a special case of *linear intelligence* ... semantics a special case of the *acquisition and utilization of knowledge* and pragmatics a special case of the *construction and implementation of plans and goals*.[48]

and set out into virtually uncharted territory.

Notes

1. White, 1789.
2. Kelly, 1979.
3. Tytler, 1791 ix.
4. Nida, 1964; 1966; 1974.
5. Malone (1988) and also Biguenet and Schulte (1989) whose collection of papers on the process of translation has, none the less, the title *The craft of translation*.
6. Malone, op. cit., 2.
7. Crystal (1987) is an exception but, it may be noted, the encyclopedia deals with 65 'thematic topics' of which one is 'translating and interpreting'. Translation itself merits a mere 4 pages out of a total of 412 pages of text; on a par with the discussion of 'spelling'. None the less an increase of interest in translation on the part of linguists (even at the 1 per cent level!) must be taken as a positive sign.
8. Dubois, 1973.
9. Meetham and Hudson, 1972, 713.
10. ibid.
11. Kipling, 1940, 605.
12. Halliday, 1978, 110.
13. ibid.
14. The diagram is from Hatim, 1984, 148.
15. Newmark, 1982, 113.
16. Newmark, 1976b.

17. Brislin, 1976, 79. The quotation (from I. A. Richards), refers, as Steiner (1975, 48) makes clear, to the specific problem of translating Chinese philosophical concepts into English and not to translation in general.
18. Savory, 1957, 48.
19. Newmark, 1976b.
20. Tytler, 1791.
21. Tytler, op. cit., 7.
22. Tytler, op. cit., 79.
23. Tytler, op. cit., 8f; original emphases.
24. Meetham and Hudson, 1969, 242.
25. Johnson-Laird, 1983; Smyth *et al.*, 1987.
26. Derrida, etc.: see Culler, 1983; Norris and Benjamin, 1988.
27. Steiner, 1975, 45.
28. House, 1977, 1.
29. Shannon, 1949.
30. Metham and Hudson, op. cit., 713.
31. Newmark, 1988, 21.
32. de Beaugrande, 1978, 26.
33. Bassnett-McGuire, 1980, 37.
34. ibid.
35. de Beaugrande, op. cit., 135.
36. Wilss, op. cit., 218.
37. See Bell, 1976, 42–44; Clancey, 1988, 49–68 for further discussion.
38. Richards *et al.*, 1985, 292.
39. See the discussion on idealization, generalization and the relationship of data to theory in Bell, op, cit., 197–202.
40. See Bell, 1981, 75f. on such a view in language teaching, Wilss (1983), who applies the distinction to translation theory and Bell (1990), who argues for an applied linguistic orientation towards the use of translation in foreign language teaching.
41. The quotation is from Kjolseth (1972) where it refers to the sociology of language.
42. Bell, 1985, 286; Crystal, 1981, 124; Richards *et al.*, 1985, 15; Vásquez-Ayóra, 1977, 1. It might be noted here that the sub-title of Catford, 1965 is, significantly, *an essay in applied linguistics*.
43. Steiner, op. cit., 47. The emphasis is as in the original.
44. Newmark, 1988, 285. Original asides in the text are indicated by round brackets and those we have inserted ourselves by square.
45. Jakobovits, 1970, 184f.
46. Weaver, 1989, 117f.
47. de Beaugrande and Dressler, 1981. xiv f; original emphases.
48. de Beaugrande, 1980a, 164; original emphases.

2 Translating; modelling the process

In this chapter, we present a model of the translation process which will be continually refined and explained throughout the book. The chapter is divided into three sections.

The first section is dedicated to a consideration of the *knowledge* and *skills* required by the translator; an attempt at the specification of **translator competence.** If it is, in any sense true, that 'any old fool can learn a language. . .but it takes an intelligent person to become a translator',[1] it seems important to investigate what this 'intelligence' might consist of.

The second section shifts the focus to the *process* itself and presents an integrated model of translating which draws on the linguistic and psychological knowledge we have touched upon in Chapter 1 and shall develop in subsequent chapters, in particular, the general principles of text-processing (the focus of Chapter 6). A number of models already exist[2] and the one presented here inevitably owes a substantial debt to them.

The final section is a brief essay in applying the model to the translation of a text, not in order to hold up a particular methodology as the ideal nor to suggest that our own translation is, in any sense, 'better' than any other but merely to show, in a very small-scale and practical way, that the theorizing may actually have some value as a means of focusing attention on the stages and issues involved. This is not to deny the need for 'quality control' in translation (whether operated by readers of translated texts or as part of the monitoring of the process itself by the translator) but to put the issue aside at this stage, particularly since so much has already been written on the topic.[3]

2.1 The translator: knowledge and skills

The question we wish to ask now is: 'What is it that translators need to know and be able to do in order to translate?' We are seeking, in other words, a specification of 'translator competence'.

We may begin by making the perhaps obvious point that the translator processes texts and, given that we have just spent some time outlining the knowledge and skills required in (implicitly, monolingual) text-processing, we already have a good deal of the answer to our question. The translator must, as a communicator, possess the knowledge and skills that are common to all communicators (this much by definition) but, and this is the issue in this section, in two languages (at least). What, we need to ask, does the translator's knowledge-base contain? One answer has been suggested in the following terms:

> ... the professional (technical) translator has access to five distinct kinds of knowledge; target language (TL) knowledge; text-type knowledge; source language (SL) knowledge; subject area ('real-world') knowledge; and contrastive knowledge.[4]

Add to this the decoding skills of reading and encoding skills of writing (which will be discussed in the Chapter 6, Section 6.3) and we have a plausible initial listing of (at least some of) the areas which need to be included in any specification of the translator's competence. It will be noted that this is, not surprisingly, very similar to that suggested in handbooks for translators and commonly accepted by the trainers of translators in designing their programmes and selecting and assessing their participants.[5] But before we move on to attempt to specify this competence, we need to modify the list and delimit the scope of our discussion.

To begin with, we would argue that the knowledge-base applies equally to *all* translators, professional or amateur, technical or non-technical, simply because translation is translation whoever does it (this is, of course, by no means to deny the likelihood of the professional doing a far better job) and because 'real world' knowledge is not the special preserve of the 'technical' translator but the possession of all communicators.

Further, we would question the extent to which the five kinds of knowledge are, in any useful sense, 'distinct'. On the contrary, we see substantial overlaps, particularly between TL, SL and text-type knowledge (a point which will re-emerge during the discussion of text-processing in Chapter 6). What links these, and is therefore of prime importance in any objective consideration of translation, is the all-embracing linguistic knowledge on which all else depends; precisely the topic which will occupy us throughout this book.

It seems indisputable that (as we suggested in Chapter 1, Section 1.2.1) the translator must know (a) how propositions are structured (semantic knowledge), (b) how clauses can be synthesized to carry propositional content and analysed to retrieve the content embedded in them (syntactic knowledge), and (c) how the clause can be realized as information-bearing text and the text decomposed into the clause (pragmatic knowledge).

Lack of knowledge or control in any of the three cases would mean that the translator could not translate. Without (a) and (b), even literal meaning would elude the translator. Without (c), meaning would be limited to the literal (semantic sense) carried by utterances which, though they might possess formal cohesion (being tangible realizations of clauses), would lack functional coherence and communicative value.

That, however, is only part of the specification we need. While we would re-affirm our desire not to subscribe to the notion of the 'good translation', which has dominated translation theory for two centuries, we would not allow our rejection of that position to lead us also to preclude the study of the 'good translator' as one element of 'an integrated, interdisciplinary, multimethod and multilevel approach'[6] to the description of the process.

The notion of the 'good translator' is inherent in any discussion of translation. Translator-trainers must believe in some implicit set of characteristics which typifies such an individual – their syllabuses and selection and assessment procedures require this to be the case – and an explicit statement of this assumed knowledge and skill would, if defined in operational terms ('What does the translator need to know and do in order to translate?'), constitute one particular and very valuable kind of specification of translator competence.

We have, so far, made some headway in outlining, in a relatively informal way, some of the kinds of knowledge we would expect the translator to possess and would probably accept some statement like the following as an initial definition of the task which faces us:

> Given the goal of linguistics to match the native speaker's competence, an applied linguistic theory of translation should aim at matching the bilingual native speaker's translation competence.[7]

This would necessarily involve seeking an integration between the linguistic knowledge of the two languages with specific and general knowledge of the domain and of the world via comparative and contrastive linguistic knowledge. Some attempts have been made to provide such contrastive information, for French and English,[8] and for a number of language pairs but we are still a long way from a comprehensive database and still have to resolve substantial theoretical problems before we reach such a point.[9]

We also need, before we proceed, to state the level of abstraction at which we are operating. Are we seeking to locate translator competence in (1) some 'ideal translator' or 'ideal bilingual' or (2) the actual human translator? Are we, in different terms, to work within a 'linguistique de la langue' or a 'linguistique de la parole?'.[10]

We shall consider both of these alternatives (and a third, more sociolinguistic, approach), hint at the implications each has for a definition of translation theory and for methodology, but discussing the second, the 'expert system' in rather greater detail, since we consider it to be both intellectually challenging and practically useful.

2.1.1 Ideal bilingual competence

One approach would be to focus on the competence of the 'ideal translator' or 'ideal bilingual' who would be

> an abstraction from actual bilinguals engaged in imperfectly performing tasks of translation ... but (unlike them) operating under none of the performance limitations that underlie the imperfections of actual translation.[11]

In this we would be following exactly Chomsky's view of the goals of linguistic theory and his proposals for the specification of the competence of the 'ideal speaker-hearer'[12] and would, therefore, be led to a definition of translation theory such as:

> translation theory is primarily concerned with an ideal bilingual reader-writer, who knows both languages perfectly and is unaffected by such theoretically irrelevant conditions as memory limitations, distractions, shifts of attention or interest, and errors (random or characteristic) in applying this knowledge in actual performance.

In methodological terms, such a view of the goals of translation theory would lead us to adopt a deductive rather than an inductive approach to the discovery of translator competence: introspection, by the translator, into his or her own mind in search of the knowledge (and, perhaps, the process) by means of which the product is created.

One interesting technique for tapping such knowledge might be to have translators keep diaries of their experiences and to interview them about these. Such a method of investigation is already widely used in cognitive science[13] and increasingly in applied linguistics, particularly the study of reading[14] and ought to provide a particularly revealing way of tapping the contents of the 'black box' (see Chapter 1, Section 1.3.3).

This would be to operate just as transformational generative grammarians do, as they perceive formal linguistic relationships in the mind, with all that such an approach implies.

2.1.2 Expertise

An alternative to the 'ideal translator' model would be to adopt a less abstract approach and describe translation competence in terms of generalizations based on inferences drawn from the observation of translator performance.

A study of this type suggests an inductive approach: finding features in the data of the product which suggest the existence of particular elements and systematic relations in the process.

Shorn of any kind of normative orientation, this kind of approach would not only re-establish the traditional inductive procedure of 'explaining' features of the translated text in terms of processes carried out by the translator in producing it but would also have the effect of operationalizing the otherwise merely anecdotal discussion of the 'craft' of translating.[15]

We might now, given the renewed interest in computer-assisted translation, begin to make the attempt to

> ... study... the craft of the human translator as an expert system. [Since] translators are experts [we ought to begin] studying the process of translation from this point of view.[16]

The expert system is a specialized software package which is 'intended to allow users to benefit from the knowledge of an expert human consultant. This knowledge is typically built into the system as a collection of rules, held as data, which may be updated with use'.[17]

Expert systems are used to give advice to users, to communicate knowledge contained in the database to them and to organize that knowledge in novel ways. Already a number of domains, including aspects of agriculture, banking, engineering, law and medicine possess such systems[18] so we might confidently expect applications to translation before too long. We shall outline just what systems of this kind contain and then hint at the general shape of one for translation.

An expert system contains, in essence, two basic components[19]:

1. A **knowledge base** which contains the combined knowledge and expertise of the domain (or, more likely, the sub-domain). In medicine, for example, this would include lists of illnesses together with their associated symptoms.

2. An **inference mechanism** (also known as an 'inference engine'); software which can use the knowledge base to reason or make inferences about the information contained there. In medicine this mechanism would compare symptoms reported to it with those listed in the database and match symptoms with likely illnesses.

In addition, an expert system would need (a) a *user interface* which would allow a dialogue to be held between the system and the user, (b) a *monitor* which would keep track of this dialogue (recording the sequence of questions and answers, for example) and (c) a *knowledge acquisition system* which allows the knowledge base to be up-dated. Even so, the fundamental elements remain (1) the database of knowledge and (2) the means of accessing it.

Clearly, the next task for anyone who accepts the notion of translator competence as an expert system would be to set about attempting to model it.

We would envisage a translator expert system containing the kinds of knowledge and skills we discussed in the previous chapter, i.e. minimally the following:

(1) a **knowledge base** consisting of:
  (a) *source language knowledge*; the syntactic rule systems of the code, its lexicon and semantics and its text-creating systems
  (b) *target language knowledge*; equivalent to that in the source language
  (c) *text-type knowledge*
  (d) *domain knowledge*
  (e) *contrastive knowledge* of each of the above;
(2) an **inference mechanism** which permits:
  (a) the *decoding* of texts, i.e. reading and comprehending *source language* texts
  (b) the *encoding* of texts i.e. writing *target language* texts, e.g. a writer's assistant system which helps with the writing.[20]

We are painfully aware of the vagueness of this specification and have only included it to show the direction in which the (partial) mechanization of the process of translating will need to go and because we are enthusiastic about the notion of the expert system for both practical and theoretical reasons.

From the applied perspective, the expert system provides a means of harnessing the enormous potential of information technology not only as an aid to more efficient translating but also for the investigation of the translation process and the re-assessment of the assumptions underlying translator training.

From a more theoretical standpoint, the expert system and the more general area of artificial intelligence have profound intellectual implications for the testing out of linguistic theories, particularly those which claim psychological validity.[21]

2.1.3 Communicative competence

A final alternative (only hinted at earlier) would be to deny the competence-performance dichotomy which we have been implicitly accepting and redefine our objective as the specification of a multicomponent 'communicative competence' which would consist, minimally, of

> four areas of knowledge and skills; grammatical competence, sociolinguistic competence, discourse competence and strategic competence.[22]

These four components cover essentially the same areas of knowledge suggested earlier, though with some shifts of emphasis:

1. **Grammatical competence**: knowledge of the rules of the code, including vocabulary and word-formation, pronunciation/spelling and sentence structure i.e. the knowledge and skills required to understand and express the literal meaning of utterances.
2. **Sociolinguistic competence**: knowledge of and ability to produce and understand utterances appropriately in context, i.e. as constrained by topic, the status of the participants, purposes of the interaction, etc.
3. **Discourse competence**: the ability to combine form and meaning to achieve unified spoken or written texts in different genres. This unity depends on cohesion in form (the way in which utterances are linked structurally to facilitate interpretation of text) and coherence in meaning (the relationships among the different meanings in a text; literal meanings, communicative functions or social meaning).
4. **Strategic competence**: the mastery of communication strategies which may be used to improve communication or to compensate for breakdowns (caused by limiting factors in actual communication or to insufficient competence in one or more of the other components of communicative competence).

This approach would lead us (adapting Hymes' definition of communicative competence as we did Chomsky's definition of linguistic competence) to attempt to specify 'translator communicative competence':

> the knowledge and ability possessed by the translator which permits him/her to create communicative acts – discourse – which are not only (and not necessarily) grammatical but... socially appropriate.[23]

A commitment to this position would make us assert that the translator must possess linguistic competence in both languages *and* communicative competence in both cultures, consisting of:

(1) knowledge of the rules of the code which govern usage *and* knowledge of and ability to utilize the conventions which constrain use.

(2) knowledge of the options available for the expression of all three macrofunctions of language[24] *and* knowledge of and ability to use the options available for making clauses count as *speech acts*[25] in conformity with the community ground-rules for the production and interpretation of a range of communicative acts (i.e. discourse)

in order to

> create, comprehend and use context-free TEXTS as the means of participation in context-sensitive (situated) DISCOURSE.

2.1.4 Summary

In the first chapter of this book, we made a number of assumptions about translation theory, one of which was that its traditional goals were no longer appropriate and that the time was ripe for a new statement and a shift of paradigm.

We indicated there that the ground-rules for translation theory appear to have been laid down almost exactly two hundred years ago and can be encapsulated in the title of the first chapter of what must surely have been the earliest attempt to formulate a theory of translation (we make no apology for repeating the quotation): 'Description of a good translation: general rules flowing from that description'.[26]

Our initial objection to this orientation derived, as we said, (1) from the emphasis on the description of the translation (the **product**), when we would press for descriptive effort to be concentrated, for the short term at least, on the **process** and (2) from the normative implications of 'good translation' and 'general rules'.

We would still find the definition unacceptable if it were changed merely to remove the normative – if the orientation were to the objective description of the text – since that would define an aspect of descriptive linguistics rather than translation theory.[27]

More acceptable, clearly, would be a focus on the description of the process and/or the translator. These two, so it seems to us, form the twin issues which translation theory must address: how the process takes place and what knowledge and skills the translator must possess in order to carry it out.

If we consider, as we have been in this section, the second of these – knowledge and skills – we come to a specification of translator competence. It is particularly striking that, within the context of the four-component model of communicative competence (which applies to all communicators), the translator seems to stand out as a *par excellence* example of the application of the fourth type: *strategic competence*.

What, after all, are translators doing when they struggle with the text other than coping with 'limiting factors in actual communication' (typically, ambiguities in the source text) and compensating for 'insufficient competence in one or more of the other components of communicative competence', i.e. grammatical, sociolinguistic, discourse?

What, too, is the translator-trainer doing other than attempting to reduce the areas in which the trainees are dependent on their strategic competence by extending competence in the other three and making the application of the skills derived from their strategic competence more efficient and effective?

We now have some idea of the knowledge and skills on which the translator depends in the process of translating and are ready to turn to the modelling of the process itself.

2.2 Translating; the model

This model rests on a number of assumptions about the nature of the process and the characteristics it must have if it is to explain the phenomenon of translation satisfactorily. It derives from work in psycholinguistics and in artificial intelligence on real-time natural language processing.[28]

It also represents an updated version of earlier models of the translating process itself[29] and an amalgamation of elements of other models which we shall present later; text-typologies and text-processing (Chapter 6, Figures 6.1 and 6.4 and information-processing (Chapter 7, Figures 7.1 and 7.2).

2.2.1 Components and processes

Let us begin with the assumptions; we assume that the process of translating

(1) is a special case of the more general phenomenon of **human information processing**;

(2) should be modelled in a way which reflects its position within the **psychological domain** of information processing;

(3) takes place in both **short-term** and **long-term memory** through devices for decoding text in the **source language** (SL) and encoding text into the **target language** (TL), via a non-language-specific **semantic representation**;

(4) operates at the linguistic level of **clause**, irrespective of whether the process is one of the analysis of incoming signals or the synthesis of outgoing ones (monolingual, reading and/or writing, or bilingual, i.e. translation);

(5) proceeds in both a **bottom-up** and a **top-down** manner in processing text and integrates both approaches by means of a style of operation which is both **cascaded** and **interactive**, i.e. analysis or synthesis at one stage need not be completed before the next stage is activated and revision is expected and permitted;

(6) requires there to be, for both languages

(i)   a **visual word-recognition system** and a **writing system**

(ii) a **syntactic processor** which handles the options of the MOOD system and contains a

(iii) frequent lexis store (FLS), a **lexical search mechanism** (LSM), a **frequent structure store** (FSS) and a **parser**, through which information passes to (or from) a

(iv) **semantic processor** which handles the options available in the TRANSITIVITY system and exchanges information with a

(v)   **pragmatic processor** which handles the options available in the THEME system, and there is also an

(vi) **idea organizer** which follows and organizes the progression of the speech acts in the text (and, if the text-type is not known, makes inferences on the basis of the information available) as part of the strategy for carrying out plans for attaining goals, devised and stored in the

(vii) **planner** which is concerned with creating plans for reaching goals of all kinds. Some of these plans may involve uses of language such as text-processing. This might include translating a text and this decision might well have been made even before its first clause had been processed.

We shall now take these components, expand the specification of what is involved at each stage and show how the components interact to create the dynamic process of translating. (Figure 2.1 gives an outline of the process.)

First of all, even at the risk of repeating what has just been said (in the fifth of our assumptions about the nature of the process), we should be absolutely clear about the nature of the process and the model we are using to describe it. The process is *not* a linear one in which stage follows stage in a strict order. It is an *integrated* process in which, although every stage must be passed through, the order is not fixed and back-tracking, revision and cancellation of previous decisions are the norm rather than the exception. If we keep this in mind and the fact that the process – even in outline – is somewhat complex, we can make divisions into stages and steps which will, we hope, clarify the model for us.

So, in the interests of greater clarity, we shall divide the process into **analysis** (in Section 2.2.2) and **synthesis** (in Section 2.2.3) and, within them, three distinguishable areas of operation: (1) **syntactic**, (2) **semantic** and (3) **pragmatic**, which co-occur, roughly, with the five stages which will be presented during the discussion of writing (Chapter 6, Section 6.3.2) – (1) *parsing*, (2) *expression* and (3) *development*, *ideation* and *planning*.

The intention is to work through the model, simulating the translation of a clause.

2.2.2 Analysis

2.2.2.1 Syntactic analysis
The first major stage in translating is, of necessity, reading the text. This requires there to be a visual word recognition system which can distinguish words from non-words in the source language text (SLT). We envisage processing as beginning with such recognition concentrated – as we suggested earlier – on the clause and converting the

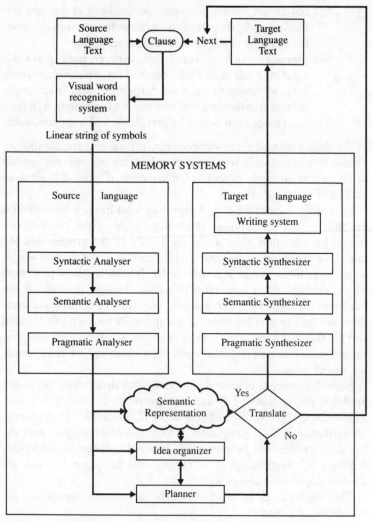

FIGURE 2.1 Translation process: outline model

physical stimuli into a 'whole' which is perceived as a linear string of discrete symbols.

This initial processing, which we envisage as being handled by mechanisms for recognizing and coding the distinctive features of the letters, and so forth (the kinds of processing we shall be describing in Chapter 7), supplies the input for the syntactic processing of the clause. We shall provide no more than a skeletal outline of what is involved here (since Chapter 4 is concerned with modelling the systems which organize meaning at the level of the clause), making use of a very simple example:

The dog bit the man.

This is taken into the syntactic processor for analysis and the clause is decomposed into syntactic structures; the clause structures available as options within the system of MOOD (see Chapter 4, Section 4.2.2).

The *default* track through the processor would be for the clause (still in the form of a string of symbols) to pass through both the *frequent lexis store* (FLS) and the *frequent structure store* (FSS) without recourse to either the *lexical search mechanism* or the *parser*.

A typical example of this would be the direct transfer of the meaning of the SL clause by means of a fixed TL clause, e.g. the first clause of the English children's story

Once upon a time there was. . .

transfers directly into Italian as

C'era una volta. . .

We should, at this point, explain the nature and function of these steps in the process. To begin with, a general point might be made about the FLS and the FSS; both have the function of relieving the **short-term memory** (STM) of unnecessary storage by allowing large amounts of data to by-pass the **parser**, in the case of structure, and the **lexical search mechanism**, in the case of lexis, and be directed immediately to the semantic level during analysis or the writing system during synthesis.

We would expect both stores to be constructed under the same kind of constraints; the notions of changing repertoires and both quantitative and qualitative differences between individuals applying in both cases (see the specification for the FSS below).

(a) *Frequent lexis store*

This is the mental (psycholinguistic) correlate of the physical *glossary* or *terminology database*, i.e. an instant 'look-up' facility for lexical items both 'words' and 'idioms'.[30]. The contents of such a store would include items of first and second order of informativity (see Chapter 5, Section 5.1.3 on this); (a) items such as *a, and, I, in, is, it, of, that, the, to, was* (which constitute some 20 per cent of the first 20,000 words in the average adult vocabulary) and (b) other frequent items such as *all, as*, *said*, *look*, *who* (i.e. a further 238 words which make up the next 40 per cent).

However, given that most linguists would accept that

> there is no very sharp line between grammar and vocabulary: the vocabulary, or lexis, is simply the open-ended and most 'delicate' aspect of the grammar of a language [and] the distinction between grammatical and lexical is really only one of degree[31]

and that a psycholinguistic model of language production (and, of necessity, translation) must contain a

(b) *Frequent structure store*

> a set of operations. . . that involves the exploitation of frequently occurring structures [which] undoubtedly are stored in memory in their entirety as is a lexical item like *dog* or *eclipse* . . .[with] direct access to phrases and sentences. . . nearly as rapid as it is for individual words.[32]

One or two points should perhaps be made here about the characteristics of the FLS and the FSS.

We imagine there to be one FLS and one FSS for each language the translator knows. It is to be expected that, for any language, the contents of the FSS will contain a majority of entries which are the shared common property of the speech community, but it is equally to be expected that each language user (even monolinguals but particularly bilinguals) will have a different configuration of items which can change over time. An analogy would be the repertoires of musicians which, even for the same instrument, differ qualitatively and quantitatively from each other and vary over time, even for the same individual.

The FSS for a user of English will consist of combinations of Subject, Predicator, Complement, Object and Adjunct which between them cover the major options available in the MOOD system of the language, i.e. the unmarked organizations of the six clause patterns (illustrated below) in their indicative – declarative and interrogative – and imperative form.

At phrase level, the FSS would also contain the major available options from the fundamental **m h q** set (see Chapter 4, Section 4.2.2 for an explanation of these symbols). We shall show the kinds of frequent structures that occur at the level of phrase later and concentrate here on the level of clause structure in the declarative mood (see Chapter 4, Section 4.2.1 for details).

Complex though English clause structure may appear, it rests on a simple foundation of six key clause types:

S P	*They ran*
S P C	*They are hungry*
S P O	*They hit Fred*
S P O O	*They gave Fred $1,000*
S P O C	*They elected Fred President*
S P O A	*They put the plates on the table*

Clearly, Adjuncts can be added to each of these – the last is unique in having an obligatory A – in almost all positions and recursively. Equally, even in the declarative, there are stylistically striking re-arrangements which are available, e.g. the passive

S P A	*Fred was hit by them*

which are striking precisely because they are *marked* (see Chapter 4, Section 4.3.2 on thematization) and are, therefore, probably not in the FSS.

The incoming string is passed initially to the FSS and then to the FLS. The ordering is important, since it is not unusual for a reader to be able to parse a clause without understanding the meanings of the words in it. Let us suppose, though, that the syntactic structure of the clause is not matched in the FSS and is passed on to the

(c) *Parser*

This has the task of analysing any clause for which analysis appears necessary. Once this has been done, the clause can continue through the process to the next step of the syntactic processing stage; accessing the FLS.

If the lexical items in the clause can be matched with items already stored in the FLS, it exits the syntactic stage and enters the semantic for further processing. This, as we pointed out earlier, is the default route; the clause – now analysed into its syntactic structure – passing through the FLS without delay. What could hold it up would be, at its most extreme, comprehension of the *structure* but not of the *content*, e.g. a text such as

the smaggly bognats grolled the fimbled ashlars for a vorit

where the SPOA clause structure (the symbols and terms used here are explained in the Appendix, Section 1 and, in detail, in Chapter 4, Section 4.2) is transparently clear as is the sequence of phrases – NP VP NP PP – and their own structure {m m h} {h} {m m h} {p c} and even the form classes of the lexical items; [d e n] [mv] [d e n] [p d n].

It is even possible to infer something about the items themselves;

bognats and *ashlars* are countable, possess the attributes of being *smaggly* and *fimbled* respectively and *bognats* are, it seems, able to *groll ashlars* either for a period of time (how long, we might wonder, is a *vorit?*) or some client (i.e. on behalf of a *vorit*). All this information derives from the reader's syntactic knowledge and, unfortunately, still does not tell us (a) what the function of all the elements is (*for a vorit*, for example) nor (b) what the words themselves mean. For that, we must turn to the

(d) *Lexical search mechanism*
This has the task of probing and attempting to 'make sense' of any lexical item which cannot be matched with items already stored in the FLS.

We are all very much aware of the frustrating 'tip-of-the-tongue' phenomenon which often afflicts the translator; the inability to 'find the right word' or, at times, *any* word at all (we shall return to this issue in Chapter 3, Section 3.1.1). The LSM provides the means of trying to make sense of an unknown word.[33] It would be possible to work through each of the lexical items in the text above but the point might be as easily made by focusing on one of them: *ashlar*.

Unless the reader knows that the dictionary definition of *ashlar* is 'a carefully finished and well-fitting building stone', the lexical item cannot pass through the FLS and must be processed by the LSM.

Faced by this difficulty, the reader can adopt one of a number of strategies: (a) attempt to assign a meaning to the item on the basis of its surrounding *co-text* (the words around it; see Chapter 3, Section 3.3.1 on this), (b) ignore the item and hope that increasing information of a *contextual* kind will provide a meaning or (c) search in memory for similar items; making use, that is, of some kind of internal *thesaurus* (see Chapter 3, Section 3.2 on this). This third approach may lead to a tentative meaning; *a hybrid tree*, i.e. a cross between an ash and a poplar. It is not too difficult to suggest an explanation for this.

No meaning can be found for the word as a whole but what appear to be its two component halves seem to be made up of a known word – *ash* – and the 'second half' of another known word: *poplar*. The fact that this is an example of faulty segmentation (carried out twice!) is not the point. It is the result which is important; a classic 'portmanteau' word: *ash* + *poplar* = *ashlar*.

In this instance, the reader finds a meaning (initially, presumably, several meanings) for *ash* but none for *lar*. However, the 'tree' meaning of *ash* leads on to a survey of the concept 'tree' and the finding of *poplar* there as an example of the concept.

At this stage, the reader has identified two types of tree but, realizing that the initial syllable of *poplar* is missing, takes the step of assuming that *lar* is some kind of abbreviation of *poplar* and so the whole word must also refer to a kind of tree.

However, such a tree might reasonably be expected to possess characteristics of both the ash and the poplar and must, therefore, be a hybrid: an ashlar.

The process (see Appendix, Section 2 for an explanation of the symbols used here) might go something like this:

1. enter item:	*ashlar*:	no entry in FLS
2. segment item:	*ashlar* = *ash* + *lar*	
3. check concept[1]:	*ash*	**isa** (example of) *tree*
		isa (example of) *dust*
check concept[2]:	*lar*	no entry in memory
4. question[1]:	x + *lar*	**isa** tree?
answer:	*pop* + *lar*	**isa** tree
question[2]:	x + *lar*	**isa** dust?
answer:		no entry in memory
conclusion;	*ash*	**isa** (example of) tree
	poplar	**isa** (example of) tree
therefore	*ashlar*	**isa** (example of) tree

Let us reiterate – without apology – that what has just been suggested is a *model* of our *theory* (our own individual way of coming to an understanding) of the kinds of question-and-answer procedures which we believe best explain what can be observed happening. There is no claim being made that this is actually what happens in the mind of the reader or translator engaged in such lexical searches; it might but we do not know.

None the less, it is clear that readers (and translators) deal with many of the stages of text-processing – both reading and writing – through established **routines**; favourite ways of tackling a particular task. These routines have to be structured (otherwise they would not work) and stored in memory in a manner which permits access to them (otherwise they could not be re-used). The cognitive scientist would suggest (as we shall in Chapter 7, Section 7.2.3) that these routines form **schemas** (or, if one prefers the Greek plural, schemata), **scripts**, and preferential **strategies**.

We imagine the FLS and FSS as themselves constituting schemas of a type which is specialized for dealing with linguistic problems. This seems to be a notion which is helpful in explaining the speed with which communicators are able to process texts and particularly welcome in the context of explaining translation.

We are now ready to move on to the next stage in the analysis: the semantic. But before doing so, it might be wise to recapitulate what has happened so far and indicate just what it is that is being 'output' by the syntactic processor.

What entered the syntactic analyser as a string of symbols now leaves it as syntactic (MOOD) structure. The information entering the semantic analyser can now be symbolized in terms of S P C A sequences with their phrase structures and their lexical fillers plus, at least provisional, lexical meanings attached to the lexical items and a tag indicating whether the items are common ones or not.

We shall display the syntactic information as a tree-diagram (see the Appendix, Section 1 for an outline of the procedure used here) running from (1) the syntagmatic chain sequence of the clause (Subject Predicator Object), through (2) the paradigmatic choices which realize each place in the chain (Noun and Verb Phrase), (3) the syntagmatic chain of the 'fillers' of the clause 'slots' (the structures of the phrases; modifier head main verb) and (4) the paradigmatic choices which realize them (determiner, noun, transitive verb) to, finally, (5) the actual words which realize the categories *determiner*, *noun*, etc.:

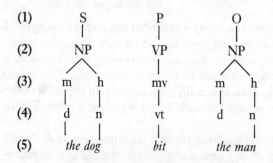

We do not wish to pre-empt what will be said in Chapter 4 but it seems useful to state here (with Halliday) that the clause is 'the product of three simultaneous semantic processes. It is at one and the same time a representation of experience, an interactive exchange, and a message'[34] and now enters the semantic analyser with information of this second kind (MOOD), i.e. that it is indicative and declarative and, in terms of its *literal meaning*, a statement. That is all. Whether it counts as a statement for either the sender or the receiver has yet to be discovered and what comes next is the analysis of the clause in terms of its *content* by the semantic analyser and its *purpose* by the pragmatic.

2.2.2.2 *Semantic analysis*

The semantic analyser has the task of 'concept recovery'[35]; retrieving the TRANSITIVITY relations which underlie the syntactic structure of the clause.

Just as the syntactic processor had the task of deriving structure from the linear string of symbols output by the visual word-recognition system, so the semantic processor serves to derive **content** from the syntactic structure supplied by the previous stage of analysis. It analyses out what the clause is about; what it represents; logical relationships between participants and processes (and also, if they are present, contextualizing circumstances; time, space, manner, etc.); ideational meaning; semantic sense; propositional content.

Let us return to our clause:

The dog bit the man.

In content terms, what must be discovered is what the process is which is being carried out (it might well be a relationship rather than a genuine action, if a different example had been chosen), who the participants are and how they relate to each other as participants in the process.

The information from the syntactic analyser was that the clause structure consisted of an SPO string. The semantic analyser recognizes an Actor Process Goal series in the proposition which underlies the clause in which the Subject is equated with Actor, Predicator with Process and Object with Goal.

In terms of purpose, it is difficult to infer much more, at this point, than the default assessment that this is a statement. We shall take this up again at the next stage.

In terms of the grammatical model we have been using, semantic analysis provides information about the TRANSITIVITY options which have been selected to structure the proposition which underlies the clause.

In speech act terms, we now have the propositional content but *not* the illocutionary force – the content but *not* the purpose – and *both* are needed before we can assign the clause to a particular speech act.

Now that we have a specification of the logical *form* underpinning the clause, we can move on to the analysis of the communicative *function* it serves.

2.2.2.3 *Pragmatic analysis*

The syntactic processor has, as we have just seen, two functions (the analysis of structure – MOOD – and the assigning of lexical meaning) and the semantic a single function (the retrieval of content; TRANSITIVITY). The pragmatic processor also has, like the syntactic, *two* tasks in relation to the information it receives from the previous stages of analysis:

(1) to isolate its *thematic structure*;
(2) to provide a *register analysis* of it.

The first is concerned with THEME (with the distribution of information and whether this is in a *marked* or *unmarked* order). The second is concerned with *register* (with *stylistic* characteristics including *purpose*), taking into account the three stylistic parameters of

(a) **tenor of discourse**: the relationship with the receiver which the sender indicates through the choices made in the text (see Chapter 5, Section 5.3.1)
(b) **mode of discourse**: the medium selected for realizing the text (see Chapter 5, Section 5.3.2)
(c) **domain of discourse**: the 'field' covered by the text; the role it is playing in the communicative activity; what the clause is *for*; what the sender *intended* to convey; its *communicative value* (see Chapter 5, Section 5.3.3).

Simultaneously, the clause is assigned:

(1) *Thematic structure* which shows that the sample clause has the structure:

The dog	*bit*	*the man*
THEME		RHEME

Since Subject, Actor and Theme are all equated, this is an *unmarked* structure (which is why it by-passed the FSS in the first place).

(2) *Register features*. We can apply the three stylistic parameters to the clause (assuming the highly unlikely circumstance that this text has appeared out of the blue and not embedded within a book on linguistics) and list our assessments. On the basis of the evidence we have:

(a) in terms of **tenor**, *formality*, *politeness* and *impersonality* are not marked (we shall ignore them in our tagging of the speech act as it goes forward, assuming the default to be the unmarked) but *accessibility* is extremely high;
(b) in terms of **mode**, there is no indication of *participation* or of *spontaneity* (we have no way of knowing how much effort it

took the writer to produce it; probably not a lot!) but *channel limitation* is high (written to be read), and the text is completely *public*;

(c) in terms of **domain**, the text is certainly *referential*, by no means *emotive*, *conative*, *phatic*, *poetic* or (unless we know where this particular clause comes from) *metalinguistic*.

The domain provides an indication of *purpose* (the *illocutionary force*) which, when combined with the existing information on content, suggests a **speech act** (in the case of the example we have been using; 'informing') and this label plus the rest of the information is passed on to the next stage for further processing.

The dog	*bit*	*the man*
Actor	Material Process	Goal

Speech act = informing

The information can now be passed on in some form like the following:

The dog bit the man

Speech act:	informing
Theme:	− marked
Tenor:	+ accessible
Mode:	− participation
	+ channel limitation
	(written to be read)
	+ public
Domain:	+ referential

On the basis of this information, the stylistic analyser can make a provisional assignment of the clause to a text-type. In this case, the analysis would throw up several possible text-types but would have to wait for further information, derived from later clauses in the same text, until a definitive assessment could be made.

A crucial question to ask would be: 'What kind of text would contain a clause like this?', i.e. a clause which is only minimally informative – it is not news the way 'the man bit the dog' would be – and is totally public and accessible but permits of no participation and operates within a limited channel: the written.

The register analysis might well, at this point, come up with a suggestion of a book or article on linguistics or philosophy; who else but linguists or philosophers would expect people to read such banal sentences? Let us suppose that that is the decision; linguistics/ philosophy. Two things now happen:

1. The information on the clause moves on with the stylistic specification given above and the tentative label 'linguistics/ philosophy book/article' to form a completely **language-free semantic representation**. This constitutes the whole of the meaning of the thought expressed in the clause *as apprehended by the reader*.
2. The analysis is fed the two remaining stages of analysis to which we now turn: the idea organizer and the planner.

It is crucially important to recognize the difference between the language-free *semantic representation* (a set of abstract, universal concepts and relationships, which represent the whole of the thought expressed in the clause) and the language-specific *clause* itself, organized through SPCA relationships selected from the MOOD systems of a particular language.

Let us list what has been analysed out from the original SL clause. The *semantic representation* of the clause now contains the following *syntactic*, *semantic* and *pragmatic information*:

1. *Clause structure*: MOOD and lexical choices including lexical meaning and where any of the lexis is uncommon, a tag to that effect.
2. *Propositional content*: TRANSITIVITY choices; the logical relations mapped onto the syntactic structure.
3. *Thematic structure*: THEME choices including indications of markedness.
4. *Register features*: *tenor*, *mode* and *domain of discourse*.
5. *Illocutionary force* (derived from *domain*) which, when combined with *propositional content*, indicates a
6. *Speech act* which the clause 'counts as'; the simplest case being where there is a one-to-one mapping between clause and speech act (a not uncommon but far from universal state of affairs).

The semantic representation is the result of the three-way analysis of the clause (and the basis of the three-way synthesis of a new clause as we translate) and if we are even to begin to understand the process of translation, we must recognize that we do not translate a clause from language A into a clause from language B. We break down the A clause into its semantic representation and use *that* as the basis for the building of an alternative clause in another language (i.e. a translation) or in the same language (i.e. a paraphrase).

A handy analogy is that of the ice-cube (SLT) which is thawed (read) and re-frozen (translated):

> During the process of translation the cube is melted. While in its liquid state, every molecule changes place; none remains in its original relationship to the others. Then begins the process of forming the work in a second language. Molecules escape, new molecules are poured in to fill the spaces, but the lines of molding and mending are virtually invisible. The work exists in the second language as a new ice-cube – different, but to all appearances the same.[36]

For most language users (particularly monolingual readers), one would expect that, once the meaning has been extracted from the clause and converted into its semantic representation, its syntactic form would be deleted from the working memory (the STM) and its meaning alone stored (in the LTM). Translators, however, knowing that they will need to be aware of thematic markedness when they come to write the TLT, have presumably to retain some of the syntactic information, if only to be able to avoid (or insist on going through) the parser at the synthesis stage.

Simultaneously, the whole analysis is fed into the **idea organizer**. This (the equivalent of the *Central Executive* of the psychological model of human information-processing which we shall introduce in Chapter 7, Section 7.1.3) has the function of (a) integrating the analysis with the developing overall layout of the text as one of a growing series as the reader works through, (b) returning from time to time to monitor the accumulating information and (c) revising some semantic representations as necessary on the basis of new information; a procedure which is well-attested by those translators who report that they read a text right through before attempting to translate any of it.

The analysis is also absorbed by the **planner** and used in any way appropriate to facilitate reaching the current goals which preceded the reading; it is at this point that decisions are made on the value of continuing to read, and so forth and, crucially important from our point of view, on whether to translate.

Up to this point, the model we have been outlining applies equally to the monolingual reader and the translator. Indeed, up to this point, the translator *is* a monolingual reader. The next decision is whether or not to translate the semantic representation. If not, the process returns immediately to the beginning to start work on the next clause.

The decision to translate takes the idea – now stored as the semantic representation of the clause – through the reverse process. We shall follow the semantic representation through as it is synthesized into a component of a target language text and use the opportunity to present (in Figure 2.2) a more explicit and detailed model.

2.2.3 Synthesis

We take up the process at the point where the SLT clause has been converted into a semantic representation (the contents of which have already been listed) and the reader has decided on the option of translating.

It is assumed that the information stored in the *semantic representation* is sufficient to suggest a text-type within which the clause might be expected to occur, in the most unlikely event that the reader does not already know what it is; for example, in a peculiar situation such as a language examination.

The construction of a text which signals all – or the selected parts of – the contents of the semantic representation begins (once again, for the sake of clarity only, imagining the process to be linear, *which it is not*) in the pragmatic processor of the *target language*.

2.2.3.1 *Pragmatic synthesis*

The TL pragmatic processor receives *all* the information available in the semantic representation and is required to cope with three key problems (and make two further decisions for each of them: to 'preserve' or 'change'):

(a) How to deal with the *purpose* of the original. The translator may wish to attempt to 'preserve' this or to alter it. Either way, a decision has to be made on how to express purpose through the available content or – assuming that the translator's plan includes a decision to shift any of the parameters (e.g. to turn an informative text into a polemical one), through different content.

(b) How to deal with the *thematic structure* of the original. 'Preservation' or alteration of the original theme–rheme relationship demands, as in the case of 'purpose' above, a decision on the part of the translator and an awareness of the options available.

(c) How to deal with the *style* of the original. Again, there is the choice between attempting to replicate on the one hand and deciding to adopt a different style on the other.

In each of the three cases, it is within the pragmatic processor that mappings of suitable purposes, thematic structures and discourse parameters of mode, tenor and domain have to be found.

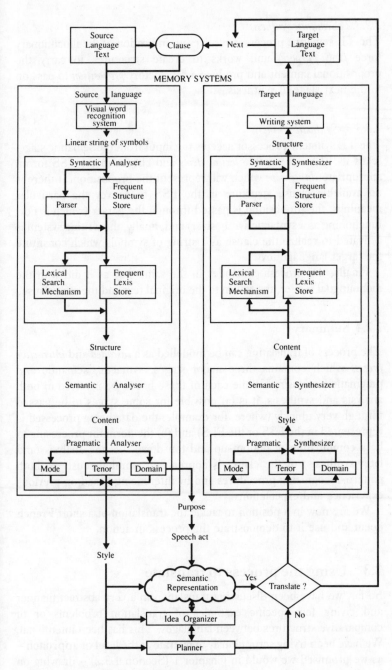

FIGURE 2.2 A model of the translation process

2.2.3.2 *Semantic synthesis*

The TL semantic processor receives an indication of the illocutionary force (the *purpose*) and works to create structures to carry the propositional content and produce a satisfactory *proposition* to pass on to the next stage of synthesis.

2.2.3.3 *Syntactic synthesis*

The TL syntactic processor accepts the input from the semantic stage, scans its FLS for suitable *lexical items* and checks in the FSS for an appropriate *clause-type* which will represent the proposition. If there is no available clause structure in the FSS to convey the particular meanings, the proposition is passed through the parser (which is now functioning as a syntactic synthesizer) and, finally, the writing system is activated to realize the clause as a string of symbols which constitute the target language text.

Finally, the process concludes in the same way as it did with the monolingual reader; the return to the original text and the next clause.

2.2.4 Summary

The process of translating can be modelled as a *cascaded* and *interactive process* which contains three major stages: syntactic, semantic and pragmatic processing. While each of these has to be involved in both analysis and synthesis, it is (a) possible for some stages to be passed through very quickly (where, for example, the data being processed is represented in the FSS or the FLS) and (b) the norm for processing to be a combination of bottom-up and top-down, i.e. the analysis (and later synthesis) of the clause is approached simultaneously by both pattern-recognizing procedures and by inferencing based on previous experience and expectations.

We are now in a position to tackle the translation of a short French poem and use it to demonstrate the process in action.

2.3   Using the process to translate

So far, we have been discussing translation in a very abstract manner and giving few specific examples of translation problems or of comparative structures between languages. This has been intentional. We have been trying scrupulously to operate at the level of **approach** – as we promised we would in Chapter 1 (Section 1.3.2) – drawing on linguistics and cognitive science to provide insights which help us in our task of attempting to make sense of translation as process rather than product and avoiding producing lists of 'translation problems' and proposals on 'how to solve them'; the very proper and necessary level of **methodology** and **technique** which can be found in readily available textbooks.[37]

Nevertheless, the validity of a theoretical model can only be tested out in actual practice and it is for this reason that we intend to bring this chapter to a close by examining a short text which we have tried to translate in terms of the model. The text is a French original and the translation is into English.

What follows is a record of the procedure used in moving from source to target language text, by one translator, in the context of decisions made about the original text and the kind of text he would select for the target language text and on one particular occasion.

The procedure is in no sense being suggested as the best or only way of tackling the text nor are the translations themselves offered as models. We intend no judgement, merely to work through the process, indicating, as we do so, what kinds of decision need to be made and what means we have at our disposal for making and realizing our decisions.

Judgements of the quality of translated texts do, of course, have to be made by translators and translator-trainers and are also made by their readers but we do not wish to become engaged, in a book which is attempting an objective description and explanation of a phenomenon, in the debate which inevitably arises over quality assessment and translation criticism.[38] This is not to suggest that, playing a different role (as translator-trainer, client or language teacher), we would be unwilling. Indeed, we firmly believe that the kind of understanding of the phenomenon which we are seeking will provide feedback which will have practical applications of this kind.

We shall approach the translation of the text *as though* the stages involved were linear and sequential. We know perfectly well that they are not and have insisted that this is the case on several occasions. None the less, we have to make sub-divisions and propose (for the sake of clarity only) three areas of focus:

(1) the *analysis* of the source language text;
(2) the organization of the semantic representations of the individual clauses of the poem into an *integrated schema* which contains the whole of the information the reader has been able to accumulate in the course of reading the text;
(3) the *synthesis* of the new target language text.

2.3.1 Analysis; reading the source language text

The text is a very short poem by Paul Valéry[39] which we wanted to translate for two particular reasons: (1) because its *content* seems to refer to a kind of behaviour in which the translator is involved – the way we search the database of our long-term memories as we try to recall information stored there (we discussed this in the previous section and will return to it in Chapter 7, Section 7.3.3) and (2) because, in *form*, it is both brief and accessible and so appears to provide a handy text on which to try out the model we have been evolving.

2.3.1.1. Text

    Je cherche un mot (dit le poète) un mot qui soit:
    féminin,
    de deux syllabes,
    contenant P ou F,
    terminé par une muette,
    et synonyme de brisure, désagrégation
    et pas savant, pas rare.
    Six conditions au moins!

2.3.1.2 Procedure

We shall deal with the text clause by clause, asking the relevant questions at each stage in the process and, as necessary, revise our interpretations and realizations.

    Je cherche un mot

Syntactic analysis: We begin by checking if the clause is in our personal internal FSS and the individual lexical items in our FLS. They are. The words are common ones, the collocations between them within the upper range of probability of occurrence (see Chapter 5, Section 5.1.3 on this) and the clause structure, too, is a very common one.

    Structure: Subject Predicator Object
    Type: indicative and declarative

There is, therefore, no need for parsing, so we can move immediately to the next stage.

Semantic analysis: There are two possibilities here, depending on whether we envisage the poet as (a) actually searching for a word in a dictionary (cf. *nachschlagen* in German) or (b) searching for a word in his own mind (cf *suchen* in German); 'word' like so many linguistic phenomena being both physical and mental entities:

> *Content* (propositional content; logical form):
> (a) Actor + Material Process + Goal
> (b) Senser + Mental Process + Phenomenon.

Pragmatic analysis: We already know that this clause comes from a poem but there is nothing particularly poetic about its form or content, so far. None the less, we can analyse it in terms of *theme*, *register* and *purpose* (illocutionary force; communicative function):

> *Theme:* unmarked
> *Register:* *tenor*; (i) accessible and (ii) unmarked in terms of other tenor features
> *mode*; written (to be read)
> *domain*; referential and, since there is the reference to the technical linguistic (and also everyday) term *mot* ('word'), metalinguistic
> *Purpose:* informative

We know, already, that this is part of a poem – it was found in a collection of poems – and have, therefore, no need to infer the text-type from the clause. Indeed, we would find it quite difficult to do so on the evidence of 'je cherche un mot' alone, except to recognize some kind of 'metalinguistic' function.

A **semantic representation** is shown in Figure 2.3.

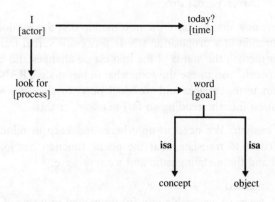

FIGURE 2.3 Semantic representation 1

In addition to what we have shown in the display, the total configuration of the semantic representation contains the speech act, stylistic and text-type information we gave above and the whole of the contents of the semantic representation is available for storage and/or translation.

We shall not take the option, at this point, of translating the clause – in reality, we might or might not do so, the opportunity is there, if we wish to take it (we shall translate in Section 2.3.3) – and will go on to the next clause:

(dit le poète)

Syntactic analysis: This three-word clause, presents us with no less than four problems: (1) we do not know if *je* and *le poète* refer to the same or different individuals, (2) unlike the first clause, this PS structure is not represented in the FSS (it looks, at first glance, like an interrogative) and therefore requires separate parsing, (3) the tense of *dit* is ambiguous (present or past; the semantic representation will require a change from *today* to *today/before* to show this), as is (4) its aspect (progressive or habitual). Parsing gives:

Structure: Predicator   Subject = Subject   Predicator
Type: indicative, declarative

and the information – the chain sequence of the clause and its phrases – is fed into the semantic analyser:

Semantic analysis: There is no ambiguity about the propositional content:

Content: Sayer Verbal Process

However, now that we have the information that this second clause is the realization of a proposition whose process is verbal rather than material or mental, the status of the first clause changes and becomes reported speech[40] or, to use the somewhat unfortunate TRANSITIVITY system term, *verbiage* and we shall need to alter the semantic representation (i.e. the reading so far) to allow for this.

Pragmatic analysis: We need to note here, and keep in mind, if and when we come to translate, that the poetic function has joined the referential and the metalinguistic and we now have:

Theme: marked
Register: *tenor:* (i) accessible and (ii) unmarked in terms of other
               tenor features

> *mode:* typical written language (written to be read)
> *domain:* referential
Purpose: informative

A revised semantic representation is called for (Figure 2.4), and, so, on to the next clause:

> *un mot qui soit: féminin, de deux syllabes, contenant P ou F, terminé par une muette, et synonyme de brisure, désagrégation et pas savant, pas rare.*

Syntactic analysis: The clause is non-finite and ought, strictly speaking, not to be in the FSS. Its length presents no problem (simple-to-process right-branching phrases) (see Appendix, Section 1 and Chapter 5, Section 5.3 on right- and left-branching structures and their implications for readability) but the parser would have to be brought into operation to recognize that the whole clause was in apposition (marked by = in the formula below) to the previous Object. The analysis would need to show that the Object of the previous clause is repeated as a noun phrase with an **m h q** structure and that the **q** is a subordinate clause with no less than six complements, some explicitly coordinated with *et* and others implicitly coordinated by sequence

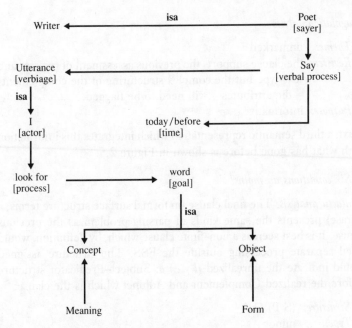

FIGURE 2.4 Semantic representation 2

alone (see Appendix on the logical sub-function of the TRANSITIV-ITY system and linkage by parataxis and hypotaxis and the symbol system used below):

Structure: [S P O = O(NP(m h q[S P C C C C &C &C]))]
Type: non-finite

This is passed on – with a note on (a) the mood of the verb (it is in the subjunctive) and (b) its modality; obligation (see Chapter 4, Section 4.2.2 on modality) – to the next stage of processing:

Semantic analysis: The clause presents no serious problems:
   Content: Carrier   Relational Process   Attributes

What is significant is the attributes and their relationship to the carrier – the *mot* which Valéry is looking for – and to each other. The range of criteria which have to be satisfied is staggering: (1) grammatical; *féminin* (2) phonological; *de deux syllables, contenant un P ou F* and *terminé par une muette* and (3) semantic criteria concerned with both usage and use; *synonyme de brisure, désagrégation* on the one hand and *pas savant, pas rare* on the other.

All this has to be passed on to the next level of analysis.

Pragmatic analysis

   Theme: unmarked
   Register: the clause supports the previous assessment of register and
               text-type but the complex structuring of the complements
               – the attributes – will need to be flagged.
   Purpose: informative

Next, a third semantic representation which integrates this information with what has gone before is shown in Figure 2.5:

   Six conditions au moins!

Syntactic analysis: The final clause (in formal surface structure terms; a phrase) presents the same kinds of parsing problem as the previous clause. It is best seen as a non-finite clause which, by definition, would need separate processing outside the FSS. The structure assigned would indicate the unrealized *il y en a*; Subject–Predicator structure before the realized Complement and Adjunct which is the clause:

Structure: (S P) C A
Type: minor

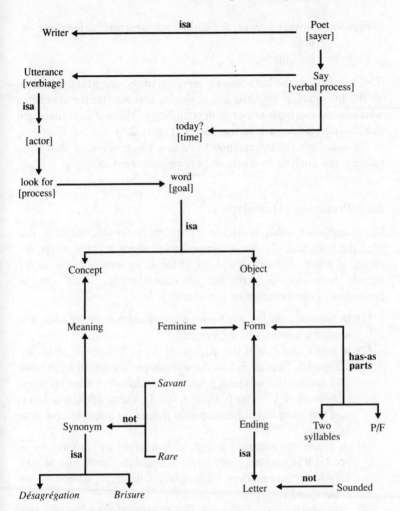

FIGURE 2.5 Semantic representation 3

Semantic analysis: This is straightforward:

   Content: Existent, i.e. 'six conditions exist'

Pragmatic analysis

   Theme: unmarked

Register: further support for earlier assessments; nothing else of
note.
Purpose: informative

This brings us to the last semantic representation; one which combines
all the information we have into a single, abstract, universal schema
which forms the basis of our understanding of the text as readers and
our transformation of it as translators (Figure 2.6).

We now have the information to reverse the process; to shift from
reading and analysis to synthesis, writing and translating.

2.3.2 Preparing to translate

Let us suppose (1) that we decide to translate (we could, of course, just
read the text) and (2) that we intend to produce a poem; there are
plenty of other alternatives and the strategic options available to the
literary translator in particular are considerable. They can be
presented as the extremes of five continua[41]:

(1) to reproduce either the *forms* (syntax and lexis) or the *ideas* (the
semantic content) of the original;

(2) to retain the *style* of the original or adopt a different style (see
Chapter 5, Section 5.3 on the stylistic parameters of *tenor, mode*
and *domain* of discourse); retain or abandon the source language
text-form (see Chapter 6, Section 6.1.3 on text-types, text-forms
and text-samples); for example, to translate a poem as a poem or
as prose;

(3) to retain the *historical stylistic dimension* of the original or to
render it in contemporary form; to translate Dante into Middle
English or into modern English (see Chapter 5, section 5.3 on
dialect and register);

(4) to produce a text which reads like an *original* or one which reads
like a *translation*;

(5) to *add* or *omit* words, phrases, clauses. . . or to attempt to
transfer everything from source to target text.

If our purpose were to promulgate commandments for the creation
of 'the perfect translation', we would commit ourselves on each of
these parameters and, possibly (but not probably), justify our decisions.
This is not our purpose nor is it the purpose of the vast majority
working in the field of translation studies; a point we made at the
beginning of the book (see Chapter 1, Section 1.1.3).

The list does give us some indication of the kind of decision-making

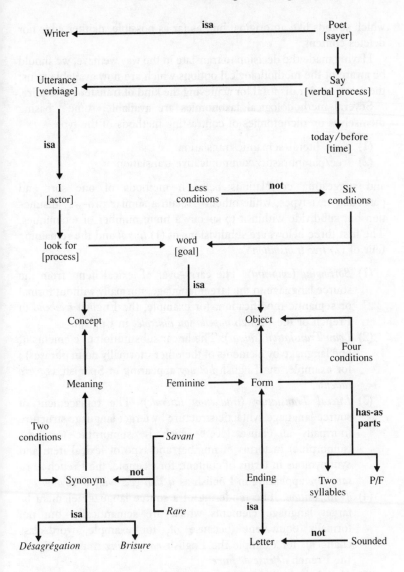

FIGURE 2.6 Semantic representation 4: overall schema

that is involved even at the beginning of the translation of a text. We shall be very cautious indeed and, on this occasion, try to be as 'faithful' as possible to our conception of the original, i.e. to reproduce its forms and meanings, its style and temporal characteristics, in a text which sounds like an original but, as far as possible, neither adds nor deletes content.

Having made the decision to translate in the way we have, we should be aware of the methodological options which are now available to us; the means at our disposal for achieving the kind of transfer we require.

Several methodological taxonomies are available, some[42] basing themselves on dichotomies of contrasting methods of the type:

(1) close/literal/semantic translation
(2) free/paraphrastic/communicative translation

and suggesting correlations between methods of one sort and particular text-types, while others[43] retain a similar two-way distinction but subdivide within it to specify a finite number of techniques. The first three below, are subdivisions of (1) *literal* and the remaining four of (2) *free translation*[44]:

(1) *Borrowing* (*emprunt*): The carry-over of lexical items from the source language to the target language, normally without formal or semantic modification; for example, the English *weekend* in French or the French *appellation contrôlée* in English.
(2) *Loan Translation* (*calque*): The linear substitution of elements of one language by elements of the other (normally noun phrases) ; for example, the English *hot dog* appearing in Spanish as *perro caliente*.
(3) *Literal Translation* (*traduction littérale*): The replacement of source language syntactic structure by target language structure (normally at clause level) which is isomorphic (or near isomorphic) in terms of number and type of lexical item and synonymous in terms of content; for example, the French *ça va sans dire* appearing in English as *it/that goes without saying*.
(4) *Transposition:* The rendering of a source language element by target language elements which are semantically, but not formally equivalent (because of, for example, word-class changes); for example the English *no smoking* transposed into the French *défense de fumer*.
(5) *Modulation:* Shifting the point of view of the speaker; for example, the French sign *complet* and the English *no vacancies*.
(6) *Equivalence:* The replacement of a stretch of source language (particularly idioms, cliches, proverbs and the like) by its functional equivalent (greeting etc); for example, English *hi* by Italian *ciao*, English *hello* (on telephone) by Italian *pronto* (literally 'ready') etc.

(7) *Adaptation:* Compensation for cultural differences between the two languages; for example, the French *santé* has a functional equivalent in the English *cheers* but none for *bon appétit*; the English equivalent is, it seems, silence!

While it is not being suggested that these techniques constitute a total answer to the problem of selecting a method or methods for translating or that the categories are watertight and unambiguous, the listing does, at least, focus our attention on the kinds of ways we can convert semantic representations into text. We shall bear them in mind as we work on our translation of the Valéry text.

2.3.3 Synthesis; writing the target language text

We begin to translate with the full resources of the semantic representations of the clauses available and with the unity of the text organized as a schema ready in memory. This schema will be similar to the one we shall be suggesting for an event in Chapter 7 (Figure 7.5). Let us recap what we have:

(1) The schema (Figure 2.6) in which all the propositional relationships are displayed and interconnected.
(2) A listing of significant text-type and stylistic information about each clause and about the text as a whole. For example, we now know that every clause is indicative and declarative in terms of its MOOD and that each is essentially informative – with a steady increase in the metalinguistic and poetic as the text develops – in terms of function and this provides us with a default path through the process; issues which do not need to be resolved and, therefore, do not take our attention away from crucial decision points.

Our decision was to try to replicate as much of the form and content of the original as possible.

The pragmatic synthesizer is accessed and the non-semantic information matched there, i.e. we have to find an equivalent text-form in the target language which meets the same speech act, thematic and stylistic criteria as the original.

Next, the configuration is converted by the semantic synthesizer into a semantic structure; a speech act with the same propositional content and illocutionary force (purpose) as the original. At this point, there are two residual problems; the lack of both tense and aspect marking in the French original and the uncertainty over the status of the process, material or mental:

1. The time reference in the French text was unmarked for both tense and aspect, i.e. it is unclear as to whether it is present or past tense and there is no indication whether the process is a habitual one or a progressive one. In some languages a single form can have even more time referents. Consider the first lines of the following brief Pushkin poem, where *liubil* has six possible translations into English:

> *Ya vas liubil; liubov yeshcho bit možet*
> *V dushe moyei ugasla ne sovsem*

The semantic sense of this is any one of the following:

$$
I \left\{ \begin{array}{l} \left\{ \begin{array}{l} \text{did} \\ \text{used to} \end{array} \right\} \quad \text{love} \\ \text{(have)} \quad \text{loved} \\ \left\{ \begin{array}{l} \text{was} \\ \text{have been} \end{array} \right\} \quad \text{loving} \end{array} \right\} \text{you;}
$$

$$
\text{(the) love} \left\{ \begin{array}{l} \text{yet} \\ \text{still} \end{array} \right\} \text{perhaps in my soul has not}
$$

$$
\text{yet} \left\{ \begin{array}{l} \text{cooled} \\ \text{gone out} \\ \text{died away} \end{array} \right\} \text{totally}
$$

For *cherche*, the English options are limited (we are relieved to say) to two: *I am/was looking for* or *I look(ed) for* but we are obliged to select one or the other and, whichever we do choose, thereby suppress the other meaning which was present in the original. On balance, we tend towards the first (and in the present) rather than the second but that is, of necessity, a personal reading without any particular general value as a model. What is crucial is the ability to recognize the alternatives that are available in the original, the choices that can be found in the target language and the realization that choices foreclose others.

2. It may be necessary to decide, one way or the other, whether we

are concerned with a material or a mental process. In some languages (e.g. German), the polyvalence (the multiple meaning) expressed by *cherche* could not be retained if the language possessed two verbs; one for looking for something *concrete* and the other for looking for something *abstract*. Fortunately, in English *look for* can serve both purposes.

The syntactic synthesizer accepts both propositions:

Actor   Material Process   Goal
Senser   Mental Process   Phenomenon

and, since there is an available structure in the FSS, by-passes the parser and outputs:

S   P   O
I   am looking for   a word

into the writing system and we move on to the next representation.

This is recalled from the semantic representation, complete with a tag 'marked theme' which the stylistic synthesizer passes on through the semantic synthesizer (which retrieves the propositional content), to the syntactic synthesizer with the requirement that it should be suitably marked stylistically. The parser (not the FSS, since we agreed, at the analysis stage, that the marked order was not stored there) builds a suitable English structure equivalent to the French original which happens to be syntactically identical:

P .   S
says/said   the poet

and is passed on to the writing system.

The next representation is not problematic as far as the pragmatic and semantic stages of synthesis are concerned. What is difficult is the selection of the verb form to carry the modality and, particularly difficult, the lexical items.

The FSS is now accessed to see if there is a structure available to express *necessity* + *existence*; there are several to choose from:

must/should/has to/ought to/needs to + *be*

We have a final clause to process (*Six conditions au moins!*) and merge with the previous semantic representation. There are no stylistic or semantic problems with the clause; the syntactic structure will be mapped onto the semantic by the parser and the remaining decisions will be lexical.

This gives us the overall schema for the poem and a complete semantic representation.

Lexical items which realize the attributes of the *mot* have now to be found in the internal lexicon:

féminin: *feminine*; but the notion is one which applies to languages which have grammatical gender and is therefore a metalinguistic term. There is, nevertheless, no alternative that we can think of.

syllabes: *syllables*; also a metalinguistic term but more common than *feminine*.

P ou F: *P or F*; also a metalinguistic term but one known to any user of English who knows the alphabet.

muette: *dumb* (literally) but, in this context, clearly, again a metalinguistic term; a written letter which is not pronounced, e.g. in *muette* itself: /mμet/ the orthographic 'e' is not pronounced in the citation form (as found in a dictionary) of the word. Among the possibilities are *silent/unsounded/unpronounced letter*. As before, in the case of *soit*, phonological considerations might well carry the day; let us hold a decision on this until more of the text is complete.

synonyme: *synonymous*; adjective from another metalinguistic term for which there appears to be no plausible single item alternative; we could try the longer *with the same meaning as* of course.

brisure: *break* or *crack*; derived from *briser* which has not only physical but medical and emotional connotations, e.g. to break rocks/heads/hearts.

désagrégation: *disaggregation, weathering* (of stone), *breaking up, dissociation*.

savant: *learned, scholarly, erudite*.

rare: *rare, unusual, exceptional*.

conditions: *conditions, requirements, requisites, essentials*.

We can, on this basis, produce a tentative translation of the whole text:

Draft translation

I $\left\{\begin{array}{l}\text{'m}\\ \text{am}\\ \text{was}\end{array}\right\}$ I looking for a word ($\left\{\begin{array}{l}\text{says}\\ \text{said}\end{array}\right\}$ the poet) a word which $\left\{\begin{array}{l}\text{must}\\ \text{should}\\ \text{ought to}\\ \text{has to}\\ \text{needs to}\end{array}\right\}$ be:

feminine

$\left\{\begin{array}{l}\text{of}\\ \text{with}\end{array}\right\}$ two syllables, containing P or F,

$$\text{ending} \begin{Bmatrix} \text{with} \\ \text{in} \end{Bmatrix} \begin{Bmatrix} \text{a silent} \\ \text{an unsounded} \end{Bmatrix} \text{letter}$$

$$\text{and synonymous with} \begin{Bmatrix} \text{crack} \\ \text{break} \end{Bmatrix} \text{or} \begin{Bmatrix} \text{disaggregation} \\ \text{weathering} \\ \text{breaking up} \\ \text{dissociation} \end{Bmatrix}$$

What we now have is the kind of display that might be expected from a computer-assisted translation package. The ground has been broken for us but there still remain a good many, crucially important, decisions for us to make; on sound patterns – whether we wish to replicate parallelisms for example – on layout and so forth, even after we have made a selection from the available lexical items. We do not intend to make these final decisions. We have decided (to use de Beaugrande's terminology) that this is, for us, a *threshold of termination* and are, therefore, about to stop.[45]

2.3.4 Summary

We have attempted (and were possibly foolhardy to do so) in this section to put our theorizing into practice by translating a short poem, not because it was a poem but because it was short and seemed good fun! What emerged can hardly be hailed as a literary masterpiece; we did, after all, stop before making most of the decisions where there were still options available. This was intentional; the whole object of the exercise was to show what questions needed to be asked and at what points. It was never our intention (though the temptation was, at times, almost irresistible) to provide final answers to those questions.

The next stage would be stylistic and, given the kind of text we have been dealing with, literary and the decisions we would reach would depend very much on personal taste. In any case, the translation can never really be finished. Even as one 'completes' the 'final' version one hears the tiny insistent voice saying: 'Hang on a minute; I've got a great idea!'[46]

2.4   Conclusion

This chapter has provided a model of the translation process and it is the modelling of that process which we believe to be the goal which translation theory should now set itself as, indeed, we have.

We have tackled three particular issues in this chapter: (1) the specification of *translator competence* (the knowledge and skills required by the translator in order to be capable of translating); (2) the presentation of a *psycholinguistic model* of the process (a model which draws its inspiration from recent work in cognitive science, text-processing and Systemic linguistics; all areas of knowledge which will be the subject of considerable discussion in later chapters); and (3) the *application* of the model to the monitoring of an actual translation; a brief poem by Paul Valéry.

It must, however, be clear that the model and its application depend on insights from linguistics and cognitive science which have, so far, only been hinted at. We shall therefore be spending the rest of the book in providing this intellectual underpinning for the model. We shall have to be, for example, far more explicit about at least five major topics:

(a) 'meaning' (word- and sentence-meaning);

(b) the grammatical structures (the logical, grammatical and rhetorical systems of code options) which organize meaning and on which the communicator draws in producing and comprehending language;

(c) textual and discoursal structure (including the nature of 'text', the components and rules governing speech acts and the parameters of stylistic variation in discourse);

(d) the knowledge and skills involved in processing texts (the recognition of text-types – or genres – and the skills of reading and writing); and, finally,

(e) the ways human beings process information (gather, store and recall it for use).

It is the purpose of the remainder of the book to be explicit about these topics and to show how they are relevant to both the practical concerns of the working translator and also to the more theoretical interests of the applied linguist.

Notes

1. Newmark, 1969, 85.
2. Kuić, 1970; de Beaugrande, 1980; Delisle, 1980; Bly, 1984; Weaver, 1989.
3. House, 1977a, 1977b.
4. Johnson and Whitelock, 1987, 137.
5. Congrat-Butlar, 1979, 45–9.

6. Kjolseth, 1972.
7. Raskin, 1987, 57.
8. For example, Delisle, op. cit., 244–6.
9. James, 1980.
10. Wilss, 1982, 13.
11. Katz, 1978, 228.
12. Chomsky, 1965, 3.
13. Gick and Holyoak, 1987.
14. Harri-Augustein and Thomas, 1984; Faerch and Kasper, 1987.
15. Newmark, 1982, 113.
16. Nirenburg, S., 1987, 10f.
17. British Computer Society, 1988, 2.
18. Holt, 1987, 89.
19. French, 1986, 415f; Holt, ibid.
20. Sharples and O'Malley, 1988, 276–90.
21. Carbonell and Masaru, 1987; Johnson and Whitelock, op. cit. The final chapter of this book deals with the modelling of the psychological mechanisms of human information processing; (a) the nature and structure of the *knowledge-base* and (b) the *addressing systems* which give access to it.
22. Swain, 1985, 37. The list below derives from the same source.
23. Hymes, 1971, 23.
24. Halliday, 1985, 37ff. These macrofunctions are the focus of Chapter 4.
25. Searle, 1969. Chapter 5 (Section 5.2) deals with speech acts and the cooperative principle on which communication depends.
26. Tytler, 1791.
27. See Cluysenaar, 1976, 16, who makes the same point in relation to stylistics
28. Harris and Coultheart, 1986; Nirenburg, 1987; Sperber and Wilson, 1986; Steinberg, 1982.
29. Bell, 1987, 1988a.
30. Crystal, 1980, 208f; Richards *et al.*, op. cit., 164f.
31. Halliday and Hasan, 1976, 281 and 6. We might also note (if we are surprised to find lexis here rather than under semantics) that Swain's *grammatical* competence includes 'vocabulary and word-formation' as part of the 'rules of the code'.
32. Steinberg, 1982, 122f.
33. Nation and Coady 1988 provide a valuable model of the 'guessing' process which corresponds well with what is presented here; a model based on the 'readings' and 'explanations' derived from an unpublished exercise carried out with undergraduate translation students at the Polytechnic of Central London. The whole issue of recall from memory is taken up again in a more general way in Chapter 7, Section 7.3.3.
34. Halliday, 1985, 53.
35. de Beaugrande and Dressler, op. cit., 43.

36. Sayers Peden, 1989, 13.
37. Darbelnet and Vinay, op. cit.; Newmark, op. cit.
38. House, op. cit.; Newmark, op. cit.
39. *Autres Rhumbs*, 1934.
40. See Leech and Short, 1981b, 318–36 on the representation of speech.
41. Savory, 1957, 48f.
42. Nida and Taber, 1974; Newmark, 1988.
43. Darbelnet and Vinay, op. cit., 47–55.
44. The definitions are, for the most part, based on Wilss, 1982, 97–9.
45. In any case, we think we have found *le mot* and, quite possibly, three: *rupture* and *fracture* both seem to fit all the poet's requirements. So does *faille*, if we read the *muette* as a schwa and have it count as a second syllable; in which case, we cannot (of course) translate *muette* as 'unsounded letter'.
46. Michael Caine's famous closing words in the film *The Italian Job*.

Part 2: MEANING

Part 2 of this book is concerned with 'meaning', since it is 'meaning' which is

> the kingpin of translation studies. Without understanding what the text to be translated means for the L2 users the translator would be hopelessly lost. This is why the translation scholar has to be a semanticist over and above everything else. But by semanticist we mean a semanticist of the text, not just of words, structures and sentences. The key concept for the semantics of translation is *textual meaning.*[1]

It is for this reason that the three chapters of Part 2, which constitute almost half of the book, are central – in both the physical and the intellectual sense – to the goal of this book. In them our attention shifts from the psychological concerns of modelling the process to the more clearly linguistic as we tackle the key issue of meaning:

(1) in terms of **semantic sense**; the domain of traditional semantics at the level of the word and the sentence (in Chapter 3) and in relation to propositional and clause structure (in Chapter 4) and

(2) as **social** or **communicative value**; the domain of pragmatics in relation to the text and discourse (in Chapter 5).

Specifically, Chapter 3 deals with what might be termed 'the naive translator's view of meaning' (word- and sentence-meaning) and is divided into three sections which discuss, in order:

(1) three approaches to the study of **word-meaning** (reference theory, componential analysis and meaning postulates);

(2) the notion of the **thesaurus** (which leads to a consideration of the distinction between denotative and connotative meaning), semantic and lexical fields and an examination of the attempt to

measure connotative meaning by means of the semantic differential; and

(3) **sentence-meaning** in relation to such notions as 'truth', contradiction, ambiguity, anomaly, entailment, implicature and presupposition, the crucial distinction between utterance, sentence and proposition and, finally, the framework for setting communication in the 'real world'; situation and context of utterance and the universe of discourse.

In Chapter 4 we take the study of meaning forward by proposing a model of language which distinguishes three major types of meaning – cognitive, interactional and discoursal – made available to the communicator through a range of **networks** and **systems** of **options**.[2]

The description is, thus, extended by focusing on the **clause** in three ways: (1) as **representation** (organized by the *ideational* macrofunction of language); (2) as **exchange** (organized by the *interpersonal* macrofunction); and (3) as **message** (organized by the *textual* macrofunction).

This expands the notion of semantic sense considerably and in three ways: (1) by moving from word level and a narrow view of what is involved at sentence level to address the issue of the structure of the **proposition** in terms of logical relations within it – actor, process, goal and circumstances; (2) by focusing on the syntactic structure of the **clause** in terms of chain and choice and structures in the chain such as subject, predicator, complement and adjunct; and (3) by investigating the **utterance** in terms of both its information structure – theme–rheme (marked and unmarked) – and its cohesive linkages.

In Chapter 5 we finally abandon the convenient fiction which coloured discussion in Chapters 3 and 4 (i.e. that the semantic sense of words and sentences can be studied in the abstract and without reference to the context of their use), to further our approach to the study of meaning by turning our attention to the investigation of **text** and **discourse**, through discussions of (a) *standards of textuality*, (b) the realization of discoursal function through *speech acts*, (c) the notion of regulative *principles of cooperation* which operate between communicators and, finally, (d) the formal structure and communicative functions of texts in terms of *stylistic parameters*; tenor, mode and domain of discourse.

In short, Part 2 moves in its consideration of 'meaning' from rather traditional notions of word- and sentence-meaning, to a more specific focus on meaning in the proposition, the sentence (or clause) and the utterance respectively and, finally, an outline of the pragmatic aspects of language in use; speech acts and text- and discourse-structure.

Notes

1. Neubert, 1984, 57; original emphasis.
2. Halliday, 1985.

3   Word- and sentence-meaning

The translator (and the second language learner) may begin by believing that the major problem is the word; it may be that there are words in the text which are new to the translator and whose meanings he or she does not know. However, it soon becomes clear that, although the meanings of words are problematic in themselves (there is no one-to-one correspondence between the items of one language and those of another), the greater problem is meaning which derives from the relationship of word to word rather than that which relates to the word in isolation.

Any act of communication (words organized into sentences and realized as utterances spoken or written) is an event created by participants (speakers, writers, hearers, readers), set in time and space and, in an absolute sense, unique and unrepeatable. None the less, speech communities operate on the assumption that situations recur and that particular selections from the language can be used again and again to refer to those situations (i.e. there are language-oriented schemas), e.g. the English word *cat* can be consistently used to refer to the domesticated mammal *felix felix*. However, the fact that we have mentioned speech communities and an individual language indicates how culture-specific such assumptions and usages are and how essential it is for the translator to understand not only the obvious semantic **sense** of a stretch of language but also its communicative **value**.

Indeed, even the 'context-free' dictionary definition of the meaning of a word actually rests on an implicit assumption of some kind of setting of use as part of a text; a text without a context runs the danger of having supernatural attributes assigned to it (that is what happens in one science fiction story, where an ancient shopping list becomes a sacred scripture!).

That said and recognizing that there are, in fact, issues to be raised about the meaning of lexical items and sentences, we shall consider some alternative approaches to word-meaning and sentence-meaning and close by distinguishing utterance, sentence and proposition; a distinction on which the next chapter (Chapter 4; logic, grammar and rhetoric) depends.

In terms of the model of translation we proposed in the previous chapter, we shall be concerned, initially, with the **syntactic** area of operation i.e. with the components of the **syntactic processor** as it 'makes sense' of lexical items (see 2.2.2 and 7.2.2).

3.1   Word-meaning: three approaches

Among the possible ways of approaching the description and explanation of word-meaning (we shall come to sentence-meaning later in this chapter), three stand out as particularly interesting: (1) *reference theory* (which would express the relationship between word and entity in some terms such as 'word X refers to entity Y'); (2) *componential analysis* (which would make use of an analogy from chemistry – 'each word contains a number of atoms of meaning'); and (3) *meaning postulates* (which would relate meaning to meaning through the conventions of set theory – 'a tiger **isa** mammal, **isa** animal', i.e. 'a tiger is a kind of mammal and a mammal is a kind of animal' or 'animal includes mammal, includes tiger': [[[tiger] mammal] animal]. We shall look at each of these approaches in turn.

3.1.1   Reference theory

Reference theory seeks to provide the answer to the question: 'What is the relationship between the phenomena observed through the senses and the words that are used to refer to those phenomena?' There are two traditional and contrary answers to the question which go back to Ancient Greece: (a) the link between the word and the 'object' to which it refers is a natural and necessary one which is determined by the structure of the universe (Plato's position) or (b) the connection is an arbitrary one constrained by no more than social convention (Aristotle's position).

It is, unfortunately, clear that the first (naturalist) position cannot be correct, in spite of the attested existence of such (English) onomatopoeic words as *cuckoo*, *hoot*, *thud*, *tinkle* and so forth, where the word 'imitates' the sound. There is, clearly, no simple one-to-one relationship of word to meaning to object.

Such examples of 'sound symbolism' are extremely rare and the overwhelming majority of words in any language demonstrate no recognizable relationship whatsoever with the 'object' to which they refer. Hence, the conventionalist would argue, the connection between the linguistic form of the word and its referent is clearly man-made rather than natural and constitutes a convenient system for labelling 'objects' by means of arbitrarily assigned and socially accepted signs.

Modern linguistics during the last hundred years has taken as its starting point in any discussion of meaning the conventionalist acceptance of the need for the relationship between word and 'object' to be an indirect one mediated by a concept (an assumption which underlies our discussion of the structure of the database of the long-term memory in Chapter 7, Section 7.2).

Building on this assumption, de Saussure[1] provides a rather more explicit model of the relationship in which the link is shown to be between the *linguistic sign* and the 'object'. The relative sophistication of de Saussure's model is that it sees the linguistic sign itself as being composed of two indivisible elements, the *concept* and the *acoustic image*, which realizes it. This might be shown diagrammatically:

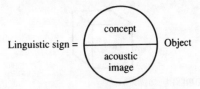

Linguistic sign = concept / acoustic image   Object

An example of this, for English, might be the relationship between the word 'tree' and the actual tree perceived by the senses which is referred to by using the word. We shall use single quotes for the word, SMALL UPPER CASE for the concept and a phonemic transcription for the acoustic image:

'Tree' = TREE / /tri:/

The value of this for us is that it suggests ways in which we can integrate linguistic models of the semantic and lexical structures of languages with psychological models of the conceptual structure of memory (see Chapter 7) and thus show parallels between the formal structures of languages and the psychological processes of perception and memory.

All very well, one might say, but what of the translator? Does the translator store the same information in different parts of memory depending on the language? If so, it seems strikingly inefficient to have the same concept represented again and again merely because its linguistic realizations are different. If not, what happens to the indivisibility of the sign on which de Saussure was so insistent? Not only does this appear to be a substantial problem in relation to translation and to bilingualism but also, though to a lesser extent, in monolingual usage where lexical 'synonyms' occur.

The problem, we would suggest, is a pseudo-problem[2] and is, to a very large degree, no more than an artifact of the modelling we are engaged in. We suspect that the 'problem' derives from the difficulty of visualizing a three-dimensional object on a two-dimensional piece of paper! In short, we now see the sign in the bilingual mind as a polyhedron with the concept *inside* it and, on each of the faces, an appropriate realization in one of the languages (see Figures 3.1 and 3.2 in which the linguistic sign for the concept 'tree' is used as an example with six languages involved; English, Finnish, French, German, Italian and Russian).

FIGURE 3.1 The concept

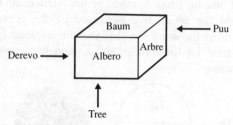

FIGURE 3.2 The linguistic sign

One advantage which this model has over the traditional two-dimensional one is that it helps to explain a phenomenon which translators find particularly annoying and frustrating; being not only unable to recall the appropriate word in a particular language but finding oneself incapable of recalling an appropriate word in *any* language. The polyhedron has, as it were, rotated so as to present us, not with a face, but with an edge and has 'stuck' like that and what we tend to say, interestingly enough, is 'I can't quite *see* it'. How extraordinary that de Saussure should have talked of an acoustic *image*! The way out of this is to imagine the use of some kind of coding in memory which allows us to 'call up' the container of the concept and, with the addition of an extra digit or two which would 'rotate' the sign so as to show the correct face to the scanning device, resolve the 'tip-of-the-tongue' difficulty we found ourselves in.

The model, which is no more than that and contains no more complex or far-fetched an idea than that of international direct dialling (IDD), gives us some interesting clues about the way the translator (or the bilingual) recalls information from different languages from memory.

However, when we compare de Saussure's sign with the models of mental representation currently being developed by cognitive scientists, it does seem to lack much of the information both at the level of the 'concept' and the 'acoustic image' that we expect and need. We require, under 'concept', the kind of information provided by the encyclopedic entry and much fuller lexical information under 'acoustic image' (these issues are taken up again in Chapter 7).

It is precisely in order to supply this information that we need now to turn to the second of our two approaches to the description and explanation of meaning: componential analysis.

3.1.2 Componential analysis

The task of 'making sense' of chaotic and continuous sensory data requires (as we shall see in Chapter 7) processes of pattern recognition and, most importantly, the segmentation of the data into discrete, codable elements. This is as true of 'making sense' of language as it is of analysing chemical substances. For example, for the chemist, *water* and *hydrogen peroxide* share the common components H and O (hydrogen and oxygen) but differ in the amount of oxygen they contain; H_2O as against H_2O_2, i.e. the 'meaning' of each depends on the components they possess and the way those components are organized.

A very similar 'atomic' and 'molecular' approach to the description of word-meaning was developed in the 1950s by anthropologists working on, among other topics, kinship systems[3] and soon extended to other systems – colour categories, plant taxonomies, diseases, etc. – and to semantics as a whole. As a *theory* which sought to isolate *universal* semantic features (features which would apply in any language) componential analysis has been a disappointment. But as a *technique* for describing at least part of the semantic system of particular languages, it is still worth considering particularly as a means of gaining insights into the similarities and differences between languages; insights which cannot but be of value to the translator and the language learner. It is in this spirit, viewing componential analysis as a technique rather than theory, that we shall outline it below.

The essential assumption of componential analysis is that the meaning of a word is the sum of a number of elements of meaning which it possesses – semantic **distinctive features** – and that these elements are **binary**; i.e. marked as present or absent (+ or −).

We might take, as an example, a set of English words such as *man*, *woman*, *boy*, *girl* and show how a componential analysis can be used to specify the **lexical entry** for each, limited (for the time being) to semantic features which create dictionary-like listings.

First of all, it is clear that the four words (or, more correctly, the four concepts they realize) do, indeed, form a set of items. They share the characteristic or feature **human**. *Man* and *woman* share the feature **adult** and *man* shares with *boy* the feature **male**. For this set, these three features are sufficient to create definitions for each which distinguish them unambiguously: *man* = 'human, adult, male', etc. The lexical entries would be:

$$man \quad \begin{bmatrix} + \text{ human} \\ + \text{ adult} \\ + \text{ male} \end{bmatrix}$$

$$woman \quad \begin{bmatrix} + \text{ human} \\ + \text{ adult} \\ - \text{ male} \end{bmatrix}$$

$$boy \quad \begin{bmatrix} + \text{ human} \\ - \text{ adult} \\ + \text{ male} \end{bmatrix}$$

$$girl \quad \begin{bmatrix} + \text{ human} \\ - \text{ adult} \\ - \text{ male} \end{bmatrix}$$

However, a fuller entry for the item would include: (a) its *pronunciation* (and, if the language has an orthography, its written form as well); (b) *syntactic information* – the form class to which it belongs (noun, verb, etc.), whether it is countable if it is a noun or transitive if it is a verb, etc.; (c) any significant *morphological information*, e.g. if it has any 'irregular' forms; and (d) its *semantic sense*; a specification of its conceptual content. Filled out in this way, each entry would include both elements of de Saussure's linguistic sign – acoustic image and concept – and, in addition, syntactic information which would be essential if the word were to be involved in the creation of sentences and used for communication.

Modified in this way, the entry for *man* might be as follows:

$$
man \begin{bmatrix} \text{/mæn/} \\ \text{'man'} \\ \text{noun} \\ + \text{ count} \\ \text{plural} = \text{/men/} \\ + \text{ human} \\ + \text{ adult} \\ + \text{ male} \end{bmatrix}
$$

How much phonological and syntactic information should be included in each lexical entry? In psychological terms, if the database is to provide enough information for the production and comprehension of grammatical sentences, each conceptual address will have to provide adequate information on the pronunciation, grammatical features and meaning of the item stored there. What, though, is 'adequate'? Part of the answer to this lies in the structure of the language in question.

In the first case (pronunciation), supra-segmental information will need to be included in addition to segmental (i.e. vowels and consonants) in languages where (1) word stress is variable in polysyllabic words (e.g. English /'permit/ [noun] versus /per'mit/ or Italian /'porto/ *I carry* [present tense] versus /por'to/ *I carried* [past tense]) or (2) where lexical items are distinguished by tone as in Chinese, e.g. /lan/ with a high rising tone *blue* versus /lan/ with a low fall-rise; *lazy*.

In the second (grammatical class), a number of distinctions would have to be included such as (1) abstract versus concrete, countable versus non-countable, gradeable versus non-gradeable for English, as would (2) grammatical gender for languages such as French and German and (3) morphological information for agglutinative or flexional languages such as Turkish and Arabic respectively.

In the third (meaning), it is not only denotative but also connotative meaning that needs to be stored, presumably as part of the individual's encyclopedic knowledge and mainly in the conceptual memory (the distinction is made between conceptual and episodic memory in Chapter 7, Section 7.3.1). Suffice it to say that somewhere and somehow in long-term memory there must be a system which allows lexical items to interact with each other, with the grammatical resources of the language and with encyclopedic knowledge, otherwise, the communicator would have no means of producing or understanding grammatical sentences or appropriate utterances and we all, clearly, do both on a vast scale.

From the translator's point of view, componential analysis has considerable attractions as a practical technique even if, as we shall show below, it suffers from a number of defects as a theory.

Consider the problem of lack of fit between the lexical items of two languages; an issue which continually faces the translator.[4] Take the difficulty of translating the German noun *Uhr*. Without help from the context, the translator cannot know whether the appropriate English equivalent is *watch* or *clock* or, even, *hour* or *time* (*die Uhr ist. . .* = 'The time is. . .'). Further, if the translation is into French, terms for no less than three kinds of time-keeping devices are available – *montre* (watch), *horloge* and *pendule* (both of which are equivalent to 'clock') – plus the translation *heure*, as in *quelle heure est-il?* ('what time is it?'). Clearly, the lexical entry for *Uhr* does not contain 'size' as a significant component as it must in English to distinguish *watch* from *clock* and in French to distinguish *horloge* from *pendule*.

There are two major problems with componential analysis, both of which reduce its usefulness: (1) that the 'features' proposed for the analysis of any item are arbitrary – not, in itself, necessarily a problem – and, hence, what may be criterial for one user may turn out to be trivial or secondary for another and (2) the binary nature of the features (possession or non-possession). This limits the application of the analysis to items which are clearly distinguishable in such terms and makes it difficult to create satisfactory lexical entries for several categories of item. Those which:

(1) belong to *multiple* rather than binary *taxonomies* – metals, for example: gold, silver, tin, copper, lead, zinc. . .;
(2) are in *hierachical relationships* with each other – measuring scales, for example: inch, foot, yard. . .;
(3) *overlap* – house, home, dwelling-place or share and divide;
(4) relate to each other by reference to some *assumed norm* – short and tall or hot and cold.

For the translator, each of these is (potentially, at least) significant. Do users of both languages, for example, categorize the same metals as 'precious'? How do they perceive units of measurement – time, space, volume, weight, etc. – or distinguish, for example, *house* from *home*?

What norms do they use; is 1.5 metres tall or short? is 25C hot, warm, cool or cold?

A partial resolution of these problems can be found in the notions of the semantic or lexical field and collocation between items (both the subject of Section 3.2.1. of this chapter) and in the third of the approaches to meaning: meaning postulates.

3.1.3 Meaning postulates

A fundamental problem for the translator is that the relationships of similarity and difference between concepts (and the words that express them) do not necessarily coincide in the languages involved in the translation. However, it is not difficult to express such relationships for a particular language in terms of simple set theory and the key notions of **inclusion** and **exclusion**; the first focusing on what concepts have in common; the second on what distinguishes them.

We can isolate three key types of relationship between concept and concept (and, therefore, between word and word).

At one end of the scale we place *inclusion* (hyponymy) and at the other *exclusion* (antonymy). As might be expected, between the two and exhibiting features of overlap – partial inclusion and partial exclusion – we find a middle term: synonymy.

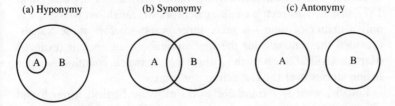

(a) Hyponymy   (b) Synonymy   (c) Antonymy

The first of these, **hyponomy**, involves total inclusion; one concept (or the meaning of one word) is included in another. For example, *animal* includes *tiger* or *wine* includes *hock*, i.e. distinguishing **example** from **class** or, in traditional terminology, the *subordinate* (hyponym) from the *superordinate* (each illustrating the two **isa** relationships discussed in Chapter 7, Section 7.2.2 and Appendix 2).

Naturally, where systems are in agreement, hyponymy presents no problems for the translator. The difficulties start when they differ. Consider, for example, Dr Johnson's famous inclusion in his dictionary of *oats* within the class *food for animals* rather than *food for men* or, even in contemporary dictionaries, *foxhunting* or *bullfighting* within the class *sport*.

The second, **synonymy**, is particularly problematic, since it involves overlap rather than total inclusion or exclusion and assumes that, in principle, either item may be selected, in any context. Absolute, 100 per cent synonymy is, as might be expected, very rare and perhaps impossible, since it would require each item to be totally interchangeable and collocate not only with the same sets as the other but with all members of those sets. Two close English synonyms – *hide* and *conceal* – illustrate this.

Leaving aside the fact that *hide* can also be a noun and assuming, therefore, that both are verbs, we find the two to be virtually interchangeable (though the game of *conceal-and-seek is clearly unacceptable!), except for correlations with less formal and more formal style respectively, i.e. it is the *context of use* rather than the *co-text of usage* which constrains the selection between them (see Chapter 5 on discourse parameters).

If there are, as we suggest there are, problems associated with differences in conceptual class organization between languages, there must, necessarily, be even more intractable problems where overlap is involved.

The Italian *canale* includes two concepts which are distinguished in English – *canal* and *channel* – by, in componential terms, the distinctive feature [artificial] which is [+] in the first case and [-] in the second. Presented with the statement by the Italian astronomer Schiaparelli in 1877 that he had seen a complex network of 'canali' on Mars, it was only a matter of time – a mere three years – before these 'canals' provided the rationale for the first story about an ancient (extinct?) Martian civilization; a mythos which has spawned countless science fiction stories over the last century or more.

Equally, what is a translator to do with the English, French and German terms for areas covered by trees? What is included in what and what are the overlaps in the series *sapling, tree, wood, spinney, grove, thicket, forest* or *arbre, bosquet, bois, forêt*, all of which refer to areas covered by trees (beginning with a single tree, of course) but the extent differs from term to term; *Wald* certainly seems to be larger than *forêt*, for example. It would, as translators are well aware, be simple (and rather unrevealing) to proliferate examples of this kind.

The third, **antonymy**, concerns exclusion rather than inclusion and, as might be expected, exclusion involves a number of relationships[5] which can be illustrated by considering the following words:

1. *true – false*
2. *gold – silver – copper – iron – tin. ...*

3. *large – small*
4. *teacher – student*
5. *one – two – three – four . . .*
6. *become – stay/remain*

It is clear that each word is not only in *contrast* with the rest of the words in the set but also that some sets consist of items which are in *opposition* and that, of these, some are *gradeable opposites*.[6]

Each of these examples serves to distinguish six major types of opposition: (1) taxonomic, (a) binary, (b) multiple and (c) hierachical; (2) polar; (3) relative; and (4) inverse.

1. **Taxonomy**: sets of items which display oppositions which are:
   (a) **binary**, where the pair of items makes up the complete set and are mutually exclusive in the sense that it would be contradictory to assert one *and* the other. Logic dictates 'if *x*, then not *y*'. If a statement (or, better, 'proposition'; see 3.3 on 'sentence meaning') is true it cannot also be false. If we assert that something is 'dead', it cannot also be 'alive'. If we declare someone to be 'male', he cannot also be 'female'.
   (b) **multiple**, where there are more than two items in the set but the order of the items is in no way predetermined. Contrast a list of 'hats' (*beret, boater, bonnet, bowler, cap, Homburg, fedora, skullcap, sombrero, top-hat, trilby*, etc.) with a list of 'units of measurement' (*inch, foot, yard, mile/millimetre, centimetre, metre, kilometre*, etc.).
   (c) **hierarchical**, where items are arranged as an organized taxonomy which may be open-ended (e.g. numbers, colours) or cyclic (e.g. days of the week, months of the year).
2. **Polar**: where the contrasts are placed at opposite ends of a scale such that each is distinct from the other but the degree of distinctness is gradeable. For example, while we cannot say (except figuratively) 'he's more alive' or 'this gold is golder than it was', we can say 'it's hotter than it was' referring, implicitly, to intermediate terms such as *cool* or *tepid*.
3. **Relative**: where there are converse relationships between the items, such as asymmetrical social roles (*doctor–patient*), kinship terms (*son–daughter*) and even temporal and spatial relations (*before–after, over–under*).
4. **Inverse**: where the terms can become perfect synonyms of each other, if (i) one is substituted for the other and (ii) the negative is moved. For example, *some* and *all*:

Some students do *not* study linguistics

Not all students study linguistics

From the translator's point of view, taxonomic opposition (binary, multiple or hierachical) appears to present no major problems, since the items either are or are not part of the same set (in a particular language used by a particular speech community).

The difficulties arise with polar and relative opposition where the relationships are more culturally bound and variable. Kinship is a good example of this. Many languages provide one set of distinctive terms for relatives on the father's side which contrast with those on the mother's e.g. in Hindi and Urdu, grandparents are distinguished between father's father and mother (*dādā* and *dādī*) and mother's father and mother (*nānā* and *nānī*). While Italian, in contrast, makes no distinction between 'brother's/sister's son' (i.e. *nephew* in English) and 'son's/daughter's son' (i.e. *grandson* in English); both are *nipote*. Indeed, we would be wise to avoid ethnocentrism, imagining that English is, somehow, more 'logical'; consider the care with which we distinguish the sex of brother's and sister's children (*nephew* and *niece*) but are, apparently, unconcerned about the sex of parents' siblings' children; all are *cousins*.

Time relations are equally variable. In Hindi and Urdu, for example, the lexical item *āj* realizes the concept 'today'. The single item, *kal*, however, refers to both 'tomorrow' and 'yesterday' and, similarly, the single lexical item, *persā*, realizes both of the concepts 'the day after tomorrow' and 'the day before yesterday'. Clearly, the translator would find this far easier to grasp if the meaning of the terms, rather than their English equivalents, were given here. A simpler model would be that, on a time scale taking the present to be zero:

Term	Days from present
āj	0
kal	± 1
persā	± 2

However, as we shall see in the next section, even the seemingly straightforward taxonomy turns out, on investigation, to be far less certain, even in a single language.

3.1.4 Summary

In this section, we have made a start on explaining word-meaning and worked through three progressively more sophisticated approaches or models.

The first approach we considered was *reference theory* which, as we saw, is of great antiquity and regards the relationship between the meaning of a word and the entity which realizes that meaning as one of straightforward reference, i.e. the word *refers to* or *stands for* the entity. The word is, to use a different term, a *sign* and it is the notion of the Saussurean linguistic sign which lies at the foundations of linguistics in this century. We make use of a modification of the traditional linguistic sign to discuss the nature of the sign in the mind of the bilingual.

The second approach – *componential analysis* – attempts to extend the usefulness of the sign by building up lexical entries which consist of semantic and lexical (grammatical, in a broad sense) distinctive features which are binary in form and listed as either present or absent.

The third approach – *meaning postulates* – goes beyond the specification of the binary components of the individual lexical entry to one which allows us to begin modelling the grouping of entries in terms of their sharing characteristics – hyponymy, synonymy, antonymy – and leads us towards the concerns of the next section; the further extension of the notion of linkages between words (and their meanings) both in the form of semantic fields and beyond the denotative to connotative meaning.

3.2   The thesaurus

What we have considered so far – reference theory, componential analysis and meaning postulates – provides only part of the explanation of word-meaning. What is missing is the recognition that one word can, so to speak, 'call up' another, since concepts (and words) are not stored in memory in a random manner but in a way which permits linkages to be created between them to both increase the efficiency of the storage system itself and to facilitate recall and retrieval (as we shall demonstrate in Chapter 7, Section 7.3.3).

The thesaurus provides us with a model for storing groups of words (and phrases) in a number of ways: where they are (a) synonyms or (b) antonyms or (c) related in other ways. As an advance in lexicography and, indeed, in semantics, *Roget's Thesaurus* (1852) was much ahead of its time. The intention of the author was to produce: 'a system of verbal classification. . . a classed catalogue of words'.[7]

The preface to the 1879 edition (the revisions having been carried out by the original author's son) is even more enlightening since it appears to recognize the essential fuzziness of lexical systems (an issue which will engage us considerably later):

> Any attempt at a philosophical arrangement under categories of the words of our language must reveal the fact that it is impossible to separate and circumscribe the several groups by absolutely distinct boundary lines.[8]

This was turned to advantage in the Thesaurus by not only creating listings of words and phrases 'according to the *ideas* they express'[9] but showing the linkages between groupings. A typical entry illustrates this:

> **optimism**   n.   hopefulness, HOPE, CHEERFULNESS, encouragement, brightness, enthusiasm; confidence, assurance. *Ant* PESSIMISM.

The items in upper case (HOPE, CHEERFULNESS, PESSIMISM) provide cross-references to additional entries, e.g. HOPE lists (i) nouns (44 items in four sub-groups), (ii) verbs (36 items in four sub-groups) and (iii) adjectives (28 items in two sub-groups) plus the antonym 'dejection'.

The thinking behind the *Thesaurus* is highly original and the notion of classification on a semantic basis derives, as the author tells us, explicitly from the taxonomies frequent at the time in the sciences:

> The principle by which I have been guided in framing my verbal classification is the same as that which is employed in the various departments of Natural History. Thus the sectional divisions I have formed, correspond to Natural Families in Botany and Zoology, and the filiation of words presents a network analogous to the natural filiation of plants or animals.[10]

From our point of view, the *Thesaurus* is not only interesting as an early attempt to group lexical items on a semantic or conceptual basis rather than put them (as dictionaries did and still do) in alphabetical order but also that it was intended to form the basis of a Polyglot Lexicon which foreshadows the multilingual terminology databases which are now becoming so common in translating. Roget was clearly well-aware of the value of such a lexicon claiming, justifiably, that nothing else would: 'afford such ample assistance to the translator.'[11]

This takes us a little further in our attempt to specify the nature of word-meaning but there are still unresolved issues. We have moved beyond the constraints of binary componential analysis and can now see that it is the possession of shared semantic characteristics that accounts for the occurrence of each of them under the same thesaurus heading.

For example, it is the characteristics (a) animate/human agent, (b) use of legs, (c) sequential movement of legs, etc., in such lexical items as *hike, march, pace, parade, promenade, ramble, saunter, step, stroll, tramp, tread* which places them all together under WALK. Nevertheless, it is no simple matter to put our fingers on exactly what it is which distinguishes them or how they differ from a set such as *crawl, jump, run* . . . with which they share a good many semantic characteristics.

It is for this reason that we need an extension of the thesaurus model: the lexical or semantic field.

3.2.1 Lexical and semantic fields

A lexical or semantic field is broader in scope than the thesaurus, since it links words to words not only in terms of (1) meaning postulates such as synonymy, hyponymy and antonymy but also in terms of (2) syntactic occurrence (collocation) and (3) phonological characteristics: initial sound, rhyme, etc.

While the third similarity – sound – clearly has great relevance for speech-comprehension (and, many psychologists would insist, reading-comprehension as well) and for stylistics in the description of poetic language, more germane to our present concerns are the first and second: meaning postulates and occurrence.

Since we have already discussed the first of these (in Section 3.1.3), we shall comment briefly on the second (collocation) before outlining two approaches to the construction of lexical and semantic fields.

Similarity of occurrence – *collocation* – is the basic formal relationship in lexis: the chain (or syntagmatic) relationship between items (see Chapter 4 on chain and choice). A word tends to occur in relatively predictable ways with other words; certain nouns with particular adjectives or verbs, verbs with particular adverbials, etc. Chomsky's famous sentence[12]

colorless green ideas sleep furiously

shows how the selection of items from incongruous sets leads to the breaking of collocational constraints and expectations and turns an otherwise perfectly normal grammatical sentence, made up of equally normal individual lexical items, into one which we cannot accept. In contrast, we could keep the same syntactic structure and create an acceptable sentence by making appropriate selections which collocate to our satisfaction:

homeless black cats mew pitifully.

At this point, since we appear to have been using the two terms – **semantic field** and **lexical field** – indiscriminately, we should perhaps explain the difference between them.[13]

Any discussion of word-meaning inevitably involves the relating of concepts (the result of perception and its organization in the long-term memory) to lexical items (units which form part of the structure of the linguistic code). The distinction between a lexical field and a semantic field can be traced back to the point of departure of the descriptive process: the lexical item or the concept.[14].

Our own approach in this chapter has been to focus on the elements of meaning contained within lexical entries and the extent to which such elements are shared between concepts which are, it is true, realized as lexical items.

What must come next is a move from word-meaning to sentence-meaning but before we move on to sentence-meaning, we should extend the discussion of word-meaning by examining meaning contrasts of a connotational (affective) rather than a denotational (referential) kind.

3.2.2 Denotation and connotation

We have, so far, been implying that all aspects of word- and sentence-meaning are objective and shared, i.e. that this type of meaning is limited to the referential or cognitive. However, as we shall see, this is not the case and for two reasons: (1) the boundaries between words and their meanings turn out – in spite of what the dictionary would have us believe – to be fuzzy rather than precise, and (2) this applies at both the denotative and the connotative levels.

If this is the case, the notion of there being a single 'correct' reading for a text becomes most unlikely and the possibility of 'preserving semantic and stylistic equivalences' in the course of translation – one of the generally expected duties of the translator – less and less plausible as a realistic goal to aim at. We have, indeed, recognized this when we defined the **semantic representation** as containing 'the whole of the thought expressed in the clause *as apprehended by the reader*' (in Chapter 2, Section 2.2.2).

We have just used the terms **denotative** and **connotative** in relation to two aspects of meaning and now need to distinguish clearly between them.

The first refers to meaning which is referential, objective and cognitive and, hence, the shared property of the speech community which uses the language of which the word or sentence forms a part.

The second, in contrast, refers to meaning which is not referential but associational, subjective and affective. This kind of meaning, being personal, may or may not be shared by the community at large. For example, the denotative meaning of the item *dog* in English is straightforward and common property (so to speak). The connotations vary from person to person, extending, no doubt, from servile dedication to the well-being of the species to utter abhorrence and from society to society; the connotations of *kelb* for Arabs are likely to be more negative than those for *dog* for English-speakers, even though the denotation of the two words is identical.

It is important to recognize that virtually all words possess both types of meaning and the few exceptions to this appear to be words which are not 'full' lexical items ('words' in the sense of nouns, verbs, adjectives, adverbs) but grammatical operators such as *the, and, may*, etc., which possess little denotative meaning and certainly, as individual items, no connotative meaning at all.[15] On the other hand, items like *democracy, love, patriotism*, etc., seem extraordinarily difficult to define in objective terms and are clearly highly emotionally charged.

It might appear from this that denotative meaning is relatively simple to describe, at least where the words involved do not refer to abstract notions but to concrete or easily visualized objects, processes or relationships, and that the description of connotative meaning, being personal, is impossible.

There is a degree of truth in this but, as we have just suggested, even denotative meaning is not wholly shared by members of the speech community. Experiments have shown[16] that native speakers of the same language do not agree totally even on the *referential* use of terms for such everyday objects as cups, mugs and beakers; the semantic boundaries between words turn out not to be clear and sharp but fuzzy. How is it then that the individual members of the speech community are able to communicate at all with each other (let alone translate from one language to another)? To explain this seeming paradox requires us to postulate the existence of shared concepts (*stereotypes* and *prototypes*); an issue which will be taken up later (Chapter 7, Section 7.2.1) during the discussion of knowledge in relation to human information-processing and memory.

The boundary lines within the cup–mug–beaker taxonomy for a particular individual are binary (a cup is not a mug; a mug is not a beaker) but, for the community, these objects are arranged in a multiple rather than a binary manner which makes them more akin to the 'hat' set than to the 'units of measurement' set of our earlier example.

To leave the consideration of meaning, even at word-level, at this point would be to miss its important subjective and personal aspects. The words we use and the sentences we embed them in do not merely 'refer' to concepts. For each of us the words we choose have associations which mean something particular to us as individual users. They have meanings which are emotional or affective; the result of our own individual experiences which are, presumably, unique and may not form part of any kind of social convention such as we suggested as a constituent of the arbitrary relationship between word and 'object'.

It is to these connotative, affective aspects of meaning that we now turn.

3.2.3 Semantic differential

Difficult though the measurement of connotative meaning is, a technique has been developed by psychologists interested in the structure of memory; the **semantic differential**.[17] Using this, the connotative meaning of a word is arrived at (for each individual) by means of fifteen 7-point scales consisting of a range of bipolar adjectives (e.g. good–bad, etc,) expressing three factors or dimensions (evaluation, potency and activity) and judged on a 7-point scale running from +3 through 0 to -3, i.e. from the strongest positive association through neutral to the strongest negative association. Thus, a score of +3 on the good–bad scale can be read as 'extremely good', while -3 on the same scale is read as 'extremely bad'. Naturally, 0 on the scale is read as 'neither good nor bad'; the distinction might be, for a particular informant, rating this word/concept, irrelevant.

Although, of necessity, connotative meanings are personal (and not necessarily shared by other members of the speech community) and the semantic differential technique collects them one at a time, there is the possibility of amalgamating an individual's profiles for a collection of words and producing a picture of part of a semantic field and, indeed, doing the same for groups who share significant sociological and/or psychological characteristics.

The procedure for applying the semantic differential consists of (1) the individual subject rating a word – *cat, bachelor, democracy* – and so forth on each of the parameters listed above, (2) the investigator combining each of these ratings to create a profile for that word for that individual and (3) grouping the adjectives under one of three dimensions:

Evaluation: good–bad, clean–dirty, fresh–stale, pleasant–
unpleasant, beautiful–ugly

| **Potency**: | strong–weak, large–small, loud–soft, heavy–light, bright–dark |
| **Activity**: | active–passive, tense–relaxed, hot–cold, fast–slow, solid–liquid |

and thereby plotting the individual's distribution of the meaning of a word in the three dimensions of (connotative) semantic space and providing some objective support to the 'intuitive' feelings that we are likely to have about particular words or concepts; feelings which constitute part of our encyclopedic, stereotype knowledge (see Chapter 7 on this).

As an example, we shall give one subject's ratings for the words *bachelor* and *spinster* and show the difference between them in terms of the 'scores' on each of the three 5-parameter dimensions listed above.

	BACHELOR	SPINSTER	Dimensions
good–bad	+2	+3	
clean–dirty	+1	+3	
fresh–stale	+3	+3	Evaluation
pleasant–unpleasant	+3	+2	
beautiful–ugly	+1	+1	
strong–weak	+2	+1	
large–small	+1	−1	
loud–soft	+2	−2	Potency
heavy–light	+1	−2	
bright–dark	−1	+1	
active–passive	+2	−1	
tense–relaxed	−3	−1	
hot–cold	+3	+1	Activity
fast–slow	+1	−1	
solid–liquid	+3	+3	

Scores on each dimension

	BACHELOR	SPINSTER
Evaluation	+9	+12
Potency	+5	−3
Activity	+6	+1

It is clear from this that, on the evaluative dimension, this informant rates *bachelor* fairly high (9 out of a possible maximum of 15 and averaging just under +2), though not so high as *spinster* (12 out of 15 and averaging almost +2.5), and that *bachelor* is rated comparatively higher on both potency and activity than *spinster* is.

This manifests itself in judgements to the effect that spinsters are substantially 'better' and 'cleaner' than bachelors but not quite so 'pleasant'. Conversely, on the dimension of potency, spinsters come out as significantly less 'potent' than bachelors; they are not so 'strong' as bachelors, being 'smaller', 'softer' (i.e. 'quieter') and 'lighter' (in weight) than them but being as 'bright' as they are 'dark'. In terms of activity, the lower score for the spinster derives from their being assessed as much less 'active' – tending towards the passive – and less 'relaxed'. Equally, spinsters are also rated as 'colder' and 'slower' but just as 'solid' as bachelors.

Subjective though these judgements are, they do seem to support our 'intuitive' expectations about the stereotypical bachelor or spinster; expectations which may (but do not necessarily have to) form part of a shared set of community-wide (or merely group-wide) associations and values.

For the translator, it is this potential of the semantic differential which is most attractive. What the translator continually needs are specifications of the connotative word meaning systems of individual writers, speech-communities and different languages. What the semantic differential can offer, then, are comparative sociolinguistic studies of the evaluation of lexical items by individuals and cross-cultural studies of the same kind, some of which have already been carried out.[18]

3.2.4 Summary

In this section we have been extending our initial approaches to the description and explanation of word-meaning in two ways. First, we went beyond the denotative senses of the individual lexical item to models which indicated ways in which items are linked together to form 'fields' of related words and concepts and, second, we distinguished denotation from connotation and outlined a means of tapping connotative meaning.

Perhaps the most significant message in this section for translation is the recognition that the essential characteristic of the lexical systems of languages is not precise boundary-marking but fuzziness and that it is the inherent fuzziness of language which presents the most formidable obstacle to the translator.

What remains to be done is to shift our attention from the meanings of individual words to those of sentences, recognizing that words cannot really be described other than within the sentence; the words we have been discussing have all, in reality, been abstracted from assumed (though not explicitly specified) sentences. We must now return the words to their proper setting and discuss sentence-meaning.

3.3.   Sentence-meaning

The goal of semantics, in the view of the majority of linguists, is (1) to show how words and sentences are '. . .related to one another in terms of such notions as "synonymy", "entailment" and "contradiction"'[19] and (2) to '. . .explain how the sentences of (a) language are understood, interpreted and related to states, processes and objects in the universe'.[20]

Clearly, on this, translators and linguists are in substantial agreement that both orientations to the description and explanation of 'meaning' are necessary: an understanding of (1) the relationship of form to form within the code and also (2) that of the formal structures of the code to the communicative context of use. Of the two, the translator particularly needs the second.

3.3.1. Words and sentences

Part of the aim of the earlier discussion of word-meaning was to show relationships of *inclusion* and *exclusion* between concepts and, hence, between the words which express them. Similar relationships can be found (as might be expected) between sentences.

The next step is to use the notion of *equivalence* (one of the key concepts in translation theory) to relate one sentence to another and to recognize that word-meaning can only be arrived at through the study of the meaning of the word in the linguistic *co-text* of the sentence and that sentence-meaning depends, just as crucially, on the setting of the sentence in its communicative *context* (a point which was raised at the beginning of this chapter and will be taken up again in 3.3.3).

We shall be making a number of important points about 'sentence-meaning' in comparison and in contrast with 'word-meaning' by using the term 'sentence' in an informal everyday manner and by leaving the critical distinction between *utterance*, *sentence* and *proposition* until Section 3.3.2.

Faced by a text, the reader (and, therefore, the translator) has to cope not only with the semantic sense of the words (the focus of the earlier parts of this chapter) but also the 'meaning' of the sentences.

The reader needs to be able to work out whether what is stated in a sentence is true or false, whether it possesses a single meaning or is ambiguous and, indeed, whether it 'makes sense' at all.

Equally, skilled reading (an undeniable prerequisite for skilled translating) also depends on seeing relationships between the sentences of a text by making inferences about such relationships. After all, the *whole* of the 'meaning' of a text is not (and cannot be) spelled out in actual written sentences. Some sentences entail other sentences, some suggest implications, others depend on presuppositions the writer makes about the reader's knowledge and expectations.

Sentence-meaning, like word-meaning, can be approached initially through the notions of inclusion and exclusion and the discovery of the **sentence level equivalents** of hyponymy, synonymy and antonymy. We might begin by considering some examples:

1.   Tigers are animals
2.   Tigers are fierce
3.   Tigers are birds
4.   They found him a good friend
5.   Semantics killed the students
6. **A** He wrote a book on linguistics
   B He wrote a book
7. **A** What is his book about?
   B It's not about athletics!
8.   Can you lend me Leech's *Semantics*?

We readily see that these sentences group together in various ways. In the first three examples, the linkage is the **truth test**, i.e. the answer to the question: 'Is what is asserted in the sentence true or false?'

1. True, necessarily so, by virtue of the meanings of the words in it.
2. Neither true nor false; more information is needed.
3. False, necessarily so, by virtue of the meanings of the words in it.

The next two, though still concerned with the meanings of the words, are focused not on truth-value of the assertions but on the **grammatical relationships** between the words.

4. Ambiguous, since we cannot tell whether 'him' is the complement or the object of 'found'. There appear to be two equally plausible interpretations between which it seems impossible to judge, without an appeal to some additional information from the linguistic co-text or social context:

(a) 'They found him to be a good friend' (taking 'him' to be the complement), or

(b) 'They found a good friend for him' (taking 'him' to be the indirect object).

5. Nonsensical; 'semantics' is abstract and cannot, except in a figurative sense, 'kill' anyone. 'Kill' requires an animate subject. It may appear, at first sight, that this sentence is no more than another example of the type already presented in sentence 3; false by virtue of the meanings of the words in it. But it can be shown that this is not in fact the case and to do this, we need to refer to the notions of **encyclopedic** and **lexical** entries (7.2.1), since the difference between the two examples lies in the nature of the anomaly in the entries for the concepts involved.

In the first case, the anomaly is purely **conceptual**, since the encyclopedic entry for 'bird' would *not* contain the information (asserted in sentence 3) that it includes the concept *tiger* (i.e. *bird* is not a hyponym of *tiger*). In simple terms, it is just not true that a tiger is a kind of bird and our encyclopedic knowledge of the world about us confirms this.

The second case is doubly anomalous, since the anomaly is both **conceptual** *and* **syntactic**: (a) the *encyclopedic* entry [21] for *semantics* would exclude information that suggested that abstract entities could kill and (b) the *lexical* entry would include the grammatical information [noun, abstract] and that for *kill* would include [animate agent]. Thus, giving a concept which is realized by an inanimate a propositional role reserved for animates (actor or agent) produces pragmatic nonsense[22] and, at the same time, using an inanimate, abstract noun as the subject of a verb like 'kill' breaks the selection rules of the grammar and produces grammatical nonsense.[23]

The remaining three are also connected but in a very different way. Up to this point, we have been appealing to the formal linguistic **co-text** – relating word-meaning to word-meaning within each example – without explicit reference to the functional and communicative **context** of actual use.

These last three examples force us to appeal to context. In each case, communicators (speakers/writers or hearers/readers) are able to draw conclusions – make inferences – from the text; to derive B from A (as in 6), to comprehend what is implicit (as in 7), to make assumptions about the 'normal' context of the use of an utterance (as in 8).

6. A entails B, i.e. if he wrote a book on linguistics, it follows, necessarily, that he wrote a book. The converse is not necessarily the case, i.e. B does not entail A. He may well have written a book but it could have been on any subject, not just linguistics.
7. The implication of B is that the speaker is uncertain about the topic of the book.
8. The speaker presupposes that the hearer has a copy of the book, that the hearer will be willing to lend it, that asking to borrow it will not give offence, etc.

In short, the eight examples provide us with eight distinct kinds of sentence relationship[24]

1. Analytic sentence
2. Synthetic sentence
3. Contradiction
4. Ambiguity
5. Anomaly/nonsense
6. Entailment
7. Implicature
8. Presupposition

3.3.2. Utterance, sentence and proposition

We must now return to the distinction between utterance, sentence and proposition; three levels of abstraction and idealization which apply to any stretch of language we may wish to translate.

There is a **type-token** relationship between the three, such that we can envisage the most abstract (the proposition) as being an ideal underlying **type** of which there are a number of **tokens** or manifestations: a range of sentences which share the same propositional content. Equally, the same relationship holds between sentence and utterance. Each sentence can be viewed as an ideal *type* which can be realized by a range of actual utterances; *tokens* of it.

We are all aware of this distinction between the ideal and the actual in our everyday experience (a point which will be raised in our discussion of the creation of conceptual categories in Chapter 7, Section 7.2.1) in which examples abound; the written score and the actual performance of a piece of music; the written text of a play and the production on the night; a recipe and the cooked dish. Music critics, interestingly from our point of view, refer to 'performances' of a piece of music as 'accounts', 'interpretations' and 'realizations', making the same point as we are.

In linguistics, the distinction is crucial and can be exemplified by de Saussure's **langue-parole** and the similar, though not identical, distinction between **competence** and **performance** in Chomsky.

The traditional issues in translation of the relationship between 'fidelity' and 'freedom' and the choice between 'literal' and 'free' (or 'semantic' and 'communicative') seem to resolve themselves into the simple question: 'Are we translating propositions, sentences or utterances?' and, the related question, 'What is the implication of choosing one rather than the other?' This being so, it is essential to be clear in distinguishing the three concepts.

Specifically, the **utterance** can be typified as being concrete and context-sensitive. It is the utterance and not the sentence that is recorded on paper or an audio tape and it is tied to a specifiable time, place and participants. It is judged in terms of appropriateness rather than grammaticality, i.e. whether and to what extent it is constrained by social convention; whether, in terms of normal expectations of communicative behaviour, it is *acceptable*.

The **sentence** in contrast, is abstract and context-free. Unlike utterances, sentences exist (if at all) only in the mind. When a sentence is said or written down, we still tend to refer to it as a sentence. This is an unnecessary confusion. It would be wiser to recognize the difference between the substantial written-down sentence and the abstract idealized sentence of which it is a realization, i.e. the written sentence is better thought of as an utterance or a text. Think of what happens when we remember what someone said or wrote. We tend to remember it in an 'edited' and idealized form; not the actual utterance with its pauses, um's and er's, slips of the tongue, etc., but the idealized sentence of which the utterance we had heard was but one instance. Again, in contrast with the utterance, the sentence is not set in time or space nor tied to any particular participants: speakers, hearers, writers, readers. It is, however, *language specific*, since it is judged in terms of grammaticality, i.e. whether it conforms to the rules of the particular linguistic code and whether, in those terms, it is *possible*.

The **proposition** is even more abstract than the sentence. It is the unit of meaning which constitutes the *subject-matter* of a sentence (and, once realized in actual use, that of the utterance as well). It has been defined as 'that part of the meaning of the utterance of a declarative sentence which describes some state of affairs'[25] and, hence, in uttering a declarative sentence, a speaker is asserting a proposition (an important point which will be taken up again in the discussion of speech acts in Chapter 5, Section 5.2).

Being even more abstract than the sentence, the proposition is not only context-free but also language-free in the sense that it cannot be tied to any specific language. An utterance can be said or written in any language and recognized as a realization of a sentence of that particular language but the propositional meaning underpinning the utterance (and the sentence) is universal rather than language-specific.

In the analysis of the proposition, we find that the grammatical categories Subject, Object, etc., which served at sentence level do not apply and a pair of fundamental logical relationships is required: the **predicate** (state or action) and the **argument** (the entity or entities referred to by the predicate). In a little more detail, these expand into the **processes** (i.e. predicates) and **roles** (i.e. arguments) which are the focus of attention in the next chapter (specifically in Section 4.1).

Perhaps a comparison of utterance, sentence and proposition with an example will be useful here; I can say (or write) the utterance (or text; the distinction seems rather illusive) in a limitless number of ways

      A hit B with a hammer

or   *A hit B with a hammer*

or   **A hit B with a hammer**

or   A HIT B WITH A HAMMER

or whatever, realizing – making substantial – a sentence with a SPOA structure in which the syntactic 'slots' (SPOA) are 'filled' by particular lexical items; *A*, *hit*, *B*, *with a hammer* rather than others, i.e. each of these is a realization of the same sentence (however written).

We might put this a little differently; saying the utterances (and the sentence they realize) all *count as* saying

I declare it to be the case that A hit B with a hammer

and in doing this, I am making a statement, asserting the existence of three entities – A, B and the hammer – and relationships between them and a process (hitting):

A (actor) hit (process) B (Goal) with a hammer (instrument)

The essential point here is that the *Actor–Process–Goal–Instrument* relationship of the **proposition** is identical *for all languages*, no matter how it is expressed syntactically.

If we express the same proposition in a number of languages (choosing suitable personal names for A and B), beginning with French, we get the written text:

André a frappé Bernard avec un marteau

or Polish

> Andrzej uderzył Bogusia młotkiem

or Hindi/Urdu

> Aziz ne Bikram ko hātore se māra

or Japanese

> Atˢushi kun wa Benjiroo kun o tˢuchi de uchimasita

or Latin

> Antonius Brutum malleo tetigit

or Cantonese

> Akahu juhng chuih daai Bahba

or Arabic

> dharaba Ahmadu Bilala bilmitraqathi

What is crucial here is the *propositional* structure, *not* the syntactic or the lexical.

Although the syntactic and lexical variations between the languages are strikingly large, it is only of secondary importance that the syntactic structures (choices from the MOOD system) are:

S P O A   in English, French and Polish
S O A P   in Hindi/Urdu, Japanese and Latin
S A P O in Cantonese
P S O A in Arabic

The significance of this for the translator is fundamental. The fact that the proposition is universal (not tied to a specific language but underlying all languages) gives it its central position in communication and provides us with a major clue in our attempts at making sense of the process of translation. As we saw in the presentation of the model of the process, the reader's initial task (and the translator's) is to decompose the language-specific clauses of the written text into their universal propositional content. Until this is done (and additional information added to it to create the semantic representation of the clause), neither comprehension nor (necessarily) translation is possible.

In short, we are suggesting that any utterance is a token of a sentence type, which is itself a token of a proposition type.

In other words, in the terminology we used earlier in this chapter in the discussion of meaning postulates, *proposition* includes *sentence* and *utterance*, and *sentence* includes *utterance*, i.e. there is a relationship of hyponymy between the superordinate proposition and the subordinate sentence and utterance:

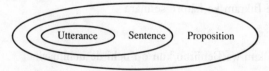

Our consideration of meaning has now reached the point where we need to move beyond the description of the formal aspects of the code and appeal outside the linguistic structure in cases of ambiguity, entailment, implicature and presupposition. This will require us to introduce three levels of location for any communicative stretch of language, i.e. the 'setting' of the interaction with its communicative functions realized by the linguistic forms of the code.

3.3.3 Situation, context and universe of discourse

We made the point at the beginning of this chapter that 'meaning' ultimately depends on the **context of use** and would re-assert that here adding that comprehension itself consists of reconstructing the context from the words of the text.

> The important thing is to set aside all the *words* of the [original] text and see the picture clearly. Having *seen the picture* the translator must write down what he sees in the simplest English. It is the idea or the picture that has to be communicated, and not equivalents of the actual words.[26]

What, though, is meant by 'context'? Three levels of abstraction can be suggested: the **immediate situation of utterance**, the **context of utterance** and the **universe of discourse**. We shall consider each in turn but preface our remarks with the comment that the relationship between situation, context and universe are related in exactly the same way as utterance is to sentence and sentence to proposition, i.e. the situation is contained in the context and the context in the universe of discourse. Thus:

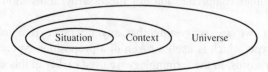

3.3.3.1 *Immediate situation of utterance*

During an act of communication individuals interact, knowledge is conveyed (i.e. sense) through selections made from the resources (the meaning potential) of the code (and other systems) and certain entities are referred to by the linguistic forms used: persons, places, things, actions, relations... and, naturally, languages differ in the ways in which they organize the transfer of information.

There is, clearly, a difference between referring to entities which are actually present at the time of speaking and those which are not and, for our present purposes, the most significant implication of this is that some meanings are totally dependent on this immediate situation of utterance (the totality of the circumstances in which the utterance was issued).

A surprising number of expressions (and even grammatical tense) turn out to be situation-bound:

(a) pronouns refer to participants in the communicative event; in Hindi and Urdu, for example, the third person singular 'pronoun' – *he, she, it* – is, in fact, a demonstrative, i.e. *wo = that*;

(b) many time expressions refer to different actual times depending on when they are uttered; *today, yesterday*...(we have already seen the Hindi/Urdu 'equivalents' of these terms);

(c) place expressions are similarly constrained; *here–there, this–that* for example. Some English dialects have a three-way system (*here, there, yon*), as do several languages (Italian had, until recently, *questo, cotesto, quello*) so are

(d) a number of verbs – *come, go, bring, take*...– and

(e) tense; for example the present tense is tied to the here-and-now of current reality, though – as we saw with the translation of the Valéry poem (in the previous chapter; in section 2.(3) – the actual form can lead to ambiguity: *je cherche* is *only* interpretable by reference to the situation of utterance.

Every one of these can be subsumed within the general category of deictic, a 'pointing expression' which refers to entities and relationships present in the situation in which it is uttered.

3.3.3.2 *Context of utterance*

The context of utterance comes next in order of increasing abstraction and generality. The relationship between the situation and the utterance can be demonstrated by observing what happens when we attempt to place an utterance (1) in its situation and (2) in its context. Consider the utterance

Pass me the oregano

If we were to ask in what circumstances this utterance was issued, satisfactory answers would be very different, depending on whether the question was about the situation or the context.

To provide an adequate answer in terms of the *situation* in which this occurred, we would need, given its uniqueness, to specify the particular participants and their behaviour, the time, place of the interaction and anything else that came to mind. Such a description would provide a listing of the components of the *aggregate* which, without a generalizing cultural dimension to them, does not lead to a specification of the situation as a *whole* (see the discussion on these terms in Chapter 1, Section 1.2.1).

By way of contrast, an adequate answer in terms of the context might be as laconic as

Cooking (a spaghetti bolognese)

The two types of 'fact' on which the description rests are of a different order from each other. The *situation* can be described in terms of *brute facts* which can be observed and reported by an uncomprehending outsider but the *context* can only be recognized by the knowing insider who can bring the brute facts together as *social facts*[27] and recognize the cultural unity in the physical diversity, i.e. that a series of situations – different from each other as they undoubtedly must be – *count as* the same; here, an event which can be labelled 'cooking' in general terms.

The immediate situation of utterance requires the *explicit* spelling out of the physical details. The specification of the context of utterance can – unlike the description of the *situation* – be much more *implicit*, since it assumes the totality of the shared knowledge possessed by the participants in the communicative act.

This 'shared knowledge' has two aspects: linguistic and social. What we are referring to here is the distinction between *linguistic competence* on the one hand and *social competence* on the other; the two coming together in the *communicative competence* of the individual member of the speech community.[28]

(a) *Linguistic knowledge* (internalized knowledge of the rule systems governing the code) includes, in particular, *co-textual* knowledge which allows the communicator to refer back and forth through the unfolding text itself. It is this kind of knowledge that allows the writer to build information into the structure of the text by marking 'new' information and distinguishing it from information which is 'old' or 'given' and the reader to recognize the structures and derive information from the text.

(b) *Social knowledge* (internalized knowledge of the conventions which constrain and regulate the application of the shared 'ground-rules' for communication in operation in a speech community) includes, in particular, *contextual* knowledge which allows the communicator to recognize that the situation of utterance is a *token* realization of a situational *type* which acts as a guide to participation (see Chapter 7 on the role of **schemas** in memory and action).

Both of these kinds of knowledge are of enormous significance for the translator.

Without the first the translator would be unable (i) to recognize the way information is distributed in a text and (ii) to identify the information focus in it. In short, comprehension (and, hence, translation) hinges on such text-knowledge. Naturally, languages vary considerably in the way they 'mark' information. English, for example, tends to interpret the distinction between 'given' and 'new' in terms of definiteness and to mark it by introducing 'new' information with a definite article *the* and all subsequent occurrences with indefinite *a*, etc.

Without the second, the translator might well be able to process text at the level of semantic sense but would be hard pressed to assign communicative value to it, since that requires contextualization which, in its turn, presupposes extra-linguistic knowledge. It is this kind of social knowledge which, for example, allows the reader to classify a text as belonging to a particular genre. It seems, then, that comprehension (and, hence, translation) hinges not only on text-knowledge but on discourse-knowledge as well.[29]

3.3.3.3 *Universe of discourse*

The universe of discourse is the third, most abstract and most general of these settings. It consists of whatever can be said about a particular subject and includes, by definition, not only what the participants know but also what they do not know and others do; all the propositions which could be constructed in relation to that subject.

What can be referred to in one topic-area will be different from that which is proper in another though there may be degrees of overlap. We may anticipate overlap between texts in a newspaper reporting on (a) soccer, (b) rugby, (c) cricket and (d) cinema with progressively less overlap as we move from (a) to (d).

Further, the 'same' genre will differ in its universe of discourse from culture to culture. We might well imagine that soccer, rugby and cricket will be treated rather similarly in British and Indian newspapers – i.e. the universes of discourse for each will be much the same; the rules of the game are, after all, identical – but expect strikingly different treatment of cinema; the western film and the Hindi film, in spite of the shared technology of production, contrast strongly in their conventions.

The notion is of particular significance for the translator, since universes of discourse cannot but be culture-specific and, to the extent that different cultures co-occur with different languages, be reflected in different lexicons.

A crucial requirement for successful communication must be for the communicators to be operating within the same universe of discourse and, therefore, the question is one which must be constantly in the mind of the translator who is required to mediate between cultures and languages.

3.3.4 Summary

In this section we have been shifting the focus from word-meaning to sentence-meaning and have made two essential three-way distinctions: (1) between utterance, sentence and proposition and (2) between the immediate situation of utterance, the context of utterance and the universe of discourse. We shall need both sets of distinctions increasingly in subsequent chapters.

3.4   Conclusion

In this chapter we have been outlining the major formal aspects of meaning. Specifically, we have been considering **semantic sense** in relation to word- and sentence-meaning.

Initially, we introduced three approaches to the modelling of word-meaning: (1) classical reference theory and its extension in the Saussurean linguistic sign, (2) the bottom-up analytical technique of componential analysis which provides information for insertion into the entries of the lexicon and (3) the top-down orientation of meaning postulates which group words (and meanings) in terms of shared elements of meaning (hyponymy, synonymy, antonymy).

Next, we (1) provided a way of extending the description of meaning which allowed words (and their meanings) to be grouped into lexical (or semantic) fields, (2) distinguished the denotative and connotative meanings of words and (3) outlined a technique – the semantic differential – for displaying connotative meaning in three-dimensional semantic space.

Then, we moved on from word-meaning to introduce the topic of sentence-meaning and the meaning relationships which hold within and between sentences (contrasting co-textually defined analytic, synthetic, contradictory, ambiguous and anomalous sentence types with contextually derived distinctions such as entailment, implicature and presupposition).

This shift led us to make two important distinctions which create links between this chapter and the next; the distinction between the utterance, the sentence and the proposition and three levels of 'setting' for utterances and for discourse (situation and context of utterance and universe of discourse).

These distinctions permit us to move the focus progressively away from the context-free formal characteristics of language as an abstract code towards the context-sensitive functional view of language as a system of resources available to the communicator for the expression and comprehension of meaning (in the broadest sense of the term).

This will entail attempting to describe what the resources of the language are which enable us to speak and write about

> the phenomena of the environment: the things, creatures, objects, actions, events, qualities, states and relations of the world and of our own consciousness, including the phenomenon of language itself; and also the 'metaphenomena', the things that are already encoded as facts and reports.[30]

We now turn to the specification of this 'meaning potential'.

Notes

1. de Saussure, 1916.
2. Not that we thought that in Bell, 1976, 120f.
3. Goodenough, 1956.
4. These examples are from Rabin, 1958, 124. Newmark (1988, 114–22) discusses componential analysis from the point of view of the descriptive linguist (as an analytical procedure) and the practising translator (as a stage in the translation process).
5. Linguists are far from agreed on how many or what type. Lyons (1977, 279), for example, makes an initial (and later expanded) three-way

distinction in which the term antonymy is used in a particular restricted sense, while Leech (1981a, 99–109), on the other hand, isolates six significant types of contrast.

6. See Lyons, ibid.; Leech, ibid.
7. Roget, op. cit., viii.
8. Roget, op. cit., ix.
9. Roget, op. cit., xiii; original emphasis.
10. Roget, op. cit., xxvi. The choice of the term 'network' is particularly apt, given that a recent labelling of word-meaning is *Word-webs; semantic networks*; Aitchison, 1987, 74.
11. Roget, ibid.
12. Chomsky, 1965.
13. Waldron, 1967.
14. This suggests two approaches:
    1. *Formalist*: the lexical item is taken as the focus of investigation and its meanings are compared and contrasted with those carried by the rest of the lexicon. The result of such an emphasis on internal relationships between items in the code leads to the modelling of lexical fields and, ultimately, to the specification of the total lexicon of the language.
    2. *Functionalist*: concepts are taken as the focus of investigation and a listing given of the lexical items which designate them. The result of such an emphasis on extralinguistic knowledge leads to the modelling of semantic rather than lexical fields and, ultimately, to a contribution to epistemology (i.e. the theory of knowledge).
15. We shall draw on this when we assign them to conceptual entries in Chapter 7, Section 7.2.2.
16. Labov, 1973.
17. Osgood *et al.*, 1967.
18. Heise, 1965.
19. Lyons, 1970, 166.
20. Bierwisch, 1970, 167.
21. Note that we are using this in the cognitive science sense rather than the linguistic. See Chapter 7, Section 7.2.2 on this.
22. See the next chapter (Section 4.1) on roles, processes and circumstances
23. In contrast with the lexical nonsense of, for example, Carroll's 'Jabberwocky'.
24. See Hurford and Heasley, op. cit., particularly units 16, 9–11 and 26, for further discussion.
25. Hurford and Heasley, op. cit., 19.
26. Tancock, 1958, 32; original emphases.
27. Searle, 1969.
28. Bell, 1976, 66 makes these distinctions in the context of a social-psychological model of communication.
29. These issues which are taken up in detail in the next chapter (in Section 4.3), in Chapter 5 and Chapter 6.
30. Halliday, 1978, 112.

4   Logic, grammar and rhetoric

In the previous chapter, we asked the question 'What does this word/sentence mean?' and concentrated on answering it by reference, in the main, to the code itself, the elements of which it is composed and the arrangements of those elements which it permits.

In this chapter we ask a different though related question: 'What resources does the code possess for the transmission and reception of particular kinds of meaning?', i.e. a question about the functions of language as a system of communication.

Let us begin by moving entirely away from language and imagine an event; a happening. We might represent this event by a simple cartoon and remind ourselves that no language or, more correctly, no speech community exists which lacks the resources to report what is going on. True, the languages of the world and the speakers of those languages would express what they say in enormously different ways but the *picture* would remain and, given that the translator's task (as we specified it at the end of the previous chapter) is 'to. . .see the picture clearly [since] it is the idea or picture that has to be communicated, and not the equivalents of the actual words' [1] there can be no report of that picture which cannot be re-reported in another language, i.e. translated.

In more formal terms, we are saying that, for any culture and any language, the immediate situation represented by the picture is by no means unusual and therefore can be accommodated within the universe of discourse, i.e. it can be spoken about (or written about, if the language has been reduced to writing). We shall use the event we discussed in the previous chapter (in Section 3.3.2), representing it in Figure 4.1.

Any report of this event which uses language will be a text (made up of one or more utterances). It might take the form, in English, of:

FIGURE 4.1 Picture of an event

Alfred hit Bill with a hammer

What might be asked about this, or any other, text? It has been suggested[2] that there are three specific questions we might ask:

1. WHAT is it about?; i.e. what is the propositional content?, what is being represented?, what does it stand for? One function of language is to convey ideas; to represent perceptions and cognitions (see Section 4.1).
2. WHY is it being sent?; i.e. what is the orientation of the sender – speaker or writer – to the exchange in which he or she is engaged? Another function of language is to facilitate interaction between communicators as they exchange ideas and goods-and-services. We can, therefore, ask (a) what kind of sentence is involved? (see Section 4.2) and (b) what kind of speech act does it count as? (see Chapter 5, Section 5.2).
3. HOW is it being transmitted?; i.e. how is the information organized? Another function (and these three functions are not to be thought of as in any kind of order of importance) of language is to arrange and focus the information content of utterances in ways which make them suitable for inclusion in stretches of discourse. Here the questions are 'What information units are there in this utterance?', 'How are they distributed?', 'Which parts are focused on?' and 'Which are new and which old information?' (see Section 4.3).

If we reduce the event to its simplest, we might state that there is a person (we have called him *Alfred*) who is hitting (or has hit) another person (we have called him *Bill*) with what appears to be a hammer.

There is, in even more general terms, an *action* (hitting), two individuals who are participating in that action – the *doer* of the action and the *goal* at which it is directed; its *receiver* – plus the *instrument* used in the action. This is, in informal terms, the proposition which underlies the picture and an answer to question 1:

Actor   Process   Goal   Instrument

These relationships were realized, in our text, by the words *Alfred, hit, Bill* and *with a hammer*. In conventional grammatical terms (and in answer to question 2), the content of the proposition has been organized as a clause with a structure in which there is a one-to-one mapping between the elements which make up the proposition and those which constitute the clause:

Subject   Predicator   Object   Adjunct

Other realizations are, of course, possible. We could have decided to focus on the sufferer of the action (the Goal or Recipient; Bill) and produced a text with a different clause structure in which the shift of the Goal to Subject position draws particular attention to him:

Subject	Predicator	Adjunct	Adjunct
Bill	was hit	by Alfred	with a hammer

This kind of alternative is achieved by manipulating the clause-making resources of the grammar to highlight or play down particular pieces of the information presented in the text, i.e. we now have an answer to question 3.

In short, we have outlined the structure in terms of (1) logic, (2) grammar and (3) rhetoric and may now be forgiven for the somewhat enigmatic title of this chapter. It was chosen intentionally to reflect the realization that the answers to the three questions we have just asked suggest a tripartite division of language study which ties us back to older, long-established practices, since it closely parallels that of the medieval **Trivium** (the undergraduate foundation course in the Middle Ages): logic, grammar and rhetoric.[3]

In terms of the model of the process (Chapter 2), we are now about to extend our specification of the components of the semantic stage, provide one for the syntactic stage and rough out part of the specification for the pragmatic. In other words, we intend to integrate and expand the notions of proposition, sentence and utterance with which we closed the last chapter by relating them to the kinds of meaning they organize: cognitive, speech functional and discoursal respectively.

The linguistic model we shall be following[4] rests on a number of assumptions:

(1) that the grammar of a language is a **system of options** which are available to the user for the expression of meaning;
(2) that any stretch of language must, if it is to be communicative, contain **all three** of the types of meaning just listed; and
(3) that each of these is organized by its own **macrofunction**; a series of networks of systems which contain the options.

Indeed, it is precisely because language is designed in the way it is that the macrofunctions exist. The purpose of language is to create **communicative texts** which convey the three types of meaning we have listed and, thereby, provide satisfactory answers to the three questions – what? why? and how? – we posed about text at the beginning of this chapter.

This chapter is, therefore, concerned with the presentation of these options and with their organization and, although each of the three sections of the chapter is dedicated to a different macrofunction (**ideational, interpersonal** and **textual**), we shall focus mainly on the first; the ideational ('logic' in the medieval sense), which organizes cognitive meaning as propositions.

We have a number of reasons for this. Firstly, the role of the proposition is, as we have seen, central to the processing of texts, since it is the proposition which underlies the diversity of sentences which can express a meaning in a particular language or in language in general and propositions which are the major constituent of the universal 'semantic representations' into which texts can be decomposed and from which texts can be created; the process which is, by definition, central to any understanding of translation.[5]

There is, if there needs to be one, a second justification for giving less space here to the interpersonal and textual macrofunctions ('grammar' and 'rhetoric'). The first is extremely well documented already and the second forms the basis of the next two chapters (Chapters 5 and 6), where it will be dealt with in detail.

Let us begin by listing the macrofunctions, the meanings they organize, the systems they use for this and the forms which their options take. The three macrofunctions are:

(1) The **ideational**, which expresses **cognitive** meaning; the fundamental 'idea-conveying' function of language. This draws on the systems and networks of TRANSITIVITY[6] to create **propositions** which convey the user's experience of the external world of the senses and the inner world of the mind (this is dealt with in more detail in Section 4.1).

(2) The **interpersonal**, which expresses **speech functional** meaning by drawing on the systems and networks of MOOD to create **sentences** which carry the cognitive and logical content of propositions and display the speaker's relationship with others to whom the messages are being addressed; speaker as questioner, respondent, etc. (this is taken up below in Section 4.2 and in Chapter 5).

(3) The **textual**, which expresses **discoursal** meaning by drawing on the systems and networks of THEME to create and realize **utterances** (or **texts**) in actual communicative events and to organize these utterances in ways which are not only able to carry propositional content but are also ordered *cohesively* – the utterances connect with each other to constitute a linguistically linked text – and *coherently*; the communicative acts themselves are rationally linked and appropriate to the context of their use (this is taken up again in Section 4.3 and also in Chapter 5).

We shall deal with each in turn in this chapter but will begin by presenting a general, overall model of the networks and systems which organize the options and specify what it is that language must be able to do in order to function as an adequate communication system.

It might be wise, at this point, to make clear the status of the model. It is intended as a linguistic model of the organization of the options provided by the language and not necessarily a psychological model of (partial) language processing. It may be that there are parallels between the two – the specification of the linguistic options and the psychological processes by which selections are made from them – and, if there are, so much the better but we are not explicitly making that claim.

Equally, we should not be misled by the necessity of presenting the elements of the model in sequence (as in Figure 4.2) into thinking that this implies a particular ordering. It is important to make clear, at the beginning, that the three macrofunctions are thought of as being activated *simultaneously* rather than *sequentially*. Indeed, the whole arrangement is best conceived of as possessing the kind of *cascaded* and *interactive architecture* we proposed for the model of translation (in Chapter 2) and shall use again in presenting a model of information processing (in Chapter 7, Section 7.1).

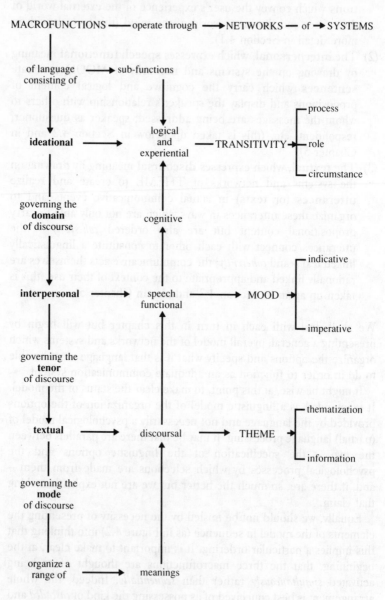

FIGURE 4.2 Networks and systems

4.1 Cognitive meaning, the ideational function and TRANSITIVITY

It may appear to be stating the obvious to say that a text cannot be translated until it has been 'understood' and, indeed, the mere assertion of this fact is fairly empty. However, its implications are far from being so. We have to ask ourselves just what it means to understand a text; what it is in a text which has to be 'understood', i.e. what the text 'means' and how the reader gains access to it.

This requires a multilevel approach which treats the text as the product of at least three types of choice which express different kinds of meaning, reflected in the content, purpose and organization of the text.

In this section, we shall focus on the first of these: the cognitive content; what the text is about.

4.1.1 Participants and processes

Consider a text like the following:

1   When the Treaty of Rome was signed on behalf of the Six in 1950, it gave Europe a long-term goal to aim at: unity.
2   After the horrors of the war, the nations of Europe hoped for peace and believed that it could be ensured by a united Europe.
3   The USA, the USSR and China were all single political units and held major positions in the world.
4   There were, of course, opposition groups but they were not, said the Europeans, significant.

What does the reader or translator know about this text? A great deal. To begin with it (1) appears to be an extract from an article or a school textbook on the early years of the EEC and (2) is written in a simple style with few unusual words or complex grammatical structures. The first of these observations concerns the text-type (a topic raised in Chapter 6) and the second signals a recognition of stylistic convention – the matching of lexical choice and syntactic structure to that – and notions of accessibility for the reader (issues which were raised earlier but will be dealt with in detail in Chapter 5).

Let us concentrate, for the moment, on the content. Let us ask, in simple terms, *who* is doing *what* to *whom* and *when* and *where* and *how* and *why?* In short, let us work out the **propositions** which underlie the text and reveal the **logical relations** which link participants, processes and circumstances together to create meaningful propositions.

There are four sentences in this passage but, as we have already suggested, we shall find it more appropriate to work at the level of clause. None the less, we can examine each sentence, dividing them – where necessary – into their component clauses.

Each sentence breaks down into two distinct propositions with Actor, Process and Goal relationships and, in some cases, Circumstances as well which can be displayed in the following ways:

1.   When the Treaty of Rome was signed on behalf of the Six in 1950, it gave Europe a long-term goal to aim at: unity.

1.1 Actor   [someone]
    Process   [signed]
    Goal   [the Treaty of Rome]
    Client   [on behalf of the Six]
    Circumstance   [in 1950]
    (time)

1.2 Actor   [the Treaty of Rome]
    Process   [gave]
    Beneficiary   [Europe]
    Goal   [a long-term goal to aim at: unity]

2.   After the horrors of the war, the nations of Europe hoped for peace and believed that it could be ensured by a united Europe.

2.1 Circumstance   [after the horrors of the war]
    (time)
    Actor   [the nations of Europe]
    Process   [hoped for]
    Goal   [peace]

2.2 Actor   [the nations of Europe]
    Process   [believed]
    Goal   [a united Europe could ensure peace]

3.   The USA, the USSR and China were all single political units and held major positions in the world.

3.1 Actor   [the USA, the USSR and China]
    Process   [were]
    Goal   [single political units]

3.2	Actor	[the USA, the USSR and China]
	Process	[had]
	Goal	[a major position]
	Circumstance	[in the world]
	(place)	

4.   There were, of course, opposition groups but they were not, said the Europeans, significant.

| 4.1 | Actor | [opposition groups] |
| | Process | [existed] |

4.2	Actor	[the Europeans]
	Process	[said]
	Goal	[opposition groups were not significant]

These analyses are not, however, entirely satisfactory. We need to make a number of modifications to the Actor Process Goal categories (and will discuss Circumstances in detail in Section 4.1.2).

The Processes in 1.1 and 1.2 are clearly **material** ones (reflecting the traditional definition of a verb as a 'doing word') and the Actors and Goals 'things'. Each of them is 'a phenomenon of our experience, including. . .our inner experience or imagination some entity (person, creature, object, institution or abstraction)'.[7] Both propositions also contain, in addition to the Goal, (so to speak) secondary 'goals': the **Client** *for* whom the Process is carried out (1.1) and the **Beneficiary** *to* whom the Goal of the Process is directed (1.2).

In 2.1 and 2.2, however, the 'processes' are not material at all but **mental**, i.e. they are concerned with the activities of the mind rather than those of the body and with *sensation* (in a broad sense; perception, affection and cognition) rather than *action*. This makes the relationship between 'actor' and 'goal' different too. More satisfactory terms here would be **Senser** and, for what is sensed, **Phenomenon**.

The next pair of propositions (3.1. and 3.2) also contains different types of participant and a different type of 'process'; a purely **relational** one; equating one participant with another – **Identifier** with **Identified** – in the first case and showing the possession of an **Attribute** by a **Carrier** in the second.

Finally, the last pair of propositions exemplify (1) a 'process' which is not a process (it is **existential**) and for that reason lacks a 'goal'; all that is indicated by the proposition is that a particular entity exists (the Existent) and (2) a particular kind of process – the **verbal** – in which the participant relationships are, once again, different; a **Sayer** who does the saying, **Verbiage** (what is said; a somewhat unfortunate term!) and, though not realized in this particular proposition, some entity towards which the 'saying' is directed; **Target**.

This rather simple (and, it must be admitted, unexciting) text illustrates six of the possible fourteen basic TRANSITIVITY options: the logical Process–Role relationships which provide the universal organization of propositions and, hence, of cognitive meaning.[8]

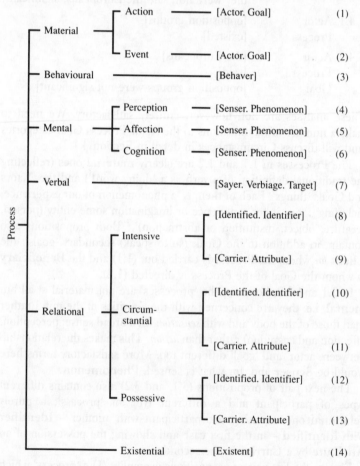

FIGURE 4.3 TRANSITIVITY systems: processes and roles

The 'simplicity' we find in the text relates, partly, to the lack of syntactic complexity in the realization of the propositions but also to the limited number of process types and the small number of circumstances surrounding them. We shall examine circumstances next.

4.1.2 Circumstances

In the previous section, we introduced the discussion of participants and processes by means of a short text. We intend to adopt the same procedure with circumstances:

> The School of Languages is situated only two hundred yards from Warren Street Underground Station. Classes normally last two hours and are available each weekday in term-time.

> Most learning is achieved by means of role-play and simulation. These are taken very seriously by staff and students who find the method more like actual communication than formal language-study was.

> As a result of the Single European Act and for the sake of our students, we have expanded our programmes in order to provide a truly Community-wide range of languages.

> We believe that learning (1) involves the teacher working with the learner and the learner with the teacher, (2) is about cooperation and (3) requires both to be equal partners in the process.

These four short paragraphs illustrate all fourteen of the options available in the TRANSITIVITY network of systems under the heading 'circumstances'. While, roughly speaking, Participant Roles provide the answer to such questions as *who/what?*, Circumstances answer questions such as *when? where? how? what with? who with? why?*, etc., filling in the detail of the immediate situation of utterance in which the Process occurs and of which the text is a representation.

They are, in a strict sense, not essential for the creation of a logically satisfactory proposition but they are crucial in providing 'background' and 'detail' without which the propositions (and the clauses which realize them) would be very bare and uninteresting.

We shall not concern ourselves with the rest of the propositional structure in this text but concentrate on the circumstances.

The circumstances signalled in paragraph 1 are all (with the exception of the first and last, which are location; in space and time respectively) concerned with **extent**:

(a) *spatial*: answering the question 'how far?' with an expression of *distance*; 'two hundred yards from Warren Street Underground Station';

(b) *temporal*: answering the question 'how long?' with an expression of *duration* of time 'two hours' and 'how often?' with one of *frequency*, 'each weekday'.

The circumstances illustrated by paragraph 2 are of **manner**:

(a) *means*: answering the question 'how?' with expressions of *agency*; 'by means of role-play and simulation'.
(b) *quality*: also answering the question 'how? but with an expression of *quality of behaviour*; 'very seriously';
(c) *comparison*: answering the question 'like what?' with expressions of *similarity* – 'more like actual communication' – and *difference* – 'than formal language study'.

Paragraph 3, however, provides examples of **cause**:

(a) *reason*: answering the question 'why?' with an expression stating the *cause* of the process: 'because of the Single European Act';
(b) *behalf*: answering the question 'who for?' by stating *for whose sake* the process is being carried out: 'for the sake of our students';
(c) *purpose*: answering the question 'what for?' with an expression of *intention*: 'in order to provide. . .'.

Finally, paragraph 4 supplies examples of the three remaining types of circumstance: **accompaniment**:

(a) *comitative*: answering the question 'who with?' with an expression which indicates that the process is one in which two participants are presented as *equally involved* 'with the learner and. . .with the teacher' in contrast with
(b) *additive*: where the question 'who with?' would be answered in a way which gave one of the participants *precedence*; 'The student as well as the teacher'.

matter: answering the question 'what about?' with an expression of *content*; 'about cooperation'.

role: answering the question 'what as?' with a statement of the role being played: '(as) equal partners'.

Figure 4.4 displays the options in *circumstances*.

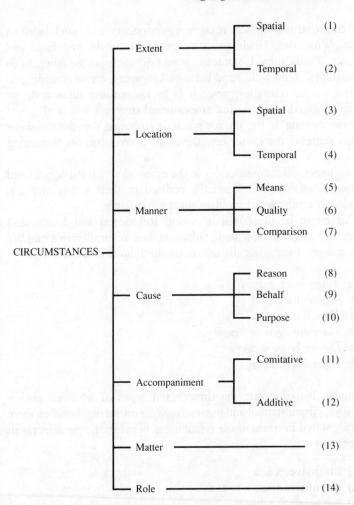

FIGURE 4.4 TRANSITIVITY: circumstances

4.1.3 Logic and the translator

The source text on which the translator works is a material object in which the TRANSITIVITY choices have already been made and have been realized through the syntactic and lexical systems of the language in which it is written. The text consists, therefore, of *clauses* which are *explicitly* present and *propositions* which are only present in an *implicit* sense.

In addition, although there is a mapping of propositional structure onto clause structure, there is no necessary one-to-one match between Actors, Processes, Goals and Circumstances on the one hand and Subjects, Predicators, Complements and Adjuncts on the other. Such 'mismatches', both within and between languages, are of considerable interest to the translator, since it is by recognizing them and, for example, inferring underlying propositional structure where elements of it are 'missing' in the surface syntactic structure, that the translator 'makes sense' of the source text; the prime prerequisite for translating it.

Languages differ considerably in the extent to which Participant and Process relationships are actually realized in their syntax and this constitutes a substantial problem for the translator.

This might be illustrated by taking **Relational** and **Existential Processes** as an example and comparing their realization in a number of languages, basing our discussion on the following six sentences:

1b *A tiger is an animal*
1b *A tiger is fierce*
2a *There is a tiger*
2b *There are tigers in Bengal*
3a *The tracks are a tiger's*
3b *Tigers have stripes*

Examples 1–3 illustrate the three major types of *relational process*; intensive, circumstantial and possessive. The distinction between them is easily stated in terms of the relationship between the participants in the process

(1) **intensive**; x is a
(2) **circumstantial**; x is at a
(3) **possessive**; x has a

and, within each, two types of participant relationship;

(a) **identifying**: *identified* + *identifier*, where 'x' and 'a' are reversible, since the relationship between them is one of *equation* and
(b) **attributive**: *carrier* + *attribute*, where 'x' and 'a' are not reversible.

We can comment on each of the six examples in turn:

1. **Intensive**
    1a *A tiger is an animal*; the equation of *tiger* and *animal* allows two

realizations of the relationship in terms of either

(i)   class-membership: 'a tiger is an animal' (belongs to the class *animal*) or

(ii) example: 'that is a tiger' (an example of a tiger).

1b *A tiger is fierce*; the lack of equation between 'tiger' and 'fierce' indicates that it is the attributes or characteristics of the entity that are being referred to.

2. Circumstantial

The circumstantial differs from the intensive (and, as we shall see, the possessive) in that the relationship is not between the entity and other entities but between the entity and its setting.

2a *There is a tiger*: a tiger is located at a particular point in space and identified by being there.

2b *There are tigers in Bengal*: an attribute, but not a defining characteristic, of tigers is to be located in Bengal.

3. Possessive

3a *The tracks are a tiger's*: the tiger 'owns' the tracks and is identifiable as a tiger (rather than, say, as a lion) by virtue of having made them.

3b *Tigers have stripes*: the possession of stripes is expected of tigers but they are not a defining characteristic any more than being located in Bengal is.

There is, of course, a final type of process we need to consider exemplified by a sentence like

There are tigers: which is *existential* in that it does no more than assert the existence of tigers. It should not, of course, be confused with a *locative* which also uses 'there' (as example 2 above) but as a deictic rather than, as it is here, a 'dummy'.

It will have been noted that, in English, *be* can be used to express all three sets of relationships (or, more correctly, five of the six realizations of them), although there is quite a range of alternatives available in English which fulfil similar functions; equatives such as *equal, represent, stand for* . . . attributives such as *get, look, seem, sound, turn* . . .

Other languages tend to make use of forms of *be* as well. Some can show the equative intensive relationship – as Russian can in the present tense – by mere juxtaposition of the two roles e.g.

Ivan, saldat i.e. John is a soldier.

Hindu/Urdu uses forms of **hona** (e.g. *hai*) in the relational processes in a way which closely parallels English usage:

1a intensive identifying: for both (i) class-membership and (ii) example:
   (i) *sher jānwar hai*: the tiger is an animal/tigers are animals
   (ii) *wo sher hai*: that is a tiger
1b intensive attributive:
   sher bimār hai: the tiger is sick
2a circumstantial identifying:
   wāhā sher hai; there is a tiger
2b circumstantial attributive:
   sher Bengāl mē hai: there is a tiger/there are tigers in Bengal
3a possessive identifying:
   pag sher ki hai; the track is a tiger's
3b possessive attributive:
   sher ki dhariā haĩ: the tiger has stripes/tigers have stripes

and the existential: *sher hai*: the tiger exists.

There appears, on the face of it, to be little problem in translating these relationships between Hindi/Urdu and English. There are, however, hidden difficulties:

In Hindi/Urdu and in several other languages (including Arabic, Hebrew, Japanese, Russian, Turkish and the Celtic languages), a form of *be* is used for the possessive relationship as well, as we have seen in examples 3a and 3b above, so a literal translation of

   sher ki dhariā haĩ =   tiger + to stripes are: to the tiger are stripes

Further, Hindi/Urdu makes a distinction between *permanent* and *transitory* attributes by adding *hotā* in the first case but using *hona* alone in the second:

   (i) *sher jangli hotā hai*:   the tiger is fierce
                                 tigers are fierce

(ii) *sher purānā hai:*   the tiger is old

In other languages (Portuguese and Spanish, for example), there are also two forms of *be* but their use is different from the languages we have been considering so far. In Spanish the forms are:

1. *ser*   for the intensive: *Juan es español*:
                                  Juan is Spanish
2. *estar* for circumstantial: *Juan está aquí*:
                                  Juan is here

However, the two forms can also be used to distinguish – as in the Hindi/Urdu case with (*hota*) *hona* – the degree of permanence of the attribute, e.g.

1. *ser*:   *Juan es simpático*:
            Juan is friendly (permanently)
2. *estar*: *Juan está simpático*:
            Juan is friendly (temporarily)

We are left, then, with a little unease about the universality of the processes proposed by the model. There seems to be a degree of fuzziness between some of them, particularly circumstantial and possessive; perhaps the fuzziness is more apparent than real and a function of language-specific syntactic and lexical choice – selections from the MOOD systems – rather than a flaw in the notion of the universal proposition; the product of choices made in the system of TRANSITIVITY.

4.1.4 Summary

The TRANSITIVITY system is that part of the grammar which provides options – fundamentally, roles and processes and circumstances – for the expression of cognitive content as required by the ideational macrofunction.

This section has been concerned with providing an outline of the system of TRANSITIVITY options and examples of it in action in other languages, as a first step towards a fuller specification of the overall grammatical system.

What follows next, is an equivalent outline of the MOOD systems which convert propositions into clauses.

4.2   Interactional meaning, interpersonal function and MOOD

In the recent discussion of the TRANSITIVITY systems, it became clear that one of the translator's major problems was to analyse the surface syntax of a text with its explicit clause structures in ways which permitted access to implicit, underlying, universal meaning carried by the propositions. Clearly, given that we also saw that there is no simple one-to-one relationship between syntactic and propositional structure, any theory of translation worthy of the name will have to outline the options available in the syntax (more correctly, in the MOOD system) for a particular language and refer, comparatively and contrastively, to others. That is the goal of this section.

First of all, we need to be clear about the role of the MOOD system. The TRANSITIVITY system (as we saw) is concerned with organizing the content of propositions. It is not concerned with the way that content is presented. That is the purpose of the MOOD system whose options present the relationships organized as propositions by the TRANSITIVITY system and constitute the syntax of a particular language.

Further, the MOOD system is, in contrast with the universal TRANSITIVITY system, language specific and there is, obviously, no way that the whole of such a system can be presented in one third of a single chapter and that is not what will be attempted here.[9] What can, however, be done is to show the relationship between communicative exchanges and syntactic forms and, in this way, alert the translator to the mechanisms which link the highly abstract and universal proposition with the totally physical and context-dependent (and, therefore, language-dependent) utterance or text.

Interactional meaning (or, alternatively, 'speech functional meaning') is the active aspect of the cognitive, since it consists[10] of the knowledge used by the communicator as *intruder* into the speech situation in contrast with communicator as *observer* of situations.

Cognitive meaning involves the representation, in propositional form, of the entities and events. Interactional meaning, in contrast, consists of the 'role relationships associated with the situation, including those that are defined by language itself, relationships of questioner–respondent, informer–doubter and the like'[11] as language is used to participate in, rather than merely observe, events. In this, the function of the MOOD system is to structure **sentences** (more correctly, 'clauses'; the two will be distinguished in a moment) which 'count as' **speech acts** which facilitate social exchanges.[12]

Let us consider the following text:

The cosmonauts reached Mars in 2023.
They were representatives of the
United Nations. They tested the
atmosphere and sent Ground Control
the historic signal; 'We have put
Man on the Red Planet'. Then they
elected the youngest member of the
crew leader of the exploration
party.

In terms of TRANSITIVITY, the text contains a mixture of Actor, Material Process, Goal and Identified, Equative, Identifier choices plus a scatter of Circumstances (location in time and in space) but what is remarkable is that these propositions are encoded into the syntax of English by representatives of all six of the unmarked positive declarative clause structures of the language. They are 'unmarked' in the sense of being 'unremarkable' and the kinds of translation we provide when asked (out of context) such questions as 'How do you say "I saw a white horse?" in French?': 'J'ai vu un cheval blanc' rather than 'C' est moi qui a vu un cheval blanc', etc. (see 4.3.3 on this).

Naturally, other options could have been selected to represent each of the propositions and those that have been selected could have been manipulated, re-ordered, expanded, contracted in an enormous number of ways, shifting the focus of attention from one part of the proposition to another (points which will be taken up later in this chapter). However, what we have in the text can be thought of as the fundamental clause structures of English which, of necessity, form part of the knowledge-base of the native and the translator and constitute (as we suggested in Chapter 2) their personal **Frequent Structure Store** for the language.

It hardly needs saying that different languages organize (and reorganize) their own clause structures differently from English and that knowledge of these contrasting MOOD systems must be part of the translator's knowledge-base.

We might examine how these structures are realized in the text, using the recognized Systemic notation: **S** [Subject], **P** [Predicator], **C** [Complement], **O** [Object] and **A** [Adjunct or Adverbial] revealing, as we do so, the 'chain' of clause 'slots' which have been filled by words and phrases. We can provide a quick analysis of the following kind:

```
            S           P       O        A
[The cosmonauts] [reached] [Mars] [in 2023]
      S       P                    C
    [They] [were]         [representatives of the
                                United Nations]
      S       P               O
    [They] [tested]      [the atmosphere]
    &      P              O
   and [sent]    [Ground Control]
                O
       [the historic signal]:
      S       P        O            A
   ['We]  [have put] [Man] [on the Red Planet']
                  S       P              O
    [Then] [they] [elected] [the youngest member of the crew]
                  C
    [leader of the exploration party]
```

This analysis is, naturally, far from complete – the structure of the phrases which (so to speak) 'fill' the structural clause 'slots' remains to be specified – and, in any case, the text itself is limited in the options it exemplifies, since every one of the clauses is a simple, positive declarative; the range of options is, of course, far larger than that (we provide an outline of the model we are using in the Appendix and shall deal with the specification of the clause options in the next section, phrase options in 4.2.2 and focus on aspects of both, with particular reference to the problems of the translator, in 4.2.3).

There is good reason to begin with the clause, since it is the fundamental unit of communication and the essential locus of operation of the MOOD system, each of whose sets of options organizes the linguistic coding of a different kind of 'exchange' and serves the crucial function of making human interaction (and, hence society as we know it) possible.

The clause, (1) encodes the universal context-free proposition into a language-specific co-text sensitive form, (2) possesses a flexible structure which allows the communicator to distribute the information contained in the proposition through a range of alternative sequences and to focus the attention of the receiver onto different parts of it and (3) acts as the abstract type for the realization of individual context-sensitive utterances and texts.

4.2.1 Communicative exchanges and clause options

It can be argued[13] that, in essence, communication involves the exchange of either (1) goods-and-services or (2) information and that the communicator (the speaker or writer) can adopt one of two roles in relation to the 'matter' being exchanged; either (1) to give it or (2) to demand it. Granted that there are many different ways of giving and demanding and a huge range of goods-and-services and information which can be exchanged but, if we accept these parameters as fundamental, communication resolves itself into an attractive, simple fourfold taxonomy which can form the basis of a model which can be elaborated later:

(a) $1 + 1 =$ Giving $+$ goods-and-services
(b) $1 + 2 =$ Giving $+$ information
(c) $2 + 1 =$ Demanding $+$ goods-and-services
(d) $2 + 2 =$ Demanding $+$ information

Without pre-empting the discussion in Chapter 6, we can assign speech acts to each of these by asking: 'What would we call what the speaker was doing in each of these cases?' Possible answers would (among others) be:

(a) Making an offer: 'Would you like a coffee?'
(b) Making a statement: 'I've made the coffee'
(c) Issuing a command: 'Give me a coffee!'
(d) Asking a question: 'Have you made the coffee?'

So far so good, but the question which arises next raises the central issue of this section; the options available in the MOOD system for the expression of these speech acts. We ask: 'What kinds of sentences can count as the above?' The answer, as we shall see in the next chapter, turns out to be very complex. No simple one-to-one correlation between syntactic structure and communicative value exists nor should we expect it too. Even so, we can show how the four types of exchange (and the speech acts we have derived from them) can be carried by *unmarked* choices from the MOOD options (the type of sentence or clause) which would be likely to co-occur with them (the very ones we actually chose in our examples): (a) Interrogative, (b) Declarative, (c) Imperative and (d) Interrogative respectively.

This is not to suggest that, for example, all declaratives signal 'giving information' i.e. that there is an isomorphism between communicative value and syntactic structure. What is being suggested is (1) that there are unmarked relationships between social value and syntactic structure and communicative value just as there are between syntactic structure and logical relationships and (2) these relationships are encoded into grammatically possible clauses through combinations of three fundamental clause structures – **Subject**, **Predicator** and, standing for both *complement* and *object*, **Complement** – which, through the sequences they offer, provide the options of the system of MOOD.

We can give examples (numbered below) of the six basic combinations in a short simulated dialogue and display the system in Figure 4.5 (the same numbers also refer to possible outcomes of selections displayed in the figure).

A We need a gromet   (1)
B What's a gromet?   (2)
   What do you mean 'gromet'?   (3)
   Is it a kind of rubber washer?   (4)
A Yes. That's right.
B Let's just use insulating tape   (5)
A Pass me the tool-box   (6)

The numbered sentences exemplify MOOD selections which are (1) **indicative + declarative**, (2), (3), (4) **open interrogative Squ** and **non-Squ** and **closed interrogative** respectively and two **imperatives**; (5) **inclusive** and (6) **exclusive**.

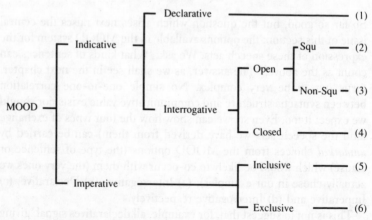

FIGURE 4.5 MOOD systems

Some comments might be made about the system shown as Figure 4.5. First of all, how is it that we are able to make these distinctions? What we are, in fact, doing is recognizing the patterning of the SPC elements and attaching syntactic labels to them rather than responding to the semantic sense or the communicative value of the clauses.

Thus the order S. . . implies *indicative* in contrast with the lack of S, which signals the *imperative*. Similarly, SP signals *declarative* while, conversely, PS signals the *interrogative*.

There is also the important distinction, in examples 3–4, between 'open' interrogatives, in which the '*Wh*' word (shown as '*Squ*' in Figure 4.5) can be either the Subject or not, and 'closed' interrogatives which are signalled by some form of *do* (in the case of lexical verbs) or by inversion of the Subject and the auxiliary (in the case of auxiliary verbs; modals, *be*, *have*, *do*, etc.).

Finally, in 5 and 6, two types of imperative can be distinguished: the first (the inclusive) marked by 'let's' and the second (the exclusive) marked by the initial Predicator and no Subject.

What marks the dialogue as somewhat artificial is the bluntness of the statements, questions, etc. What is missing is some indication of the speaker's assessment of what is being said. We might expect some qualification of the statement, some more tentative way of putting the question, some softening of the imperative, i.e. clauses which are different in *form* but the same in their *function*.

Let us imagine a slightly different dialogue, also simulated and with numbers which refer to Figure 4.6.

B	Here's a gromet	(1)
A	It could be one	(2)
	It probably is	(3)
	Yes. It must be one	(4)
B	I've never used one before	(5)
	Though Sue sometimes does and	(6)
	Iain usually does	(7)
A	I always use them	(8)
	You have to use them for a job like this	(9)
B	OK, OK I'll let you!	(10)

The crucial feature of this dialogue is the appearance (in sentences 2–4) of some kind of **modal** element, signalled by a modal verb (e.g. *could* and *must*) or a modal adverb (here, *probably*). The system of modality is an extremely important one, since it gives the communicator the option of expressing an opinion about the extent to which the assertion is (a) probable and (b) usual.

In the first clause, there is no assessment of either kind; the speaker does not raise the issue. In the second, third and fourth clauses, conviction and the statement of that conviction grows through possibility, to probability, to certainty.

In 5–8, assessment takes place but in terms of 'usuality'[14] rather than probability, moving from totally unusual (*never*) through the increasingly usual to totally usual; *always* (we shall be discussing the implications of modality for the translator in Section 4.2.3).

In 9 and 10, we have examples of obligation and inclination; a system of *modulation* rather than *modality*, since it is concerned with *proposals* rather than *propositions*. In the first instance, A justifies the use of the gromet by reference to some (unstated) safety regulation or code of good practice. In the second, B expresses the degree of willingness he feels in accepting A's insistence on the use of the gromet.

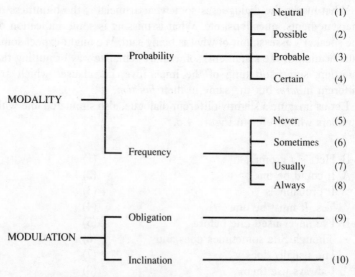

FIGURE 4.6 Modality and modulation

To conclude, we might make the point that we have carefully avoided saying that, for example, the open interrogative seeks information and is answered by the provision of that information and that this contrasts with the closed interrogative which seeks confirmation and is properly answered by 'yes' or 'no' or some equivalent expression. These are matters which are more correctly dealt with as part of a discussion of speech acts (see Chapter 6) rather than here where we are intentionally limiting ourselves to an outline specification of the syntactic resources themselves: the options which are available to the communicator for the encoding of propositions and also for use as communicative acts.

We also take it as axiomatic that (1) the structures we have been discussing can be extended in an enormous number of ways – by the expansion of the 'fillers' in each 'slot', by the embedding of further clauses within the main clause, by the coordination of additional clauses and/or phrases, by the addition of Adjuncts and so forth – and that (2) this knowledge, too, forms part of the language user's competence.

Since the clause is the carrier of the totality of the content of the proposition, we have been concentrating on an outline of the options at that level. We recognize, of course, that a grammar provides options at all of its levels – morpheme through to sentence – (and contributes to structuring beyond sentence level) and that a comprehensive model of the grammar (which would be of enormous size and beyond the scope of this book) would attempt to cover them all exhaustively.

None the less, even though we intend no such comprehensive treatment, we still feel obliged to give some attention to the smaller units, particularly the phrase.

Phrases certainly possess systems of their own (number, case, gender in the head of the NP, for example), and although these are of less general interest than those of the clause, they can and often do carry important information, particularly at the level of specific detail.

It is to the phrase and the important notion of *chain* and *choice* to which we now turn.

4.2.2   Chain and choice: phrase options

In our outline of the MOOD systems of English we have been concentrating on *clause structure*. What has been avoided (intentionally) is any consideration either of structure above or below the level of the clause or of the elements which fit into that structure. Some of these omissions can be rectified now.

We should begin by recognizing a crucial distinction in the grammatical model we are using: that of **chain** versus **choice** (alternatively, *function* versus *form*, *slot* versus *filler*, *syntagmatic* versus *paradigmatic*); syntactic *structure* versus the *forms* which realize that structure.

The analogy of the 'fruit-machine' might help here. The 'fruit machine' allows for the mechanization of a game of chance in which the player gambles on particular strings of symbols occurring in sequence. The machine contains three drums, each of which rotates at a different speed and carries a number of symbols: bells, cherries, grapes, lemons, oranges, pears, etc. There are, then, two axes:

(a) the *syntagmatic axis* of *chain*; the three positions at which the drums can stop revolving; the equivalent of the options of the MOOD system in the grammar and
(b) the *paradigmatic axis* of *choice*; the 'list' of symbols which can appear in those positions; the equivalent of the options available in the lexicon (words *and* phrases).

The MOOD system of the grammar provides a chain or structured sequence of functional positions or relations which are 'realized' or 'filled' by formal items (a) at the level of the clause by phrases and (b) at the level of the phrase by words. Just as the clause has its SPCA structure, so too phrases have their own structures; for the moment, *modifier* (m), *head* (h), *qualifier* (q).

The chain in the clause typically contains functions and forms such as:

Subject (S), *Object* (O) and *Complement* (C), typically 'realized' by formal items such as *noun phrases* (NP) 'filling' S, O and C 'slots'.

Predicator (P), realized by *verb phrases* (VP) 'filling' P 'slots'.

Adjunct (A), realized by *adverbial phrases* (AdvP) and *prepositional phrases* (PP) 'filling' A 'slots'.

For example:

The crew	tested	the atmosphere	carefully
S[NP]	P[VP]	O[NP]	A[AdvP]

Equally, phrases also contain chains and choices, e.g. in the NP, AdjP and AdvP; **modifier** (m), **head** (h), **qualifier** (q), 'filled' by formal items (normally words), as in the example below, by a determiner, an adjective, two nominals and a prepositional phrase:

The	excited	space	scientists	from Earth
NP [m(d)	m(adj)	m(n)	h(n)	q(PP)]

The suggested *modifier – head – qualifier* structures fit NP, AdjP and AdvP well enough but require re-definition for the other phrases in the case of:

(1) *verb phrases* as **auxiliary – main verb – extender** and
(2) *prepositional phrases* as **before–preposition – preposition – completer**[14] with, in principle, an unlimited number of items (including zero) 'filling' the modifier (or auxiliary) and qualifier (or extender) 'slots'.

With this information we can specify the contents of the FSS at phrase-level for English.

4.2.2.1 *Frequent structure store; phrase level*

At phrase-level we should expect modifier–head–qualifier structures, the mhq being redefined in the case of (1) verb phrases as auxiliary–main verb–extender and (2) prepositional phrases as before preposition–preposition completer[15] with, in principle, an unlimited number of items (including zero) 'filling' the modifier (or auxiliary) and qualifier (or extender) 'slots':

Noun phrases:

(m) h (q)   the man $\begin{Bmatrix} \text{from Kew} \\ \text{outside} \\ \text{who rang} \end{Bmatrix}$

Adjective and adverbial phrases:

(m) h (q)   quite $\begin{Bmatrix} \text{fast} \\ \text{quickly} \end{Bmatrix}$ enough

Verb phrases:

(a) mv (e)   can look up

Prepositional phrases:

(bp) p c   almost to France

We were careful to qualify the point about the unlimited number of 'fillers' in various parts of the structure by adding 'in principle'. In practice, processing would break down if there were too many but, more interesting from our point of view is the fact that, given a series of 'modifiers' and 'qualifiers', there is some constraint over which can occur where. In the case of the verb phrase, the order is rigid:

modal +	have +	be +	mv
may	have	been	going

Noun phrases have a greater degree of flexibility, though the fixed part of the series can be typified by

determiner	ordinator	epithet	nominal	head
the	last	hungry	Siamese	cat

That there is a typical order and that this is not necessarily the same from language to language requires us to imagine such ordering as part of the FSS.[16]

4.2.2.2 *Order of modifiers in NP*

One way of discovering the unmarked order for modifiers in a noun phrase would be to try making up arrangements of items drawn from a set of data.

For example, taking the headword *cat* and a small number of modifiers: *a, chocolate, Siamese, small, young*, we quickly arrive at the unmarked order

   a small young chocolate Siamese cat

and recognize the string of formal items as a determiner followed by no less than four *epithets*:

   d   e   e   e   e   h

The question still remains: Why *this* order rather than another? The answer seems to lie in the nature of the epithets themselves. They refer, in order, to: size, age, colour and origin. To shift the order would result in varying degrees of markedness (the determiner occurring in any but initial position, for example, would be ungrammatical as, one suspects, (3) and (4) are) or, as in (2), a change of meaning from a reference to colour (i.e. a type of Siamese cat which has chocolate-coloured points) to one which is made out of chocolate:

(1). *a young small chocolate Siamese cat*
(2). *a small young Siamese chocolate cat*
(3). *a chocolate Siamese small young cat*
(4). *a young chocolate small Siamese cat*

and so forth.

Nor are we finished if we merely say that the determiner must come first in the string. What order do the following (all of which precede the epithets) come in?: *all, other, their*. The native-user of English comes instantly to the decision:

> *all their other cats*

on the basis of knowledge which suggests that determiners can be sub-divided into (at least) *pre-deictic, deictic* and *post-deictic* (we introduced the notion of *deixis* briefly in Chapter 3, Section 3.3.3 as part of the discussion on *immediate situation of utterance*).

All this, and a great deal more, is known by the competent user of English[17]; it goes without saying that such knowledge must also be available to the translator and it is to a consideration of some aspects of MOOD, which may be of particular relevance to the translator, that we now turn.

4.2.3 Grammar and the translator

In this section we shall take up two issues which have been addressed earlier in relation to MOOD in English: (1) the ordering of epithets in other languages and (2) the expression of *modality* with particular reference to German.

4.2.3.1 The ordering of epithets

We have already suggested that part of the information stored in the FSS would include the typical unmarked order for epithets and that this is not necessarily the same from language to language. Compare, for example, the same content in English, German and French[18]:

d	e	e	n
a	fast	red	car
ein	schnelles	rotes	Auto
but:			

d	n	e	e
une	voiture	rouge	rapide

We might leave this topic by making the possibly obvious point that the English order, as given, is certainly unmarked but what if the epithets are switched?

d	e	e	n
a	red	fast	car

seems possible, though marked. Can this be replicated in German and French in the same way?

ein schnelles rotes Auto
une voiture rapide rouge

4.2.3.2 *Modality*

We saw earlier (in Section 4.2.1) that part of the MOOD system provides options for expressing opinions on the probability of a proposition being true and its frequency (i.e. how reliable the assertion is and how usual what is asserted).

We isolated eight levels of assessment: four for each. In actuality, these are points on a continuum running from *possible* and *probable* to *almost certain* and from *never* through *sometimes* and *usually* to *always*.

Clearly, it is essential for the translator to be able to recognize the strength with which the writer of the SLT holds an opinion and to be able to render that in an appropriate manner in the TLT.

English realizes these through modal verbs but also through a range of modal adjuncts and so does German, but German also has a substantial number of *modal particles* for which there are no automatic equivalents in English.

A small word like *doch* in German illustrates just how complicated translation is. By using *doch* the speaker (or writer) turns a response into a retort and its connotation is of 'complacent superiority or challenge: by the way you talk (or act) one would think you didn't know (or were ignorant of the facts)'[19],e.g.

Have you been to the exhibition at the Royal Academy?

I *never* go to London.

Ich fahre doch nie nach London.

Notice that we are reduced to italicizing the *never* in English because there does not appear to be a suitable *lexical* item, i.e. in *speech* the modality would be signalled by intonation: a rise-fall. Indeed, even where it is possible to find lexical equivalents they are rarely one-to-one and may also require substantial syntactic re-adjustment. For example, *Ist doch klar* . . . might by translated as *it's obvious* . . . but another option would be. . . *you ought to know that*, the choice depending on the surrounding co-text and context. Nor, we might add, is *doch* unique. There are over a dozen more:

(1) *mal* and *aber* to show that the speaker is impressed; favourably or unfavourably:

> *Das ist mal (aber) eine Überraschung für dich*
> That's a disappointment for you

(2) *schon* and *auch* with the same function in exclamations:

> *Was der Kerl auch (schon) für Einfalle hat!*
> *What strange ideas this fellow has!*

(3) *ja* in statements to indicate that the speaker/writer believes that the hearer/reader is aware of the facts being stated:

> *Du hinkst ja* – you're limping

or to express irony or sarcasm:

> *Du verstehst ja viel davon* – a lot *you* know about it

It would be possible to continue and survey the uses of *eben, denn, eigentlich, etwa, bloss, nur, sogar, noch, überhaupt*. . . but the point has surely been made.

4.2.4 Summary

In this section, we have shown how interactional meaning is carried by the interpersonal macrofunction of language drawing upon the options available in the systems of MOOD. The essential point was made that the role of the MOOD system is to provide the means for converting the abstract, universal, observer-oriented representations of entities and events in the form of propositions into equally abstract but language-specific, communicator-oriented clauses which underlie the ability to express meanings and to participate in communicative acts.

We have outlined the options available in the system and listed half a dozen clause-types which we believe to be typical of English and, therefore, part of the competence of the translator working from or into the language and, hence, included in any specification of that competence.

What follows is an examination of the enabling options of the THEME systems which convert clauses (plus their corresponding propositions) into utterances and texts which are actually issued in the course of communication – spoken or written – and structured so as to present information in a marked or unmarked manner.

4.3 Discoursal meaning, the textual function and the THEME system

Discoursal meaning consists of what we know about the structuring of utterances (or texts). This includes such linguistic knowledge as articulation and the use of writing systems and lexico-semantic knowledge involved in the creation of cohesive texts. It also includes knowledge which allows the speaker to organize speech acts into coherent communicative discourses; linguistic knowledge combined with such social knowledge as knowing when to speak or write, to whom, what about and how (all this stored, presumably, in the logical and encyclopedic entries of the LTM database; see Chapter 7 on this).

It is the role of the textual macrofunction of language to organize such discoursal meaning by placing both cognitive and interactional meaning in context and making 'the difference between language which is suspended *in vacuo* and language that is operational'.[20] The macrofunction provides the speaker with the means (through the systems of THEME) to create and issue **utterances** and **texts** which are 'any instance of language that is operational, as distinct from citational (like sentences in a grammar book, or words in a dictionary)'.[21] Without it the speaker would be unable to produce anything but a random collection of sentences. Through it what is produced is 'any passage, spoken or written, of whatever length, that [forms] a unified whole'.[22]

The orientation of the textual macrofunction is in contrast with the ideational and the interactional towards the concrete and physical. While the ideational macrofunction is concerned with context-free propositions (the propositional content of the speech act), and the interpersonal with the context-free **sentence type** (i.e. with linguistic rather than logical structure), the textual is concerned with the realization of **sentence tokens**, i.e. context-sensitive **utterances**.

In **speech act** terms, it is the **illocutionary force** rather than the **propositional content** which is signalled by the **textual macrofunction** and, in **discourse** terms, the **mode of discourse** rather than its **domain** or its **tenor** and the texts it structures are judged – inevitably, given their context-dependence – purely in terms of **acceptability**.

The THEME system operates through two systems both of which are concerned with the placing of **information units** in the structure of the clause and providing a range of options which allow clause structure to be manipulated so that varying degrees of **prominence** can be achieved by the information contained in the clause. The two systems are:

1. THEMATIZATION: this organizes the initiation of the clause (its communicative point of departure) and acts to direct the attention of the receiver of the message to the parts the sender wishes to emphasize. The key elements involved in this are **theme** and **rheme**.
2. INFORMATION: this organizes the completion of the clause (its information focus) and, like THEMATIZATION, also directs attention to parts of the message. The key elements involved are information **distribution** and information **focus**.

4.3.1 Organizing information; text structure

There has been, and still is, a degree of confusion in linguistics over the definitions of 'text' and 'discourse'.[23] Our own usage hinges on the distinction proposed by Widdowson[24]; a **text** is 'sentences in combination', in contrast with **discourse** which is the 'use of utterances in combination'.

A little more explicitly, we might contrast text – a 'structured sequence of linguistic expressions forming a unitary whole'[25] – with discourse as a 'structured event manifest in linguistic (and other) behaviour'.

We can go further, defining text as the 'verbal record of a communicative act'[26] and distinguish **text-as-product** from **discourse-as-process**.[27] We realize that this is a somewhat conservative position to adopt.[28] It does, however, at least have the merit of allowing us to concentrate here on text – a product of the linguistic system – and leave until the next chapter elements which are products of all the communication systems available to human beings and not just the linguistic: (1) discourse (Section 5.2) and (2) speech acts and parameters of stylistic variation (Section 5.3).

How, then, are **texts** distinguished from **non-texts**? Three characteristics have been suggested. For a text to demonstrate 'texture' (i.e. to be a text) it must possess (1) generic structure (it must belong to a recognizable genre or register, both notions we shall take up again in the next chapter), (2) textual structure (it must reflect the selection of options from the THEME systems; theme and information) and (3) internal cohesion.

The first of these characteristics – generic structure – belongs conceptually outside the linguistic system itself and within the larger semiotic systems of communication in general; it belongs, in short, with a discussion of discourse. The remaining two, however, are particularly germane to our present interests – outlining the form and function of the systems which organize discoursal meaning – and will, therefore, be discussed next.

But, before we look in detail at THEME and, more briefly (since it is a topic taken up in the next chapter) at cohesion, it would be well to state clearly what we believe text to be.

We see text as a combination of sentences linked by both syntactic and (more importantly) semantic means (through and with the linguistic co-text): **cohesion**. Text is only text by virtue of the network of lexical and grammatical links which hold it together. It is 'the basic linguistic unit, manifested at the surface as discourse'[29] and *signalled* by choices from the **theme** and **information** systems of the grammar. These systems manipulate linguistic structure to distribute and focus information; the theme system through the lexico-grammatical structure of the clause and the information system through the phonological structure of the tone group.

4.3.2 Thematization

The two THEME systems provide options for the expression of discoursal meaning as required by the textual macrofunction. Specifically, these options allow the structure of the clause to be manipulated in ways which permit the *focus* to be shifted between the various parts of the message, e.g. the passive in English making the Goal rather than the Actor the Subject of the clause and thus focusing on and giving prominence to the Goal of the Process rather than the Actor.

Theme itself contains two sub-systems: **thematization** and **information**, each of which, it will be noticed, are involved in information distribution but in different ways.[30] The first is concerned with the distribution of information in the clause and, specifically, the initiation of the clause – its 'communicative point of departure' – and acts to direct the attention of the receiver of the message to those parts of the structure of the signal which the sender wishes to emphasize.

The second, in contrast, is concerned with the distribution of information in the context of the **tone group**. We shall concentrate here on the first of these systems, since the focus of the second is speech and our own is essentially writing.[31]

In contrast with the propositional terms, Participant and Process, used in the discussion of the TRANSITIVITY system or the syntactic (syntagmatic, functional, chain) terms SPCA used in the MOOD system at clause level, thematization makes a single distinction: **Theme** versus **Rheme** (concepts originated by the Prague School in their work on 'functional sentence perspective' in the mid-1920s).

We shall use the term 'theme' in this section in a strictly technical sense which distinguishes it from 'topic' (on 'topic' and 'comment', see Chapter 5, Section 5.2.3). The Theme is the initial unit of a clause and the Rheme the remainder.[32]

Exceptions which are not taken into account when locating theme are the occurrence, as the first unit of the clause, of (a) initial 'linkers' as *and* and *or*, (b) 'binders' such as *because* and *if*, (c) evaluative disjuncts such as *fortunately*, *frankly*, *ideally* and (d) conjuncts such as *yet*, *though*, *then*, etc.[33]

The options available in thematization are displayed in Figure 4.7 with, as usual, the numbers in it corresponding to those of the examples we are about to give.

4.3.2.1 *Unmarked theme*

The 'expected', 'unmarked' and 'unremarkable' theme of a main clause – shown in italics – is illustrated by any one of the following:

1 (a) *He* bought a new car
   (b) *Did* he buy a new car?
   (c) *What* did he buy?
   (d) *Buy* a new car!

In terms of syntactic structure, these are realizations of:

(a) Subject in an active declarative clause
(b) Auxiliary in a closed interrogative

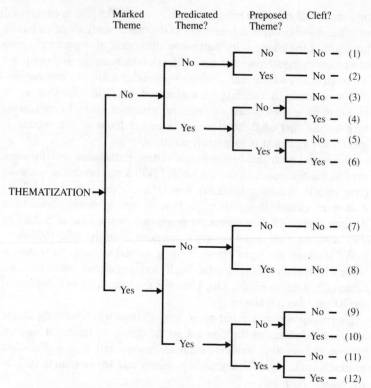

FIGURE 4.7 THEME systems: thematization

    (c) Wh – element in open interrogative
    (d) Predicator in an imperative

Any deviation from this (apart from the cases we noted earlier) constitutes **marked theme** which can be realized by means of fronting and/or predication and/or preposing (see below).

4.3.2.2 Marked theme

We shall illustrate marked theme in English – signalled by predicating, preposing, clefting or fronting of the theme and combinations of these options (other languages have, of course, different ways of marking theme) – with the following sentences, all of which, it will be realized, contain exactly the same propositional content (i.e. the Actor–Process–Goal is identical):

    (1) The dog bit the man

(2) The dog bit the man, it did
(3) The one that bit the man was the dog
(4) It was the dog that bit the man
(5) The one that bit the man was the dog, it was
(6) It was the dog that bit the man, it did
(7) The man was bitten by the dog
(8) The man was bitten by the dog, he was
(9) The one that was bitten by the dog was the man
(10) It was the man that was bitten by the dog
(11) The one that was bitten by the dog was the man, it was
(12) It was the man that was bitten by the dog, it was

We may comment on each of these options since, as will have been noticed, the stylistic effect – the appropriateness for a particular communicative context – differs quite considerably from example to example.

(1) This is the 'neutral' unmarked selection. The attention of reader (or hearer) is not caught in any way by the order in which the clause is organized. There is, in fact, a one-to-one correspondence between the elements of the propositional content (the selections from the TRANSITIVITY system) the syntactic units (selected from MOOD) and the Theme–Rheme ordering (selected from the THEME system) which is precisely why the clause, realized in this form, is unmarked:

Actor	Process	Goal
Subject	Predicator	Complement
Theme		Rheme
The dog	bit	the man

(2) Here the theme has been **preposed** by repeating it. There are, of course, alternative ways of doing this:

(a) The dog, it bit the man
(b) It bit the man, the dog did

(3) Here the theme has been **predicated** by selecting not a 'cleft sentence' structure (see (4) below) but a 'pseudo-cleft' with the structure:

$$S = NP = m\ h\ q\ [= \text{relative clause}]$$

(4) In this instance, predicating the theme has again been selected but, in contrast with the example we have just seen, taking up the option of the 'cleft sentence' where the theme is given the structure:

$$\text{it BE Theme} \left\{ \begin{array}{l} \text{who (m)} \\ \text{which} \\ \text{that} \end{array} \right\} \text{Rheme}$$

(5) This example combines predicated with preposed theme and, within the predicating options, the 'pseudo-cleft'.

(6) Here the selections are the same as in the example above – predicating and preposing – but with the 'cleft-sentence'.

(7) This example introduces the third major option: the theme has been **fronted** (also termed 'thematization', 'topicalization' and 'marking'). This has been achieved by deviating from the unmarked order, i.e. by putting, in the example we have given, the Goal in Subject position. Again there are alternatives depending on which part of the proposition is the focus. We could (a) focus on the Goal as in the example, or (b) the Process:

bit the man, the dog did

(8) Fronting with preposing.

(9) Fronting with predicating and the 'pseudo-cleft' selected.

(10) As above except for the choice of the 'cleft'.

(11) Here marking has been achieved by all three sets of options: fronting, predicating and preposing of the theme, with the 'pseudo-cleft' form of the preposing.

(12) Identical to the above, except for the 'cleft' in place of the 'pseudo-cleft'.

So much for the distribution of information within the confines of the tone group or clause. What is needed next is to indicate ways in which clauses are tied together to create texts: the processes of cohesion.

4.3.3 Linking clauses; textual cohesion

When clauses are structured by making choices from the formal options in ways which focus attention on one part rather than another of the chain, the theme systems are being activated to create linkage *within* the clause. However, when the structure of clauses contains formal lexical items which serve to create linkages *between* clauses, cohesion is being used.

Cohesion – one of the seven standards of textuality[34] – makes use of formal surface features (syntax and lexis) to interact with 'underlying semantic relations'[35] or 'underlying functional coherence'[36] to create textual unity.

Cohesion is achieved in five major ways by means of sets of markers of cohesive relationships. We shall provide examples (the numbers referring to those in Figure 4.8):

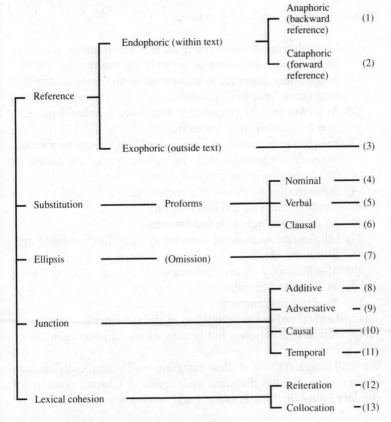

FIGURE 4.8 Markers of cohesive relationships

(1) Here's Sue. *She* has just arrived.
(2) They've gone to Spain, *the Smiths*.
(3) It's over *there*.
(4) *We* gave *them* it.

(5) Let's *do* it.
(6) I think *so*.
(7) Who's there? Fred?
(8) I got up *and* had a coffee.
(9) I woke up *but* went back to sleep.
(10) I was awake *so* I got up.
(11) I got up *then* I had a coffee.
(12) I drank *coffee* after *coffee*.
(13) There were plenty of hot drinks: *tea, coffee, milk. . .*

We may label and comment on these:

(1) **Endophoric** reference: reference to items within the text itself which make interpretation possible by making use of the *co-text*. Here reference is backwards, to an earlier part of the text; hence '*anaphoric*' reference.
(2) As above, only the reference is now forward rather than back; *cataphoric* rather than anaphoric.
(3) **Exophoric** reference: reference outside the text which makes interpretation possible only by making use of the *context* in which the text is being issued.
(4) **Substitution** by means of a *proform*; here a nominal.
(5) As above but with a verbal proform.
(6) As above but with a clausal proform.
(7) **Ellipsis**; the omission of a previously explicitly expressed form.
(8) **Junction**; additive.
(9) Also junction but, here, adversative.
(10) As above but causal.
(11) As above but temporal.
(12) **Lexical cohesion**: reiteration of the same item
(13) Also lexical cohesion but here by means of collocation.

We shall be making use of these categories and examples in the next chapter as we discuss discourse and, again, in Chapter 6 when we consider issues involved in reading and writing texts.

4.3.4 Rhetoric and the translator

Given that rhetoric – the THEME system of the grammar – is concerned with all the resources available to a communicator for distributing information in a text and focusing on selected parts of it, it is clearly impracticable to think of providing examples for all options, even for a single pair of languages; that would constitute a major work in itself. We shall therefore limit ourselves to a single issue, *markedness*, and a single pair of languages, English and French.

Consider the possible renderings into French of the proposition realized by the English clause[37]:

I saw a white horse.

(1) J'ai vu un cheval blanc.
(2) C'est moi qui a vu un cheval blanc.
(3) Mais j'ai bien vu un cheval blanc.
(4) C'est un cheval blanc que j'ai vu.

We might try literal translations of each of these into English; a process of 'back translation'.

(1) I saw a white horse.
(2) It's me/It is I that saw a white horse.
(3) But I well saw a white horse.
(4) It is/was a white horse that I saw.

Clearly there are degrees of acceptability being reflected here.

(1) is isomorphic and, presumably, unmarked in both languages and, hence, part of the FSS for both and a clause which would move through the syntactic processor at high speed whether being analysed or synthesized.

(2) is possible (i.e. grammatical) but has an awkward ring to it, which signals unacceptability for a native user of English. One would feel more comfortable focusing on the Actor with an English clause with a predicated theme and a 'pseudo-cleft' of the type:

The one who saw a white horse was me

rather than the predicated theme with a 'cleft sentence' selected by French.

(3) is not possible, as it stands (i.e. it is ungrammatical), since the information focus is on the *truth* of the assertion and would be more naturally rendered by some clause such as

I really did see a white horse

in which case we are dealing with *modality* (see 4.(3) or, alternatively, a version could be constructed which focused on the process;

> Saw a white horse, (that's what) I did

but one suspects that that is not the focus of the original.

(4) again an isomorphism between two marked forms in both the languages; focus on the Goal of the process through fronting and predicating with a 'cleft';

> It is/was a white horse that I saw

It is revealing how even two closely related languages should still diverge in their choice of options in THEME. How much greater might we expect the differences to be between more distant languages and cultures.

4.3.5 Summary

This brings to an end the outline of the third of the systems which are at the disposal of the three macrofunctions of language: the *textual*. In this section we have been concerned with specifying the nature of *text*, outlining the components of the THEME systems – information and theme – and, finally, giving an indication of the range of markers available in English (there being, of course, comparable formal sets in other languages) for linking clauses and sentences together to form texts rather than chaotic aggregates: cohesion.

4.4. Conclusion

The chapter began by building on the three-way distinction introduced near the end of the last – proposition, sentence and utterance – and used this to introduce a functional rather than a formal model of language, based on Systemic linguistics[38]. In this model, the linguistic resources of the language have been presented as being regulated by three distinct macrofunctions of language, each of which organizes a particular type of meaning through a range of options made available to the communicator, in a complex of networks and systems, for use in the encoding and decoding of messages.

The chapter, therefore, marks a major shift of focus, from form to function; from language as a closed system to language as an open system; from semantic sense to communicative value; from the context-free word or sentence to the context-sensitive utterance or text.

Most importantly, it is in this chapter that we have begun to place language in its social context, building on the three levels of setting for the communicative act (situation, context and universe of discourse) which we introduced at the end of the previous chapter, and move away from the earlier preoccupations with language as a purely abstract linguistic phenomenon or a psychological phenomenon located in the mind of the individual user and from language as an abstract context-free code isolated from the influences of space and time.

We are now at the point where we can move from the **code** and the options available in it for the expression of meaning to the actual realization of choices from among those options. We are about to leave the **text** with its thematic structures and cohesive bonds, clauses as representations of propositions (with the propositional participants and processes mapped onto the subject, predicator, complement structures of the clause) and begin to examine **discourse**: language in use, in context.

Notes

1. Tancock, 1958, 32.
2. Halliday, 1985, 37.
3. The point is made by de Beaugrande and Dressler, 1981, 15.
4. Halliday, op. cit.
5. Newmark (1988) sees similar arguments in favour of making use of 'case grammar' arguing 'Grammar is the skeleton of the text' and 'As translators, we are interested in grammar only as a transmitter of meaning' (1988, 125).
6. The ideational macrofunction operates through TRANSITIVITY (systems and networks are, following systemic convention, written in upper case), the interpersonal through MOOD and the textual through THEME and INFORMATION.
7. As Halliday, 1978, 112 puts it.
8. Halliday, ibid.
9. We are working with a Systemic model of the grammar of English; see Halliday (1985) for the most extensive current version.
10. Halliday, 1978, 112.
11. Halliday, ibid.
12. Searle, 1969.
13. Halliday, 1985, 68–70.
14. The term and the concepts are from Halliday, 1976, 86.
15. Berry, 1977.

16. Clark and Clark, 1977, 475; Muir, 1972, 30; Quirk and Greenbaum, 1973, 405.
17. Muir, 1972, 120–41, provides a summary of systems at group level.
18. Clark and Clark, ibid.
19. Schubiger, 1980, 286.
20. Halliday, op. cit., 113.
21. Halliday, 1975, 123.
22. Halliday and Hasan, 1976, 1.
23. See Riley, 1985, 22f.
24. Widdowson, 1973, 66f.
25. Edmondson, 1981, 4.
26. Brown and Yule, 1983, 6.
27. Brown and Yule, op. cit., 24–5.
28. It is, for example, in contrast with that adopted by Halliday who would accept Butler's assertion (Butler, 1985, 64) that text is both process *and* product; the product of choices made from the THEME systems and also an interactive process; an exchange of meanings.
29. Halliday, 1978, 134.
30. Information is (1) distributed, in speech, in a *simple* or *complex* manner – the boundaries of the tone group either coinciding with those of the clause or not – and (2) focused in a *marked* or *unmarked* manner. In English, the unmarked, normal focus of information (signalled by the nuclear tone) is the syllable which bears primary stress in the last lexical item of the clause and any deviation from this results in a 'marked' information focus; Halliday, 1978, 69.
31. The systems provide ways of organizing the information which distinguish the 'given' from the 'new' and by shifting the focus, create marked structures which draw the attention of the hearer to 'unexpected' parts of the message. 'Given' information is assumed by the speaker to be either already known by the hearer or to be recoverable by the speaker from what has gone before (the linguistic *co-text* and/or the extralinguistic *context*), in contrast with 'new' information which is assumed not to be recoverable in this way; Muir, 1972, 103. A useful recent discussion can be found in Butler, op. cit.. 139–48
32. Theme and Rheme appear to be roughly equivalent to the psycholinguistic terms **frame** and **insert**; see Sperber and Wilson, 1986, 88 and 138.
34. See Muir, op. cit., 97f.
35. The seven standards of textuality proposed by de Beaugrande and Dressler (op. cit., 311) are taken up in the next chapter.
35. Halliday and Hasan, op. cit., 76.
36. Widdowson, 1979.
37. Tancock, op. cit., 35.
38. Halliday, 1985.

5   Text and discourse

Up to this point, notwithstanding the approach we adopted in the previous chapter, we have been tacitly accepting two of the major tenets of twentieth century linguistics: (1) that the goal of linguistics is to specify the rules of the code possessed by some kind of idealized speaker of a language – **linguistic competence**[1] or, though not a wholly equivalent term, **langue**[2] – and, (2) that the largest linguistic unit which can be described is the sentence.

Clearly, both of these limitations work against our stated objective of building a model of the process of translation and, ultimately, creating (or discovering) a general theory of translation as both process and product.

It is self-evident that language does not exist in isolation from its users nor they from the society in which they live and it is equally evident that language, whether as knowledge or as communication, does not consist of individual, isolated sentences. We must, of necessity, extend our analysis of the code, rejecting the narrowness of focus expressed in such terms as: '. . .the structures above the level of the sentence are so varied that it is more practical. . . to focus attention on the sentence. . .'[3] and go beyond the formal structure of language as a context-free system of usage to its context-sensitive use in discourse and, as a result, take the analysis of the formal aspects of the code beyond the sentence into the text.

This raises again two issues which have exercised translators and translation theorists for centuries, i.e. the size of the unit of translation and the focus of commitment of the translator; the 'preservation' of the content or the form of the original text (both points discussed in Chapter 1, Section 1.1.2). Current thinking among translation theorists stresses the inherent impossibility of 'preserving' the original content and insists that the translated text is a new creation which derives from close and careful *reading*; a reconstruction rather than a copy:

In contrast to the critical inquiry of a text, which frequently assesses, describes, and evaluates the implications of content in a work, the translator/reader focuses on the word and sentence as process, as possibilities toward meanings. Although criticism and scholarship might already have surrounded a work by fixed opinions of interpretation, translators always have to rethink the web of interrelationships in a text before any translation becomes feasible.[4]

In this chapter we shall first pose a number of questions about the nature of texts and offer a set of criteria for judging 'textuality', then ask questions about the functions of utterances which will lead us into a consideration of the *speech act* (a notion already drawn upon in our modelling of the translation process in Chapter 2) and, finally, return to the text to specify *register* parameters which allow us to pin down the *stylistic* characteristics of texts.

This chapter, then, has the crucial role of making a link between the consideration of 'meaning' as; (a) essentially, *semantic sense* and 'meaning' as (b) *communicative value*. We have, so far, considered meaning initially in a rather conservative manner at word- and sentence-level (in Chapter 3) and, subsequently (in Chapter 4), in a somewhat more sophisticated way in terms of networks and systems of options available to serve the three macrofunctions of language – ideational, interpersonal and textual – and express three major types of meaning: cognitive, interactional and discoursal.

We shall return to the notion of 'text' and extend the rough initial definition we gave of it in the previous chapter to distinguish **text** from **discourse**. This will initiate a discussion on **cohesion** in text and **coherence** in discourse; two of the seven 'standards of textuality' (all of which will be discussed in the first section of the chapter) which give texts their 'texture' – what distinguishes text from non-text – and constitute, therefore, the defining characteristics of text.

The *text*, like the sentence, is (as we suggested earlier in Chapter 4, Section 4.3.1) 'a structured sequence of linguistic expressions forming a unitary whole',[5] in contrast with *discourse* which is a far broader 'structured event manifest in linguistic (and other) behaviour'.[6]

These definitions are, unfortunately, not entirely adequate for a number of reasons – for example 'text' and 'discourse' are used interchangeably by some linguists, while others reserve the first for written documents and the second for speech – so we would suggest definitions of the following kind (recognizing that many of the terms within them will themselves require later definition):

Text: the formal product of selections of options from the THEME systems of the grammar; a unit which carries the *semantic sense* of the *proposition* (the propositional content and locutionary force of the speech act) through *sentences* which are linked by means of *cohesion*.

Discourse: a communicative event which draws on the meaning potential of the language (and other systems of communication) to carry *communicative value* (the illocutionary force) of speech acts through *utterances* which are linked by means of *coherence*.

Once we have begun to examine texts in terms of their communicativeness, we shall find that we rapidly arrive at the point where we need to ask questions about the functions of texts (answers coming from the philosophical investigation of speech acts) and about the interconnections between textual features (selections from the code), features of the context of communication (time, place, relationship between communicators, etc.) and features of the discourse which make manifest these relationships: tenor, mode and domain of discourse.

What we have said so far about the purposes of this chapter looks back to earlier parts of the book but we should make clear that the chapter has a second purpose in addition to linking back with what has gone before. It specifies more of the knowledge the communicator must possess in order to be able to process texts (whether as sender or receiver; the focus of Chapter 6) and therefore provides a further essential element of the model of the process of translation which we outlined in Chapter 2.

5.1   Standards of textuality

In this section we shall be presenting seven defining characteristics of text; the set of standards which applies to all texts that possess communicative value, i.e. function in, and as, discourse. Each of the seven is essential and failure to comply with any one of them constitutes failure overall; the 'text' which lacks any one of these characteristics is not a text but merely an aggregate of words, sounds or letters.

The 'standards' have been proposed in order to answer a number of key questions which the reader (and translator) will need to ask about a text:

1. How do the clauses hold together? (*cohesion*)

2. How do the propositions hold together? (*coherence*)
3. Why did the speaker/writer produce this? (*intentionality*)
4. How does the reader take it? (*acceptability*)
5. What does it tell us? (*informativity*)
6. What is the text for? (*relevance*)
7. What other texts does this one resemble? (*intertextuality*)

Let us begin with a widely accepted definition of **text**:

> ... a COMMUNICATIVE OCCURRENCE which meets
> seven standards of TEXTUALITY. If any of these standards is
> considered not to have been satisfied, the text will not be
> communicative. Hence, non-communicative texts are treated as
> non-texts.[7]

We shall base this section on such a definition – recognizing, as we
do, that it extends the notion of text we have been using into that of
discourse – and work through each of the seven standards. It may be
noted, before we begin, that these standards are the constitutive
principles which define textual communication and that they are all

> *relational* in character, concerned with how occurrences are
> connected to others: via grammatical dependencies on the
> surface (cohesion); via conceptual dependencies in the textual
> world (coherence); via the attitudes of the participants toward
> the text (intentionality and acceptability); via the incorporation of
> the new and the unexpected (informativity); via the setting
> (situationality); and via the mutual relevance of separate texts
> (intertextuality).[8]

Further, we must be aware of the need to distinguish such defining
characteristics from other attributes which control textual communication once it has come into being; efficiency, effectiveness and
appropriateness have been suggested (on constitutive and regulative
rules in relation to speech acts see Section 5.2.2 and Chapter 6,
Section 6.2 on regulative rules in relation to text-processing).

5.1.1 Cohesion and coherence

The first two standards – *cohesion* and *coherence* – are distinct from each
other but share one crucial characteristic; they both have the function
of binding the text together by creating sequences of meanings. But it

is in the manner in which they do this and the nature of the 'meaning' involved that they differ.

Cohesion, the first of the seven standards, has already been described in the previous chapter (in Section 4.3.3), where we saw that cohesion consists of the mutual connection of components of SURFACE TEXT within a sequence of clauses/sentences; the process being signalled by lexico-syntactic means (see Figure 4.6 and subsequent discussion). Cohesion is, then, concerned with the manipulation of selections from the options available in the MOOD system; Subject, Predicator, Complement, Adjunct, etc. (see Chapter 4, Section 4.2.2).

Coherence, in contrast, consists of the configuration and sequencing of the CONCEPTS and RELATIONS of the TEXTUAL WORLD which underlie and are realized by the surface text; the propositional structures (Actor, Process, Goal, Circumstances, etc.) which are the creation of the systems of TRANSITIVITY (see Chapter 4, Section 4.1).

The distinction between cohesion and coherence can be readily seen in the following examples:

1. I had a cup of coffee. I got up. I woke up.
2. Burn the paper in the incinerator.
3. Generals fly back to front.
4. He found her an efficient typist.

The first is perfectly cohesive but lacks, as we know from our 'real world' knowledge, coherence; people normally wake up before they get up and have a cup of coffee. It is possible, of course, to have coffee in bed and it is also possible, though less common (it is called sleep walking) to wake up after having already got up and had a coffee; the clauses are fine but the acts are out of order.

The remaining three are syntactically ambiguous with two apparently equally appropriate interpretations:

2 (a) Predicator Object
  (b) Predicator Object Adjunct
3 (a) Subject Predicator Adjunct (place)
  (b) Subject Predicator Adjunct (manner)
4 (a) Subject Predicator Object (direct) Complement
  (b) Subject Predicator Object (direct) Object (indirect)

The code-relations alone – the cohesive linkages provided by the lexis and syntax – cannot resolve these ambiguities; reference to the co-text is insufficient. Disambiguation, in these instances, can only be achieved by reference out of the code to the context of the use of the code, i.e. by turning to real-world knowledge and by making inferences on the basis of that knowledge.

We need to know the propositional structure underlying the syntactic structure. *In the incinerator* (in 2) is clearly a realization of an **applies-to** relationship (see Appendix, Section 2 on **isa** and **applies-to** relationships) but 'applies to' what; to the *paper* (a quality) or to the *burning* (circumstance; place)?

Equally, *back to front* (in 3) is, without doubt, a Circumstance but is it *where* (place) or *how* (manner)? And is 4 to be interpreted (a) Actor Process Carrier Attribute (i.e. He found her *to be* an efficient typist) or (b) Actor Process Client Goal (i.e. He found an efficient typist *for* her)?

We are still unable to decide, until we ask the question: 'What kind of world do we think we live in?' Not, it should be noted, 'What kind of world do we think we *ought* to live in?' We may regret how things are and may attempt to change them but we have to engage in the activity of matching the world as presented to us by the text (the 'text world') with the world as we know it (the 'real world').

Is paper, necessarily, always in an incinerator ready to be burned? Our commonsense knowledge tells us that it is not and that, without further information about the specific situation of utterance (see Chapter 3, Section 3.3.3 on this), we are left with the ambiguity.

Do generals fly backwards? Not, we would suppose, in the 'real world'. The text must mean that the generals were flying back to the battle-line. Of course, it is possible to imagine alternative worlds in which generals do swoop around the sky facing the direction from which they have come but that is called 'fiction' or 'fantasy' precisely because it is not a representation of the 'known', 'real' world.

Finally, do we live in a world where a 'boss' (male) normally employs an efficient typist for someone else (female) or one where typists are normally female and expected to be found to be 'efficient'? The first seems implausible and we would be more likely to accept the second.

This appeal to our knowledge of the world and the attempt to get the text to 'make sense' in terms of it raises a number of questions which are of considerable significance for the translator: (a) *which* world are we attempting to match with the text, given the subjectivity of personal experience, the certainty that different cultures perceive (or, at least, model) the world differently?, (b) how can we act upon the realization of the highly interactive nature of text? and (c) how can we come to any principled understanding of text-processing, unless we find ways of relating 'real world' and 'text world' together in a way which 'makes sense' for us?

The next two parts of this section will begin to answer these questions and the issues will carry over into Chapter 6 as well.

5.1.2 Intentionality and acceptability

While cohesion might be seen as a typically text-oriented phenomenon and coherence less so, it is clear that notions of the 'real world' imply inhabitants of that world – users of texts who engage in discourse – and standards of textuality which refer to them rather than to the text itself. The next two characteristics – intentionality and acceptability – are, indeed, oriented in this way.

Even if a text is cohesive and coherent, it 'must be **intended** to be a text and **accepted** as such in order to be utilized in communicative interaction',[9] i.e. the *producer* of the text must intend it to contribute towards some goal (giving/demanding information/goods-and-services; see 4.2.1) and the *receiver* of it must accept that it is, indeed, fulfilling some such purpose.

The two are the converse of each other, **intentionality** being sender-oriented and **acceptability** being receiver-oriented and paralleled by the notions in speech act theory (see Section 5.2) of illocutionary and perlocutionary force and the whole framework of cooperation which marks human communication.

We shall pick up intentionality and acceptability in the next section during our discussion of speech acts and language functions.

5.1.3 Informativity, relevance and intertextuality

The three remaining standards of textuality are concerned with information structure, the relevance of the text to its situation of occurrence and the relationship of the text to other texts. We have changed the original term in the second case – *relevance* replacing *situationality* – but retain the original definition.

Texts contain information and a measure of that is the **informativity** of the text. However, the calculation is not a simple one but depends on the notions of choice and probability. A text is seen as the realization of choices made from among sets of options. There are, at each point where a choice can be made, actual choices which are more, or less, probable. The less probable and predictable a choice is, the more informative and interesting it is. Conversely, choices which are wholly predictable are uninformative and uninteresting.

However, too much information (the density of occurrence of the unpredictable exceeding some upper limit) renders the text unreadable, while the converse – too little information (the density of occurrence of the unpredictable failing to reach a threshold) – renders it readable but not worth reading. Just what the limits are is an issue which will be raised later in this chapter (in Section 5.3.1). Typically, texts will contain the highly predictable, the likely and the unpredictable and it is the balance of these which makes a text readable and also interesting (see Chapter 6, section 6.3.2 on the regulative principles which relate to this).

Three orders of informativity have been suggested, based on the assessment of a choice as falling within a range of probability: (1) upper, (2) lower and (3) outside the range.[10] We can illustrate this by examining a short text[11] in which choices at all three levels occur (each sentence has been numbered for ease of reference):

(1) Friar Sparks sat wedged between the wall and the realizer.
(2) He was motionless except for his forefinger and his eyes.
(3) From time to time his finger tapped rapidly on the key upon the desk, and now and then his irises, gray-blue as his native Irish sky, swivelled to look through the open door of the *toldilla* in which he crouched, the little shanty on the poopdeck.

In sentence (1) we have mainly second-order choices until we reach the last word; *realizer*. We only know two things about a 'realizer': (a) that it is something which 'realizes' something. This we know by analogy with *equalizer*, etc.; lexical knowledge which we bring into play at the stage of syntactic analysis as the lexical search mechanism comes into play (see Chapter 2, Section 2.2.2) and (b) that a seated man can be wedged between it and a wall.

Sentence (2) is also second-order, though *forefinger* is odd, and does nothing to resolve the problem of the 'realizer'.

Again, in sentence (3), second-order choices dominate, though *key* is third-order, as is *toldilla* – which is glossed as 'little shanty' almost immediately – and *poopdeck*, since we certainly do not expect a nautical term relating to sailing-ships.

There follows, in the original text, a four-line paragraph from which we infer that the monk is on the *Santa Maria* and is sailing with Columbus across the Atlantic on the voyage which culminated in the discovery of America. We still, however, do not know what a 'realizer' is. What follows (we shall number as if we had reproduced the paragraph just referred to) gives us more clues by providing more second-order information and, thereby, building up a clearer context for the reader to process:

> (8) The single carbon filament bulb above the monk's tonsure showed a face lost in fat and in concentration. (9) The luminiferous ether crackled and hissed tonight, but the phones clamped over his ears carried, along with them, the steady dots and dashes sent by the operator at the Las Palmas station on the Grand Canary.

Sentence (8) begins with a choice which, in the context of what has gone before, is outside the set of probable options; *carbon filament bulb*, where we might expect *guttering candle* or the like. The phrase *a face lost in fat and in concentration* is a nice example of *zeugma* (cf. *she left in a Rolls and a flood of tears*).

Sentence (9) increases the density of improbable – and, therefore, highly informative – choices; *ether, phones, dots and dashes, operator, station*. We now know what a 'realizer' is but at the expense of accepting an imagined world (the text-world) in which electricity and radio had been discovered and were in use in 1492 and (Irish) monks acted as radio operators, receiving messages in Morse from senders at transmitters on such places as the Canaries (Grand Canary being the island rather than some mythical potentate of cage-birds).

We are now in a position to provide definitions of the three levels of informativity:

1. *First order*: this level is always present in a text and is typified by choices which are obligatory or almost so; 'function words' are a good example, since they contain little actual content (we noted earlier, in Chapter 2, Section 2.3.2, the lack of an encyclopedic entry for such items), their role being logical and structural. So low is their informativity, that they are frequently omitted in such texts as telegrams and newspaper headlines and their function is easily inferred from the surrounding co-text and context.

2. *Second order*; this level represents the middle ground between first and third and arises when first-order expectations are not fulfilled i.e. where unexpected but not unlikely choices are made. For example, given a text which contains *Coffee and tea are ——*, a choice falling within the upper range of probability would be *popular drinks* (and several other possibilities which we have stored in memory). This would be true but very uninteresting; we all know that coffee and tea

are popular drinks. However, if the sentence were completed *dangerous drugs*, we would have an example of second-order informativity. A search of our memory database for *coffee* and *tea* would, no doubt, throw up the fact that coffee and tea are drugs and are dangerous, though not in the sense or to the degree that alcohol or the 'hard drugs' are.

3. *Third order*: this level is attained by choices which fall outside the expected set of options and is typified by discontinuities, where information appears to have been omitted, and/or discrepancies, where what is being presented in the text fails to match with our knowledge; i.e. there is a mismatch between the text-world and the real world, as there is in the text we have just been considering. The classic poetic example is Dylan Thomas' *a grief ago*.

This brings us to the sixth of the standards of textuality: **relevance**.

Texts not only contain information, they possess a degree of relevance or *situationality* in so far as they exist for a particular communicative purpose and link communicative acts (discourse) to the situation in which they occur. Indeed, it is crucially important for the assessment of the appropriateness of a text to know where it occurred and what its function was in that situation. For example, what are we to make of this text?:

CHINESE TAKE AWAY FOOD

Unless we know the situation in which it occurs, we cannot work out what it is. Found in a newspaper above an item of news, the text is clearly a headline. Conversely, if the text is seen outside a shop, it is, equally clearly, a sign for a fast-food outlet.

The ability to discriminate in this way depending on the situation of occurrence is, of necessity, derived from 'real world knowledge'- knowledge of contexts of utterances, schemas, frames, etc. – and is mediated by our own personal goals, values and attitudes. Indeed, it has been argued that the 'acceptability' of a text is frequently judged not in terms of 'the "correctness" of its "reference" to the "real world" but rather. . . its *believability and relevance to the participants' outlook regarding the situation*'.[12]

The passage we considered above is 'acceptable' in a science fiction story but not in a history text-book; part of our assessment of 'acceptability' relates to our knowledge of similar texts. There is, then, a need for a standard which recognizes this fact.

The final standard – **intertextuality** – refers to the relationship between a particular text and other texts which share characteristics with it; the factors which allow text-processors to recognize, in a new text, features of other texts they have encountered. What is involved here is the notion of *genre* or *text-type* (to be discussed in the next chapter) and the crucial role played by knowledge of previous texts in 'making sense' of newly encountered texts (and, we might add, making texts of new sense).

We shall not attempt to build up a text-typology at this point but will limit ourselves to making the simple point that much of our frequent appeal to 'real world knowledge' has assumed, implicitly, knowledge of the forms and functions of texts. Were this not the case, we would have been unable to use the examples we have been using to flesh out the discussion. We recognize a text such as

STOP CHILDREN CROSSING

as a direction to road-users and not as a political slogan, if we encounter it written on a circular board being carried on a black and white pole by a man or woman wearing a white coat who is stepping into the road followed by school-age children (all situationality; relevance), because we have come across such texts before. They belong to the genre 'road signs' and, for that reason, we know how to respond to them; we come to a halt before the line of children rather than rush across to them and try to prevent them from crossing the road!

5.1.4 Summary

This section has been concerned with specifying standards of textuality (the seven parameters: cohesion, coherence, intentionality, acceptability, informativity, relevance and intertextuality) to provide part of the foundation for the next chapter, which deals with text-processing. Indeed, what we have done in this section, is to reveal the elements which will be combined together later to make a dynamic model of the way readers and writers process texts.

All seven of the standards of textuality have been implicit in the model of the process of translation and in the knowledge and skills the translator possesses which allow him to translate. This section has made them explicit.

In the next section we shall continue to move away from the **microlinguistics** of code analysis to the **macrolinguistics** of code analysis 'beyond the sentence'[13] and the pragmatics of code use. Not to do so would, in Searle's words, be as unsatisfactory as 'a formal study of the currency and credit systems of economies without a study of the role of currency and credit in economic transactions'.[14]

Searle's position is clearly stated and of profound significance for a theory of translation (and, indeed, for linguistics as a whole):

> speaking a language is performing
> speech acts [which are] made
> possible by and performed in
> accordance with certain rules for
> the use of linguistic elements. . .
> The unit of linguistic communication
> is not the symbol, word or sentence
> . . .but rather the production or
> issuance of the symbol or word or
> sentence in the performance of the
> speech act. . . Speech acts are the
> basic or minimal unit of linguistic
> communication [and therefore] an
> adequate study of speech acts is a
> study of *langue*.[15]

For these reasons we wish to examine the speech act next.

5.2   Speech acts and the co-operative principle

We can ask two contrasting questions about language:

(1) 'What is language like?' (i.e. what are its formal characteristics as a context-free code?); the internal aspect of language.
(2) 'What is language for?' (i.e. what are its functions as a context-sensitive communication system?); the external aspect of language.

Until we reached this chapter, our focus has been essentially on the first of these questions as we considered the internal aspects of the code – propositions, sentences and texts – and the psychological processes which activate them.

The approach we adopted in the previous chapter marked the beginning of the shift of emphasis by presenting language as a system of communication and the code itself as a network of options for the expression of meaning. This brings us closer to responding to the second question through the description of the speech acts, utterances and discourse which are the units of the external aspect of language and to the specification of the knowledge required by the skilled communicator (and, therefore, by the translator).

Specifically, and to begin with, we shall turn our attention to the speech act, since we need to show the relationships between communicative events (or speech events or discourse) and speech acts which are realized through utterances.

We have already distinguished (in 3.3.2) proposition, sentence and utterance and have hinted (in 4.3) at the nature of the text and (in the previous section) have begun to build up a list of specifications for textuality. We have, in addition, made a distinction, within the general concept of 'meaning', between semantic sense and communicative value (Chapters 3 and 4).

The next step is to describe and explain the notion of the *speech act* which, since it contains both types of meaning, constitutes (as we saw in Chapter 2, Section 2.2) one of the major inputs to the *semantic representation* into which the clause is decomposed and from which the new clause is constructed in the process of translation.

The term 'speech act' derives from work in philosophy[16] on 'ordinary language' (initiated in the 1930s by Wittgenstein) in which the attempt is made to adduce logical rules which would show the relationship between the utterance and the behaviour of **speaker** (S) and **hearer** (H) and the **acts** (A) and **events** (E) experienced by them in the course of interpersonal communication.[17]

Specifically, the question answered by the concept is 'What does this particular utterance *count* as?', e.g. a number of sentences which all share the grammatical characteristic of being formally imperative in mood have different functions, i.e. count as a different speech act[18]:

Give me that book	[ORDER]
Pass the jam	[REQUEST]
Turn right at the corner	[INSTRUCTION]
Try the smoked salmon	[SUGGESTION]
Come round on Sunday	[INVITATION]

One answer[19] was to propose that there are five types of speech act:

commissive	commits S to some A, e.g. threat/promise
declarative	changes state of affairs in the world, e.g. wedding ceremony
directive	gets H to perform A, e.g. request suggestion/command

expressive   S expresses feelings and attitudes to something, e.g. apology/complaint

representative describes states or events in the world, e.g. claim/report/assertion

A number of questions which have particular significance for the translator now arise: (a) How do we make utterances count as particular speech acts? (b) How do we recognize what kind of a speech act a particular utterance is? (c) Is there a finite set of universally available speech acts? (d) Whether there are or not, how are we to cope with the fact of differences in realization of 'the same' speech act from language to language? In short, are there rules (universal or only language-specific) which we draw on as S and H? Searle says 'To perform speech acts is to engage in a rule-governed form of behavior'.[20]

A light-hearted example might be appropriate here. Why, we might wonder, do we ask 'Is that a threat or a promise?' and, when we do, why do our hearers often laugh? It is obviously not as simple as it appears; if it were, translation would be a great deal easier than it is. Unfortunately, some utterances seem or are intended to count as particular speech acts but speaker's intention and hearer's interpretation of that intention fail to coincide. We shall try to resolve this problem as part of a discussion of *indirect* speech acts (in Section 5.2.2) but it is to the issue of the component parts and the rules which link them to which we turn next.

5.2.1 Components and rules

According to Searle, the speech act consists of two parts:

(a) *Propositional content*: the conceptual content; the nucleus; what the act is about; what is referred to; the ideational macrofunction realized as a proposition; the literal meaning (also locutionary act/meaning); the semantic sense of the act.
(b) *Illocutionary force*: the communicative value the speaker intends the act to have; the function it is intended to serve; the intentionality of the text. Mirroring this there is, inevitably, the value the hearer puts on the act; the *perlocutionary* force; part of the acceptability of the text.

The proposition (the nucleus) is converted into a speech act which contains a particular illocutionary force by the action of an operator; some function-indicating device(s) including (in English at least):

(i)   Word- and sentence-stress
(ii) Intonation
(iii) Word order
(iv) Mood in verbs
(v)   'Performative' verbs: *apologize, assert,*
          deny. . .
(vi) The context itself; the norms for the interaction

In written English, of course, the first two in the list do not apply.

We might take three speech acts with which we shall be concerned during the discussion of text-processing in the next chapter – (a) *defining*, (b) *exemplifying* and (c) *commenting* in the context of a written didactic text – and suggest the indicating devices for each of them:

(a) *Defining*

(i)Word order: X (is thought of as) Y
              X consists of Y
              We think of X as Y

(ii)Mood in verbs: We may define X as Y
                      might
                      can
                      could
                      must

(iii)'Performative' verbs: We *define* X as Y

(iv)The context itself; the norms for the interaction

(b) *Exemplifying*

(i)Word order: For example, X is Y
              Y is an example of X
              An example of X is Y

(ii)Mood in verbs; We can exemplify X by Y

(iii)'Performative' verbs: *exemplify*

(iv)The context itself; the norms for the interaction

(c) *Commenting*

(i)Word order; X is Y

(ii)Mood in verbs: We might comment that. . .

(iii)'Performative' verbs: *comment*

(iv)The context itself; the norms for the interaction

For the translator, the problem is to match the operators by finding equivalents between the languages involved. We have already seen (in Chapter 4, Section 4.3.3) how crucial the fourth of these – modality – is and, throughout the book, have been recognizing the fundamental significance of the last; context and norms.

Searle suggests[21] that this process of conversion is regulated by two fundamentally different types of rule (constitutive and regulative), both of which we have met in the previous section during the discussion of textuality and, earlier (at least implicitly), in the outline of the model of the translation process (in Chapter 2, Section 2.2).

(a) *Constitutive rules* which define behaviour which is thereby brought into existence, e.g. the rules of a game define otherwise chaotic behaviour as that game and without the rules the behaviour might occur but would not be so named. Also, the constitutive rule is – unlike the second type of rule; the regulative – essentially descriptive and can be formulated as an *equative*: X *counts as* Y.

(b) *Regulative rules* which control pre-existing forms of behaviour, e.g. the rules of etiquette control (or regulate) social interaction but social interaction antedates the creation of the rules and is in no sense brought into being by those rules. Further, the regulative rule is essentially *prescriptive* and can be formulated as an *imperative*; *do* X or *if* Y, *do* X (and their negative forms).

Five regulative rules appear to be needed for the creation of message forms which count as speech acts with particular communicative values:

1. *General rules* which apply to all speech acts and require – inter alia – that 'normal conditions' be in force; Speaker (S) and Hearer (H) share the same code, S is (unless there is evidence to the contrary) assumed to be serious, sober, telling the truth, etc.

2. *Propositional content rules* which define what concepts can be used; the participants – speakers and hearers – and processes – acts (A) and events (E) – and their setting in time (past/present/future).

3. *Preparatory rules* which are concerned with the notions of advantage and disadvantage, the likelihood of the act or event happening in the natural course of events and the beliefs speakers and hearers

have about these notions; promises, for example, are distinguished precisely by the speaker's and the hearer's belief that the proposed act will be beneficial or harmful.

4. *Sincerity rules* which require the Speaker to be committed to carrying out the act.
5. *Essential rules* which state the 'essence' of the act i.e. that the utterance 'counts as' speech act x or y or z.

We can illustrate these rules in action by looking at 'threatening' rather than (as Searle does) 'promising'.

In order for an utterance to 'count as' a threat, rules of the following kind appear to need to be adhered to:

1. *General rule*: normal input and output conditions prevail
2. *Propositional content rule*: S refers to a future A of S.
3. *Preparatory rules*:
   (a) H would prefer S to not do A rather than do it.
   (b) S believes H would prefer this.
   (c) It is not obvious to S and H that S will do A in the normal course of events.
4. *Sincerity rule*: S intends to do A
5. *Essential rule* S intends that the utterance will place him under an obligation to do A

We might notice here that the only significant difference between the 'threat' and the 'promise' is the status of the A in the preparatory rules; for S to 'threaten' to do something which H would prefer S to do and for S to believe this and for it to not be obvious to both that S will do A in the normal course of events is not a threat but a promise.

The distinction between 'warning' and 'threatening' involves similar but more complex forms of the rules in that the active agent in the event is H rather than S. The propositional content now refers to a future act of H not of S. In the preparatory rules in (a) it is S who would prefer H not to do the act, in (b) H presumably is initially ignorant of S's preference and, indeed, it may well be that H appears to be about to do A in ignorance of the consequences; hence the warning. The sincerity rule and the essential rule are also different for 'warning': S intends H not to do A and in issuing the utterance S is committed to the truth of the assertion that (s)he would prefer H not to do A.

We can now answer the question we posed earlier about the difference between threats and promises; it all depends on the assumptions and expectations of S and H. Here is the significance of speech act theory for the translator. The General rules and those relating to Propositional content may well be universal (the concept of the semantic representation requires this) but the remaining rules, dependent as they are on notions of 'preference', the 'normal course of events' etc. must be relative and rooted in the conventions of individual (or groups of) languages and speech communities. Once again we have an example of the ease with which semantic *sense* of the proposition can be comprehended and translated in contrast with the intractability of communicative *value*.

5.2.2 Indirect speech acts

Not all speech acts are as 'direct' as those we have been discussing; there is often a mismatch between 'sentence meaning' (locutionary force; literal meaning; semantic sense) on the one hand and 'utterance meaning' (illocutionary force; indirect meaning; communicative value) on the other. As Searle says

> in hints, insinuations, irony,
> and metaphor. . .the speaker's
> utterance meaning and the sentence
> meaning come apart in various
> ways. One important class of
> such cases is that in which the
> speaker utters a sentence, means
> what he says, but also something
> more. . . In such cases a sentence
> that contains illocutionary force
> indicators for one kind of
> illocutionary [speech] act can be
> uttered to perform, IN ADDITION,
> another type of. . . act[22]

and gives the example of the interrogative/question or declarative/ statement heard as a request, e.g. 'can you reach the salt?' or 'I would appreciate it if you would get off my foot' where, as he points out, it takes some ingenuity to imagine a situation in which these utterances would not be requests.[23]

Being able to make valid requests and to recognize valid requests in the utterances of others constitutes a part of an individual's communicative competence and derives from a knowledge of the community ground rules which constrain and facilitate communicative interaction (see Chapter 2, section 2.1.3 on this in relation to translator competence).

Consider indirect requests[24] beginning with the conditions under which an imperative is heard as a request:

> If A addresses to B an imperative specifying an action X at time T1 and B believes that A believes that
>
> 1 (a) X should be done for a purpose Y (need for the action)
>   (b) B would not do X in the absence of the request (need for the request)
> 2 B has the ability to do X
> 3 B has the obligation to do X or is willing to do it
> 4 A has the right to tell B to do X
>
> then A is heard as making a valid request for action.

The significant feature of this set of conditions is the series of terms – *need, action, request, ability, obligation, willingness, right* – none of which refers to linguistic categories or concepts, i.e. they do not form part of models of the code. They belong, rather obviously, to models of society rather than of language. They are non-linguistic and, indeed, anthropological/sociological and therefore constitute (as did the notions we discussed earlier as we distinguished *promising, threatening* and *warning*) part of the social context of language use; relative rather than universal features of crucial imporance to the translator.

We can extend the discussion of indirect requests from the *imperative = request* combination to interrogatives and declaratives which function as requests. Labov and Fanshel[25] give the following rule:

> If A makes to B a *request for information* or an *assertion* to B about
>
> (a) the existential status of an action X
> (b) the time T1 that an action might be performed
> (c) any of the preconditions for a valid request for X as given in the Rule for Requests
>
> and all other preconditions are in effect, then A is heard as making a valid request of B for the action X.

(a) *Existential Status*

Have you dusted yet?

You don't seem to have dusted this room yet.

(b) *Time Reference*

When do you plan to dust?

I imagine you will be dusting this evening.

(c) *Preconditions*

1a Need for action:

Don't you think the dust is pretty thick?

This place is really dusty.

1b Need for the request:

Are you planning to dust this room?

I don't have to remind you to dust this room.

2   Ability:

Can you grab a dust rag and just dust around?

You have time enough to dust before you go.

3a Willingness:

Would you mind dusting around?

I'm sure you wouldn't mind picking up a dust rag and just dusting around.

3b Obligation:

Isn't it your turn to dust?

You ought to do your part in keeping this place clean.

4   Rights:

Didn't you ask me to remind you to dust this place?

I'm supposed to look after this place, but not do all the work.

Naturally, it is possible to challenge any of the speaker's assumptions, e.g. I could deny the existential status of X; 'I *have* dusted' or the time reference. 'I'll do it tomorrow' or any of the preconditions, 'It doesn't look bad to me', 'You don't need to remind me I'll do it later' etc. But the key point is that we tend to accept the conventions, even if we challenge their applicability at a particular time. Communication depends on *cooperation* and the withdrawal of cooperation leads rapidly to breakdown. This is certainly the case whether we limit our search for 'rules' to those which apply to individual speech acts (direct or indirect), as we have been doing here, or widen our focus to incorporate sequences of communicative acts.

Indeed, our initial attempts, when faced by something incoherent, is to try to make sense of it by using one or other of the strategies just suggested; i.e. rather than accept that the speaker/writer is being intentionally perverse, we assume that (s)he is (in spite of appearances to the contrary) trying to cooperate and to adhere to some kind of cooperative principle which regulates communication.

5.2.3 The co-operative principle

Grice,[26] discussing conversation but implying a wider applicability, suggests just such a 'rough general principle which participants will be expected (*ceteris paribus*) to observe' the Cooperative Principle:

> Make your conversational contribution such as is required, at the stage at which it occurs, by the accepted purpose of direction of the talk exchange in which you are engaged.

He goes on to distinguish four categories from which he derives a number of specific maxims:

Quantity
1. Make your contribution as informative as is required (for the current purposes of the exchange).
2. Do not make your contribution more informative than is required.

Quality
1. Do not say what you believe to be false.
2. Do not say that for which you lack adequate evidence.

Relation
1. Be relevant.

Manner
1. Avoid obscurity of expression.
2. Avoid ambiguity.
3. Be brief (avoid unnecessary prolixity).
4. Be orderly.

An interesting suggestion, which connects well with translation, has been made; that these conventions are close equivalents to the constraints which operate in intra- and inter-lingual code-switching, i.e.

> the usage conventions by which
> two codes are categorized. . . have
> conversational functions
> that are equivalent to the
> relationship of words and referents.
> This implies that both message form
> and message content play a role in
> implicature. . . Basic referential
> meanings are shared by all speakers
> of a language. . . are stable over time
> and can be preserved in dictionaries.
> Code usage [though, is] subject to
> change. . . so that sharing of basic
> conventions cannot be taken for
> granted. This accounts for the fact
> that listeners in code switching
> situations may understand the
> literal meaning of an utterance but
> differ in their interpretations of
> communicative intent.[27]

The parallel with translation is clear. We may equate the two codes with the two texts (SLT and TLT) and replace the phrase 'listeners in code switching situations' with 'readers acting as translators' and recognize in this an answer to the question of the universality of the speech act. There is, we now realize, a fundamental difference between the *propositional content rules* and the *essential rules* on the one hand and the *preparatory* and *sincerity rules* on the other.

> Searle's propositional content
> and essential rules express
> the kind of information that
> falls properly within the
> grammar's representation of the
> *lexical meaning* of performative
> verbs and other syntactic devices
> for indicating illocutionary
> force, whereas his preparatory

and sincerity rules express
essentially different information,
that is, *facts and guidelines*
that speakers use in working out
utterance meanings on the basis
of *assumptions* about each other's
beliefs and intentions.[28]

In other words, the first are concerned with context-free propositional
structure – semantic sense – while the second are concerned with
context-sensitive and language-specific communicative value. Grice
even goes so far as to define *meaning* in terms of illocutionary force;

the effect that a sender intends
to produce on a receiver by means
of a message[29]

There is, then, some hope for the universality of the speech act at the
propositional level but not at the level of illocutionary force; a
realization which helps to explain how the translator can often replicate
the *content* of a text with ease but finds much greater difficulty in
coping with grasping and re-presenting the writer's intentions.

5.2.4 Summary

In this section, we have been addressing a number of issues which
resolve themselves into a single question; what criteria can be used to
specify individual communicative activities – such as 'threatening' or
'promising' or 'defining' – and what means are there for regulating
them?

This has led us to a consideration of the speech act; a) its
components – the propositional content and illocutionary force – b) the
constitutive rules which define it and c) the regulative rules which
control it. From this came the recognition that there are indirect
speech acts which are regulated by rules of a far more social nature;
co-operative principles shared by communicators.

The ground is now laid for a discussion of text-processing (in the
next chapter) and for the further filling out of the model of the
translation process in the next section when we extend the specification
of the parameters of *register*; a major constituent of the information
stored in the semantic representation.

5.3   Discourse parameters

This section is concerned with issues which were introduced at the very beginning of the book (in Chapter 1: section 1.1) or have been implicit in earlier chapters: (a) the nature of variation in language and the way this variation reflects variations in the users of the code (realized as dialect variation) and the uses to which the code is put (realized as register variation).

Figure 5.1 can provide a visual model of user and use variation and form the basis of more detailed discussion of each parameter. First, briefly, user-based (dialect) variation. Any individual can be grouped with others by virtue of sharing with them particular quantifiable demographic characteristics which are, for most people, if not actually permanent, extremely long-lasting: gender, ethnicity, occupation, level of education, age at a given time, place of origin... One would therefore expect that the individual's speech, and to some degree writing too, would carry indications of age (temporal dialect), of geographical origin (regional dialect) and social class membership (social dialect).

Turning to the contrasting axis of use rather than user, we expect to find textual markers of the relationship between addresser and addressee(s), of the channel(s) chosen to carry the signal and of the function played by the text as an example of human communication. What we are looking for are realizations of conventions shared by the speech community for doing certain kinds of communicating; conventions which constrain the choices available to the individual and, to a degree, mask his or her individuality. There are, indeed, many types of discourse – particularly, though not exclusively, written discourse – in which the options are so severely limited that the writer's personality is totally submerged and (s)he is left with no choices which can be appropriately made which permit satisfactory communication and, at the same time, allow the writer to demonstrate any individuality.

It may have been noted that we were careful in what we have just said to hedge our assertions by using a term like 'expect' and this qualification was intentional. The problem with discussing linguistic variation in texts – and sociolinguistic variation in the broadest sense – is that while the linguistic features present in the text are categorically there or absent (they are, after all discrete units), the sociological, social-psychological and psychological characteristics we are attempting to match them with are not discrete but spread out along a continuum of more-or-less. We shall therefore need to make statements which express expectations of co-occurrence; probabilities

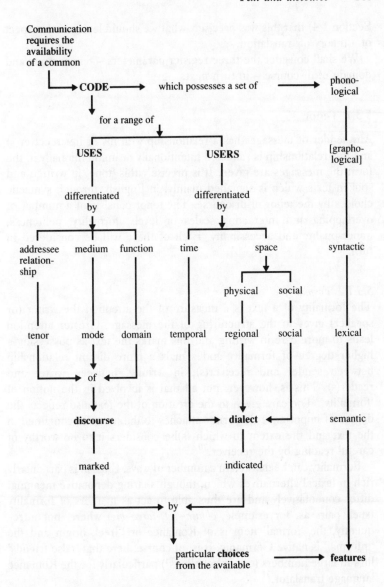

FIGURE 5.1 Variation: use and user

which are more effective as post facto 'explanations' of what has occurred than as weakly predictive statements of what will occur. This should come as no surprise. We made the point earlier (in Chapter 1,

Section 1.4) that this was precisely what we should legitimately expect of a theory of translation.

We shall consider the three register parameters – tenor, mode and domain of discourse – in turn next.

5.3.1 Tenor

Any sender of messages has a relationship with his or her receiver(s) and this relationship is reflected intentionally or unintentionally in the form the messages are given. It is precisely this 'tone' in written and spoken texts which is signalled mainly, in English, through syntactic choices by the tenor of discourse. The tenor consists of a number of overlapping and interacting scales or levels: formality, politeness, impersonality and accessibility. Each of these will be considered in turn:

5.3.1.1 Formality

The formality of a text is a measure of the attention the writer (or speaker) gives to the structuring of the message. Greater attention leads to more care in writing and this marks the text as possessing a higher degree of formality and signals a more distant relationship between sender and receiver(s); in writing, between writer and reader(s). This is, however, not all that is involved in the notion of 'formality'. The care given to the creation of the text also reflects the degree of importance the writer attaches to the message contained in the text and the extent to which (s)he considers it to be worthy of careful reading by the receiver.[30]

Formality can be marked in a number of ways. English is particularly rich in lexical alternatives which, though sharing denotative meaning, differ connotatively and are thus able to act as markers of formality (such pairs as, for example, *obtain–get*, *large–big*) where, not infrequently, the 'formal' item is of Romance or Greek origin and the 'informal' is native Germanic. It is, of course, here that 'false friends' lurk in large numbers (or big battalions?) particularly for the Romance language translator.[31]

There are, equally, syntactic choices. Parenthetical (or left-branching) structures marking formality, in contrast with informality-marking progressive (or right-branching) structures. Contrast:

1. *Left-branching*:
   King Caractacus' court's ladies' nose-powdering boy.

2. *Right-branching*:
   The boy who put the powder on the noses of the ladies of the court of King Caractacus.

There are good psychological reasons for the first being judged more formal than the second. The first takes far longer to encode and to decode and, therefore, requires more attention to be given to it by both the sender and the receiver whose short-term memories are sorely tried by the weight of information they are attempting to process. We shall take up this issue of processing again (in Chapter 6).

5.3.1.2 Politeness

Politeness reflects the social distance in the addressee relationship between sender and receiver. In this we can see two dimensions at work: (a) horizontal which is a measure of the distance between social groups and (b) vertical which reflects power relationships connected with status, seniority, authority. Clearly, the greater the distance – horizontally or vertically – between participants, the greater the degree of politeness we may anticipate in the options taken up and realized in the text.

Many languages indicate politeness through their address systems, selecting some form equivalent to the French *tu* or German *du* for the non-polite (i.e. where politeness does not apply; between social equals) and a form equivalent to the French *vous* or German *Sie* for the polite. Some languages go further – Italian has, for example, tu, voi and Lei in ascending order of politeness – and others make no such distinction in the pronoun system, e.g. English has only *you* and politeness is now signalled by the use of titles, etc.

Other markers of politeness in English (which will be partly paralleled in other languages) can be seen in the way directives are 'softened' by adding 'please' to imperatives or by structuring them as conditionals and the like.

5.3.1.3 Impersonality

Impersonality is a measure of the extent to which the producer of a text – speaker or writer – avoids reference to him/herself or to the hearer/reader. Such avoidance is far commoner in written than in spoken texts and, within written texts, in those in which the message – the cognitive content – is felt to be of greater importance than the participants in the exchange.

Typical examples can be seen in academic, bureaucratic and legal writing where the impersonal manner is signalled by comparatively high frequencies of occurrence of *it* as subject, passive constructions, abstract nouns and, when they occur, references to *the present writer* or *we* rather than *I* and to *the reader, the student, the claimant* etc. rather than *you*.

5.3.1.4 *Accessibility*

While formality reflects the attention the sender has given to the structuring of the text, accessibility shows the assumptions the sender has made about the knowledge he or she shares with the receiver; assumptions about the universe of discourse (see Chapter 3: Section 3.3.3 on this). The more the writer assumes is shared, the less needs to be made explicit in the surface structure of the text and more inaccessible the text becomes to the reader who lacks the assumed shared knowledge.

In the main, accessibility is a function of lexis. All specialisms have their own technical terminology which the newcomer to the field has to learn but the problem is not simply one of vocabulary; inaccessibility may well depend not so much on the words but on the concepts which they realize in the text, concepts which may be presented together with a novel method of argumentation. To comprehend a physics text one has to begin to think like a physicist.

5.3.2 Mode

The four parameters we have just discussed were all concerned with the reflection of relationships between the producer of the text and the text itself or the receiver of the text. In what follows, we shall be examining features which signal the choice of channel which carries the signal. We shall see that in each of the four scales what is being measured derives from the nature of the medium being used and not from any characteristics of the participants in the act of communication.

As in the case of tenor, four scales need to be considered within the general category of mode of discourse: channel limitation, spontaneity, participation and privateness.

5.3.2.1 *Channel limitation*

Communication may involve single or multiple channels. Speech, for example, operates in both the visual and the audio channels and, if the participants are close enough to each other, the tactile as well but writing is limited to the single, visual channel.

Given this limitation of channel, written texts are required to be a good deal more explicit in the signalling of meanings than spoken texts are. In speech, the information focus can be shifted by means of variations in intonation and the speaker's intention (the illocutionary force of the speech act realized by the utterance) is, more often than not, indicated by means which are not, strictly speaking, linguistic: intonation, gesture, facial expression. Since these additional channels are not available in writing, the writer is therefore forced to 'flag' parts of the text with adverbials which indicate how they are to be read e.g. 'fortunately. . .', 'to be frank. . .', etc.

5.3.2.2 *Spontaneity*

At one end of this continuum is the completely spontaneous utterance – spoken or written – which is produced on the spur of the moment without any premeditation or planning (other than that which is required by the processes of language production) and at the other, the utterance which is the result of a long period of deliberation, preplanning and editing of successive versions. The continuum nature of this scale is important to stress. While the channel limitation phenomena we have just been discussing are relatively easy to comprehend in all-or-none terms (the channel is either unitary or multiple), spontaneity is clearly far more a matter of degree; any text can be the product of more, or less, planning (a point we shall take up again in Chapter 6).

Speech is typically unplanned and, for this reason, typically non-fluent with pauses, 'ums' and 'ers', false starts and incomplete utterances as indications of this. Written language does not display such features. If a writer were to discover that a sentence was incomplete, the line (even the whole page) can be rewritten and the reader will never know what had happened.

Because the planning of written texts can extend over long periods of time during which revisions can take place, writing tends to be not only more fluent than speech but also syntactically more complex, presenting a wider range of choices from the MOOD systems and arrangements of them from the THEME systems. Indeed, the complexity extends to the lexis as well, since many writers consciously avoid repetitions of the same item and seek out replacement synonyms when they feel that they are repeating themselves.

5.3.2.3 Participation

Again, the continuum nature of this scale needs to be stressed. At one end there is the pure monologue and at the other the seemingly chaotic jumble of the genuine relaxed dialogue. What is at stake here is the extent to which feedback is permitted between sender and receiver. In face-to-face communication, feedback is normally continuous and, for the most part, non-verbal. In writing, there is no feedback or, if there is, it may come months or years later in the form of a review or a letter to the author.

None the less, the written text may well contain features which simulate participation by stimulating activity on the part of the reader. Examples would include occasions where the writer anticipated problems the reader might have and attempted to resolve them before they arose 'at this point an example may be helpful', 'the diagram on page 11 illustrates this', etc., or where the writer, assuming that a reader might wish for additional discussion on a point or access to other authorities, provides footnotes and references.

5.3.2.4 Privateness

This last mode category concerns the number of recipients intended for a particular text; the more addressees the less private. Naturally, the privateness scale overlaps considerably with some of those of the category of tenor in particular, accessibility and is signalled by the same kinds of feature. This should come as no surprise; we made the point at the beginning of the section that scales overlap and we have recognized all along that a particular element of the linguistic system can be selected and perform multiple functions.

Finally, it would be tidy if speech and writing were at opposite ends of a neat continuum where speech was typified by no channel limitation, by being impromptu, dialogue and private, in contrast with channel-limited, prepared, monologue, public writing. This is, of course, far from the truth. As Figure 5.2 shows, the continuum is very much more-or-less and the apparently clear-cut distinction between the two modes turns out to be much more fuzzy than might have initially been expected.[32]

5.3.3 Domain

The domain of discourse is revealed by choices of features of the code which indicate the role the text is playing in the activity of which it forms a part. We have already seen (in Chapter 2, Sections 2.2 and

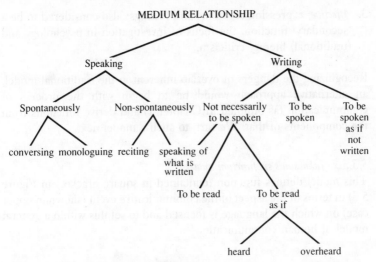

FIGURE 5.2 Types of medium relationship

2.3) how the pragmatic processing stages of the translation process drew upon *domain* to complete the specification of the *speech act* and how this information became central to the entry for the clause in its *semantic representation*.

Domain is intimately connected with function; in a narrow sense, the use of language to persuade, inform (or some other speech act) or, more broadly, in relation to some more general kind of meaning (e.g. an emotive function which stresses connotative meaning) or, in a very much broader sense, domain can refer to such macro-institutions of society as the family, friendship, education and so forth.

We shall limit ourselves, at this point, to the first of these interpretations and consider two models in turn, building on the second to isolate six major functions.

5.3.3.1 The traditional model

The traditional model of language functions suggested that language played three major roles:

1. *Cognitive*: expressing concepts, ideas, thoughts: commonly seen as the 'primary' function of language: the focus of investigation in philosophy and linguistics.
2. *Evaluative*: expressing attitudes and values: often thought of as a 'secondary' function: the focus of investigation in anthropology, sociology and social psychology.

3. *Affective*: expressing emotions and feelings: also considered to be a 'secondary' function: the focus of investigation in psychology and (traditional) literary criticism.

Recognizing the dangers of overlap inherent in the traditional model, an alternative approach would be to begin with the process of communication (as outlined in Chapter 1) and derive functions from the components of that. We turn to such a model next.

5.3.3.2 Jakobson's six function model

This model defines function (contained in square brackets in Figure 5.3) in terms of the aspect of the communicative event (shown in upper case) on which the language is focused and to set this within a general model of human communication[33]:

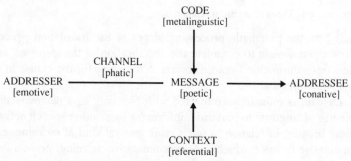

FIGURE 5.3 Domain of discourse: language functions

The notion of 'focus' is very helpful. Adult utterances (in contrast with those of pre-school children) are typically ambiguous (i.e. multifunctional) and to think in terms of *the* meaning or function of an utterance (or text) is naive. The problem is to discover the primary meaning (the focus) and this resolves itself into asking 'whose meaning?'; the meaning/focus intended by the addresser (the sender) or that decoded from the text by the addressee (the receiver)? Fortunately, we do not need to address this question yet (we shall in the next chapter) and can continue with an explanation of the model in spite of the ambiguity of reference.

Referential function. Here the focus is on the denotative content of the message; the subject-matter. As its name suggests, this function is oriented towards referring to entities, states, events and relationships which constitute the 'real world' of our experiences and are represented in the propositions which underlie texts. We have met this function already in the discussion of *cognitive meaning* and the *ideational macrofunction* of language (in Chapter 4, Section 4.1). Since it is concerned with the face-value, semantic sense of utterances, this function has, as we noted earlier, tended to be thought of as *the* function of language by the linguistically unsophisticated but, given that language is typically multifunctional, it is difficult to find an example of language in use which is *only* referential. The best we can do, for this and the remaining five functions, is to give an example which is *mainly* referential:

Here's the 14a.

Said in the bus queue, this has a referential function. It indicates the presence of an entity; a number 14a bus. But even this is potentially functionally complex. The semantic sense (or locutionary force) of what has been said is clear enough but what of the speaker's intention (the illocutionary force)? The intention could be to warn the rest of the queue that the bus was coming so that they could be ready to board it when it stopped (a conative function). Equally, given that the rest of the people in the queue can also see the bus, the actual giving of the information is redundant; the function might be a solidarity-marking one (a phatic function) and so on.

Emotive function. If the focus of attention is the sender, the meaning which is being highlighted is connotative rather than denotative; subjective rather than objective; personal rather than public. References to states of mind, feelings, health and the like all have this as their primary function. For example:

I'm tired

Emotive but also useable as a warning, an apology, an excuse. . .

Conative function. Where language is being used to influence others, we have a conative function. Very clear examples are imperatives and vocatives both of which have the explicit intention of altering the actions of another, if only by stopping them and attracting their attention. Examples might be:

Alex! Come here a minute!

Not that we should naively assume that there is a one-to-one correlation between the linguistic form imperative and the delivery of a speech act which counts as a directive. The conative function is frequently carried by features from the code which appear to be innocently signalling something quite different. Persuasion is a subtle art and, no doubt, at its most successful when it is not recognized as such by the recipient; no wonder the advertising industry in capitalist societies finds it necessary to publish a code of conduct for the regulation of its members.

Phatic function. We have dealt with functions which derive from a focus on the content of the message, on the sender and on the receiver(s) and now, with the phatic function, come to focus on the channel; on the fact that participants are in contact. The role of language of this type is to signal that one could communicate (greetings and channel-clearing signals such as 'hello' on the telephone) typify this or that one is, for the moment, not willing to discuss any particular topic; in Britain, at least, the weather and the unsatisfactory nature of public transport serve as suitable phatic topics.

It may appear that the phatic is referential but this is only true in the secondary sense that it is difficult to communicate in language without referring to something. Consider the following simple greeting ritual:

A   Hello. How are you?
B   Fine thanks. How are you?
A   Fine. See you later.
B   Yes. OK. See you.

The 'how are you?' looks like a genuine enquiry about B's physical and mental state of health and all competent users of English know that the only acceptable answer to the 'question' is one which precisely does not provide that kind of information; a recital of one's aches and pains tends to generate annoyance rather than sympathy.

But what of the context? What if A were B's doctor and they are in his surgery? Clearly, the conversation would be inappropriate and the doctor would be rightly annoyed that B was wasting his time and that of other patients. If the two meet at a party though. . .

Poetic function. In this case, the orientation is towards the message and the selection of elements from the code which draw attention to themselves and, hence, to the text. The poetic use of language has, traditionally, made use of unexpected collocations and marked thematic structures and patterning – at both the syntactic and the phonological level – which is striking through its repetitiveness or though the breaking of expectations of repetition. Rhyme- and rhythm-schemes are a clear example of this; consider the strict conventions of the limerick or the Petrarchan and Shakespearian sonnet forms.

There are, it should be recognized, 'poetic' uses of language which are an everyday occurrence; genre such as story-telling and joke-telling, children's rhymes, football shouts. The poetic function is not the preserve of the poet alone.

Metalinguistic function. This final function derives from an orientation to the code; language being used to talk about language. Dictionaries and grammars have, par excellence, a metalinguistic function as, indeed, has the whole of discourse in the discipline of linguistics itself; for example, this book.

There are, as we might expect, metalinguistic utterances and texts which are produced by people who are not professional linguists. Communicators not infrequently check their speech as they go along, particularly when verbalizing the search for an appropriate lexical item:

> Perhaps we should look into opportunities
> for fu. . .fu. . .funding. No that's not it.
> I've lost the word. What do you call it
> when a company gives a student money to
> do research? Sponsorship. That's it. Yes.
> Sponsorship.

5.3.4 Summary

In this section we have been trying to make explicit linkages between, on the one hand, selections of options available from within the systems of the code (the TRANSITIVITY, MOOD and THEME systems outlined in Chapter 4), which are realized in TEXT and, on the other, situational variables (differences between (a) *users* of texts time and both physical and social space and (b) *uses* to which texts are put; differences in addressee relationship, medium and function). To achieve this required the setting up of a descriptive level between that of the code itself and the situation of its use; the level of DISCOURSE.

Within discourse, we noted the distinction between user-based varieties of language – *dialect* – and concentrated on use-based variation – *register* – within which we examined the three major parameters and their subdivisions: (1) tenor of discourse: formality, politeness, impersonality, accessibility, (2) mode of discourse: channel limitation, spontaneity, participation, privateness, (3) domain of discourse: referential, emotive, conative, phatic, poetic and metalinguistic functions.

5.4 Conclusion

This chapter has filled out some of the areas which had to be presented in short order earlier in the book, when we presented the model of the translation process. We now have at our disposal substantial information about the code and the way choices from it are structured into texts, have introduced the important notion of the speech act and have drawn together linguistic and situational variables in discourse.

The way is now clear for a shift of emphasis from text-as-product to text-as-process and for a specification of the knowledge and skills required of the competent communicator as a creator and interpreter of texts and a participant in discourse.

Notes

1. Chomsky, 1965, 3.
2. de Saussure, 1915.
3. Cook, 1969, 39.
4. Biguenet and Schulte, (eds),1989, ix.
5. Edmondson, 1981.
6. ibid.
7. de Beaugrande and Dressler, op. cit., 3.
8. de Beaugrande and Dressler, op. cit., 37; original emphasis.
9. de Beaugrande and Dressler, op. cit., 113; original emphases.
10. de Beaugrande and Dressler, op. cit., 141f.
11. Farmer, P.J., 1952, 1.
12. de Beaugrande and Dressler, op. cit., 179; original emphases.
13. Hill, 1958.
14. Searle, 1969, 16.
15. ibid.
16. Austin, 1962; Searle, 1969.
17. The definition is based on Crystal, 1980.
18. The examples are from Richards, *et al.*, 1985.

19. Searle, op. cit.
20. Searle, 1972.
21. Searle, 1975, 138–40.
22. Searle, op. cit., 59; original emphasis.
23. ibid.
24. Labov and Fanshel, 1977.
25. ibid.
26. 1975, 45f.
27. Gumperz, 1982, 94.
28. Katz, 1977, 224; emphasis added.
29. Grice, 1957.
30. The recognition of this in sociolinguistics can be seen in Labov's vernacular principle: Labov, 1972, 78.
31. Kirk-Greene (1981) lists over 2500 'French false friends'.
32. The diagram is from Gregory, 1967.
33. Jakobson, 1960.

Part 3:   Memory

We began this book with an outline of the issues involved in translation and, in particular, in the building of an applied psycholinguistic model of the process itself. A model was proposed (in Chapter 2) and elements of that model have been expanded as we have gone along taking in (a) 'meaning' at word and sentence level (semantic sense), (b) language as a system of options for the expression of meaning, and (c) textuality and discourse; speech acts and parameters of stylistic variation in discourse (communicative or pragmatic value).

What has been assumed but not discussed openly has been the whole issue of the processes of information storage and retrieval (short-term and long-term memory) and their relevance to text-processing.

One of the very few issues on which there is substantial, if not universal, agreement among translators and translation theorists is the centrality of the text and its manipulation through the process of translation (this is typically expressed in terms of 'replacing' a text in one language with an 'equivalent' text in another: see definitions in Section 1.1).

This final part therefore focuses on the text and provides a general model of text-processing which fills in gaps in what otherwise would be an integrated model of translating.

Specifically, Chapter 6 takes up again the discussion of text and discourse which was begun in Chapter 5 and extends it into a model of text processing which includes the building of a tentative text-typology and the knowledge and skills which underpin the processing activities of reading and writing.

We consider the knowledge and skills involved in text-processing, including those of recognizing and producing appropriate realizations of different text-types, to be essential topics which need to be addressed both by the theorist and the practical translator.

We are convinced that translation cannot be adequately carried out without substantial (mainly unconscious) knowledge of the formal and functional characteristics of the text and of the typological set to which it belongs and fully support Wilss' assertion that the text-oriented nature of translation necessarily 'requires the syntactic, semantic, stylistic and textpragmatic comprehension of the original text by the translator'.[1]

Equally, we would fully support – and extend beyond poetry to text in general – de Beaugrande when he says:

> Most contributions on translation of
> poetry do not focus specifically on
> the process whereby the original text
> is read and understood. Yet the fact
> that a text must be read before it can
> be translated is by no means nugatory. . .
> one would be hard put to discover a
> translation of poetry that is entirely
> free of what appear to be errors. It is
> more probable that the errors derive
> from inaccurate reading than from
> inaccurate writing (although the latter
> cannot be ruled out).[2]

Either way, it is difficult to see how an adequate description of translation could avoid modelling, as part of the overall system, the analytical processes of reading and the synthetic processes of writing; hence the focus of Chapter 6.

Chapter 7 brings us to the point where we are able to be explicit about the processes of human information-processing on which the model of translation in Chapter 2 was itself premised.

Notes

1. Wilss, 1982, 112.
2. de Beaugrande, 1980, 29.

6 Text processing

In this chapter we shall be concerned with the question 'How do users process text?'. We shall approach this issue from two angles: the specification of (1) the knowledge required in order to process texts and (2) the skills required and we shall examine both issues in terms of reception (reading; which has been the implicit focus of our attention so far) and production (writing).

The reader of a text is faced by three problems concerning the text: (1) what it is *about*, (2) what the writer's *purpose* was in producing it and (3) what a plausible *context* is for its use. In order to answer these questions, and 'make sense' of the text, the reader has to draw on appropriate linguistic and social knowledge – syntactic, semantic and pragmatic – which reveals (a) the propositional content of the speech acts which make up the text, (b) their illocutionary forces and (c) the text-type of which this particular text is an example.

We have typified text-processing as being concerned with three problems – the discovery of content, purpose and context – and would see the process as skilled problem-solving. We shall end the chapter with a model of the stages which the reader and writer goes through when processing text and extend the model by focusing first on synthesis (writing) and then on analysis (reading).

Many of the aspects of processing which will be dealt with in this chapter have been introduced earlier (particularly in Chapter 2) and much of the knowledge involved has also been presented (in Chapters 3 – 5). It is the prime goal of this chapter to begin to integrate what has gone before and, in so doing, introduce Chapter 7 (in which we present a model of human information-processing). This will give us a clearer picture of how texts in general are processed and how translators draw on the particular kinds of knowledge and skill required in the particular type of text-processing which we term 'translating'.

At the end of the first section of the previous chapter we introduced the notion of intertextuality as one of the seven standards of textuality which a text was required to meet if it was to be considered *text*. We made the point there that part of the knowledge the text-processor possesses is knowledge of genre or text-types and it is the problem of text-typologies to which we turn first.

6.1   Text-typologies

One of the characteristics of text which we noted in the previous chapter was that individual texts resemble other texts and it is this resemblance which is drawn upon by the text-processor in 'making sense' of the text. This knowledge is, clearly, of crucial importance to the language user and any attempt to explain how texts are created and used must include an answer to the question 'How is it, given that each text is unique, that some texts are treated as the same?'

The question – posed in different forms – has, we quickly realize, arisen on no less than three previous occasions in our discussion: (1) in exploring the relationship between utterance, sentence and proposition (in Chapter 3: Section 3.3.2); (2) in demonstrating the manipulation of syntactic structures to create a range of thematic variations (Chapter 4, Section 4.3.2); and, most recently, (3) in defining the notion 'text' itself (in Chapter 5, Section 5.1) and will re-appear in relation to the creation of conceptual categories (in Chapter 7, Section 7.2.1).

The answers we gave earlier are germane to the one we seek now; the key concept is that of a type-token relationship; each individual text is a *token* – a realization – of some ideal *type* which underlies it just as the individual proposition underlies a set of clauses which, in their turn, underlie the infinite realizations of the utterance.

Unfortunately, the situation is not so simple. The infinity of utterances derives from a limited number of clause-types which, in their turn, derive from an even smaller number of propositions but, in a very real sense, the individual text is an utterance; a realization of something else. What, though, is this 'something else'? It is an interlinked series of clauses – the forms and order of which are only partially predictable – representing an interlocking series of speech acts (propositional content + illocutionary force) which are also predictable only to a limited extent.

The difficulty derives from the fact that a text-typology has to deal not with 'VIRTUAL SYSTEMS. . .the abstract potential of languages [but] . . .with ACTUAL SYSTEMS in which selections and decisions have already been made' and, further, such a typology 'must be correlated with typologies of discourse actions and situations'.[1]

This immediately calls to mind the form-function dichotomy which has been running through our discussions. Perhaps we could try a formal approach which focused on the topic (the cognitive content; the semantic sense) of the text and, as an alternative, a functional one focused on intention.

6.1.1 Formal typologies

Texts have traditionally been organized into informal typologies on the basis of *topic* – the propositional content of texts – making use of quantitative measures (frequency of occurrence of particular lexical items or syntactic structures) which were thought able to typify 'the language of science' and the like. Such work in *register*[2] developed into the kind of discourse analysis we described in the previous chapter and ran side-by-side with attempts at rather more ad hoc and intuitive groupings such as 'institutional', 'technical', 'literary' and so forth. In addition, where the typologies were set up as part of a programme of translator-training, they were used as a means of grading texts by ranking them along a scale of 'difficulty' and 'loss' from the extreme of poetry, through other literature, other texts and scientific and technical to mathematical texts which appear to be the least 'difficult' and in which there is virtually no 'loss'.

There are a substantial number of difficulties in working with such a typology but one is immediately obvious and significant. There is a fundamental problem of definition. What is meant by 'poetry', or 'literature' and how are 'scientific', 'technical' and 'mathematical' distinguished? There is, clearly, a substantial degree of overlap which suggests that content, *per se*, is inadequate as a discriminator. 'Poetry', for example, can presumably be about anything. It is how the poet treats the topic which marks it as 'poetic'. Perhaps, then, it is the formal characteristics (the linguistic structures) which are the defining characteristic. Such an approach will work with some highly ritualized genre (some types of poetry, for example) but not in the case of the majority of texts where again, and now at the formal level, there is overlap. Many of the linguistic characteristics of poetry, for example, recur in non-poetry, e.g. advertising copy. This suggests that a much more sophisticated view of 'topic' is required and this we can find in the notion of domain; the function of the text.

6.1.2 Functional typologies

A number of functional typologies have been suggested, a few[3] based on the notion of degrees of translatability but the majority[4] organized on a three-way distinction (which derives from Bühler's *organon* theory of language; language as a tool[5] depending on whether the major focus of the text is on: (1) the producer (emotive), (2) the subject-matter (referential) or (3) the receiver (conative). The typology we shall be discussing[6] labels these distinctions (1) expressive, (2) informative and (3) vocative; the poetic, metalinguistic and phatic being, presumably, subsumed under the expressive, vocative and informative, respectively.

One advantage of this typology is that it makes it possible to list text-types under each function and, in the case of the informative function, distinguish 'topic' from 'format'. For example:

Informative;   scientific   textbook

Further, it is suggested that texts can be divided into three types – literary, institutional and scientific – but it is unclear under which function 'institutional' is intended to come and the problem of overlap still remains; 'scientific ... including all fields of science and technology but tending to merge with institutional texts in the area of the social sciences'.[7]

What is still lacking is an objective statement of how the three types are to be distinguished without overlap and without an implicit dependence on native intuition. It is, after all, precisely this intuition which we wish to tap and to make explicit; it cannot, therefore, be 'given' in the argument, if we are to avoid fatal circularity.

6.1.3 Text-types, forms and samples

An extension of the three-way functional typology also proposes a three-part model: three 'major contextual foci, subsuming a number of others'.[8] This model contains a number of features which are helpful in arriving at a more hierarchical model of text-types (which begins to address the type-token problem we raised above) and, in particular, in integrating with it the three major parameters of discourse variation. Figure 6.1 illustrates how the model works.

The first major category – **text type** – is arrived at by assigning to it a particular rhetorical purpose (alternatively, the type possesses a particular communicative focus) – exposition, argumentation and instruction – and each of these major text-types contains two or three subtypes:

Text-type			
Major	Exposition	Argumentation	Instruction
Sub-type	Descriptive Narrative Conceptual	Overt Covert	+ Option – Option
Text form			Example *contract*
Text sample			Example
tenor mode domain			*formal written conative*

Note: examples are in *italics*.

FIGURE 6.1 Text-types, forms and samples

Exposition: focusing on states, events, entities and relations and sub-divided into (a) descriptive; focus on space, (b) narrative; focus on time, (c) conceptual; in terms of analysis or synthesis.

Argumentation: focusing on argument, in a broad sense, either (a) overt or (b) covert.

Instruction: focusing on influencing future behaviour either (a) with option or (b) without option.

This gives a grand total of seven text-types (e.g. instruction without option) for each of which there are large numbers of **text-forms** (e.g. for the type 'instruction without option'; 'legal contract'), each of which can be realized as a limitless number of **text samples** – actual texts – which vary in accordance with choices from among the options available in discourse; tenor, mode and domain.

An example of this might be a legal contract which has selected from (1) *tenor*; formal, polite, impersonal, inaccessible, from (2) *mode*; single channel (written to be read), non-spontaneous, non-participative, public and from (3) *domain*; conative (and referential).

What this model provides us with is the same relationship of inclusion – type and token – which we found between proposition, clause and utterance. At text-level, we now have the equivalent:

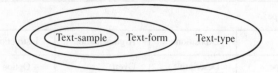

6.1.4 Summary

The importance, from both a theoretical and a practical stand-point, of creating a comprehensive and plausible text-typology cannot be over-stressed. Without the ability to recognize a text as a sample of a particular form which is itself a token of a particular type, we would be unable to decide what to do with it; we could neither comprehend nor write nor, clearly, translate.

We have considered, and rejected as excessively vague, formal typologies based on subject-matter, examined a three-way functional model which is not untypical of most current text-typologies and closed with a more sophisticated hierarchical model which seems to offer a more satisfactory framework for grouping texts and, therefore, for specifying another element in the competence of the communicator (and, by definition, the translator). It is precisely to such communicative competence (the knowledge required for text-processing) that we now turn.

6.2 Text-processing; knowledge

There is a well-known distinction between two kinds of knowledge: *procedural knowledge* (knowing how to do something) and *factual knowledge* (knowing that something is the case). In this section and the next, we propose to treat text-processing as an instance of procedural knowledge and skill in applying that knowledge; a particular aspect, that is, of communicative competence.

Initially (in this section), we intend to address the question, 'What is it that communicators need to know in order to process texts?' and then go on (in the next section) to address the related question, 'What do communicators do when they process texts?' In short, this section is concerned with the underlying knowledge which makes action possible, while the next focuses on the skilled application of that knowledge in the production and comprehension of texts; the skilled activities of (since we wish to focus on the written rather than the spoken) writing and reading.

The communicator calls upon many domains of knowledge in processing texts but the centrality of linguistic knowledge among these is in no doubt. We shall therefore ask the question: 'What is the nature of the linguistic knowledge required by the communicator?'

This is clearly a question of considerable complexity and in answering it we shall make a start by specifying three interlocking levels of linguistic knowledge (based on the approach we adopted in Chapter 4) and indicating their role in the creation of discourse.[9]

6.2.1 Syntactic knowledge

Knowledge at this level is limited to the means for creating clauses; ordered sequences consisting of the units and structures (e.g. clause: SPCA). What is involved is the knowledge of the systems of chain and choice which organize the semantic meaning provided by the proposition. In itself, then, syntactic knowledge is a matter of knowing what elements exist in a language and how they may be legitimately combined.

We can see such knowledge in operation if we try to make sense of a text whose original has been 'scrambled'; the words it contained are now presented in a random order.

Text A

in the to safely hardly all two of
said the many course almost at in
changed working of field hundred
be of views translation the years
can have

As it stands, this is not a text in the sense we have been using the term. It lacks 'texture' and fails on all seven of the criteria for judging it. True, there are stretches which have a degree of internal cohesion achieved by the collocation of words which tend to co-occur and create phrases or partial phrases; 'in the', 'hardly all two of', 'almost at', etc. We cannot even parse it, i.e. discover its syntactic structure; the realization of the choices made from the options in MOOD; where is the Subject, where the Predicator, etc.?

However, the knowledge which permits the reader to complete such exercises as this and the well-known 'cloze' tests, for example,[10] not only assumes redundancy (it is not necessary for every letter or word to occur in the text for the message to be conveyed adequately) but also semantic information about the sense of the clause. To examine this, we need to recognize that what is being called into play is not syntax alone but syntax combined with semantic information and it is this combination which gives the language user access to the literal meaning of the clause; the locutionary force of the speech act.[11]

6.2.2 Semantic knowledge

The 'cloze' text with, as in text B, every fifth word omitted and a further remodelling of text A provide our next examples:

> *Text B*
> When snow becomes compressed _____
> a long period of _____ freezing, it
> congeals into _____ and forms ice-
> streams _____ as glaciers. . . As we _____,
> the summits of many _____ are covered
> with snow _____ the year round.

This 'text' has lost its 'texture' as a result of the discontinuities created by the omitted words. It now contains seven places where there is third-order informationality; no choice has been provided from among the options available for selection at each of the points. The competent user of the language finds little difficulty in 'filling in the gaps' with items selected from the upper range of probability: *after, prolonged, ice, known, know, mountains* and *all* or lexical equivalents (other members of the set of options) of these words. It should, however, be realized that such an ability derives from semantic knowledge; what is put into the gap is what the reader believes will make sense and return missing 'texture' to the text.

Let us now take text A and reorganize it in an order which at least makes syntactic sense (text C):

> *Text C*
> in hardly two years many in the
> field can of course have changed
> almost all of the views of the
> hundred said to be working safely
> at translation

In this case, the competent reader recognizes the syntactic structure; ASPO and within the Object the relative clause acting as qualifier to the NP with 'hundred' as its head. The text 'makes sense' as a grammatical sentence and might also do so as a contribution to discourse, if there were adequate support from the context (earlier text and/or an informative setting). What is strange about this text is not the propositional structure underlying it which is impeccable

Circumstance (extent; time)	Actor	Process (material)	Goal (beneficiary)

but the uncertainty of reference which makes the text inaccessible (to us but possibly not for others). We find ourselves asking; 'What are these "two years"?', 'What field?', 'Who are these "hundred" and why are they "said" to be "working at translation" and why "safely"?'

Such issues clearly take us on to the third kind of linguistic knowledge involved in text-processing – pragmatic – but, before we move on, here is the original of texts A and C: text D:

Text D
The views of many working in
the field of translation can
safely be said to have hardly
changed at all in the course of
almost two hundred years.

6.2.3 Pragmatic knowledge

The next step is to go beyond the word and demonstrate that sentences themselves – or, more correctly as we shall see, 'speech acts' – can, to some extent, be predicted from their context just as words can. We are now in the domain of pragmatics which involves plans and goals and the textual characteristics of intentionality, acceptability and situationality – the attitudes of the producer and receiver of the text and its relevance to its context of use – all matters which take us well beyond the code (the syntax and semantics) and into the area of the use of the code for communication. Consider the following 'text'.

Text E
The user of English instantly
recognizes it, despite the
shared content, as something else:
an apology. This, as a speech act,
is one of simple reference: the

content is the burning of the
toast and my attitude to that
event is merely that of a reporter.
For example, I can refer, in a
completely neutral way, to a past
action of my own and say 'I burned
the toast this morning'. In simple
terms, a speech act consists of its
content + the orientation of the
speaker to that content and these
together give the speech act its
social meaning. This, clearly, is
more than neutral reporting of the
event. Each speech act is thought
of as consisting of two elements
(a) the **propositional content** –
what is being referred to; what it
is about – and (b) the **illocutionary
force**; the meaning the act is intended
to convey or the emphasis given to it
by the speaker. However, I could take
the same content and say 'I'm sorry I
burned the toast this morning'.

Here, all the sentences are perfectly grammatical but the overall effect
is one of chaos. The syntactic and semantic links between the elements
within the structures of the individual sentences are in no sense
problematic but this linkage is not paralleled *between* sentences, i.e.
there is no cohesion and the passage is, by virtue of this lack of
cohesion, not a text at all but a random assemblage of isolated
sentences.

How would the competent reader reorder the sentences and justify
the order (s)he selected? Presumably by (1) working out the
propositional content and the illocutionary force of each clause, i.e.
labelling each as a particular kind of speech act, e.g. the first sentence
is a statement, (2) recognizing in the text, as it unfolds, the realization
of a particular text-form which is, itself, the token of a particular
text-type and (3) reordering the sentences on the basis of expectations
of the order in which speech acts are likely to occur in this kind of text.
But, once again, we run ahead of ourselves and are in danger of
straying into the area of skills – the use of the knowledge we are

discussing here in the actual processing of texts – and feel that we should call a halt so that the processing of the text can be shown in its proper place; in the next section.

6.2.4 Summary

In this section we have been suggesting that the linguistic knowledge which underlies the user's ability to process texts can be divided (for analytic purposes) into syntactic, semantic and pragmatic knowledge, all of which play a part in the production and comprehension of texts.

In the next section, we consider how such knowledge is activated when texts are processed, apply this knowledge to making sense of text E and work our way through the text sentence by sentence in order to reveal the process.

6.3 Text-processing: skills

In the previous section, we outlined the nature of the knowledge which must underlie the ability we all possess to process texts. It must have become clear, in the course of that discussion, that it is difficult to keep knowledge and the use of knowledge separate and, indeed, they are only so distinguished in analysis and certainly not in action; the point we have reached in our discussion of text-processing. However, we shall continue in the attempt.

Perhaps a convenient place to start is to recognize that text-processing operates in both directions – reception and production; listening and speaking (or, the focus of our particular interest, reading and writing) – and that the processes involved are essentially mirror images of each other, i.e. we can explain reading and writing in terms of the same model.

There is far more involved than a simple ballistic model of the type:

Writer ⟶ TEXT ⟶ Reader

The interconnections between production and reception can be seen in Figure 6.2.

The crucial point here is that the 'text' is, as it were, a macro-speech act with its own propositional content and illocutionary force and it is clear that 'retrieving the illocutionary force of the entire text, as well as the forces of the elements making up the text, are basic principles in explicating texture. . . negotiating structure and ultimately reconstruct-

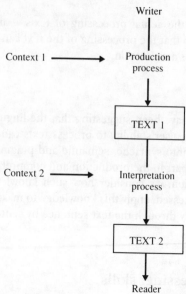

FIGURE 6.2 Writer, reader and text

ing context'[12] and that this ability is 'a precondition for efficient translation. . .'[13].

This being the case, there must be two texts (which might share a common propositional content, though even this is in doubt; see below) which differ in terms of 'force'; one (text 1) reflecting the intentions of the writer in producing the text (its illocutionary force) and the other (text 2), the result of the reader's attempt to make sense of text 1, the perlocutionary force. In other words, text 2 is the semantic representation of text 1.

Text-production and text-reception constitute the major part of the process of human communication and, as such, are inevitably subject to constraints which ensure that we are dealing not with one text but with two; the writer's text and the reader's. We can make use of part of the sociolinguistic acronym SPEAKING[14], to list the variables involved.

(1) The context (setting and scene) of writing and reading differs as between (2) writer and reader (participants) who are different individuals with different experiences of life and (3) intentions when engaged in the task of text-processing; they have differing goals (aims; general and particular) and for each the experience will have different outcomes (ends); results, intended or otherwise. Further, (4) the way in which the writer planned for the text to be taken (key) – the tenor of

the discourse – may differ drastically from the way in which it is actually taken by the reader; what was intended by the writer to be light-hearted and entertaining may be felt to be flippant and annoying by the reader. There are, however, (5) expectations (norms) concerning the behaviour of the participants as producers or receivers and these norms must, to a great extent, be shared (or at least be assumed to be shared) and realized in socially recognized text-types (genre) which are readily identified by users.

There is, then, the text produced by the writer (text 1) which is typified by the subject-matter and the writer's intentions in producing the text. Both of these factors are mediated by the context in which the text was produced, by the writer's assumptions and decisions concerning 'what constitutes a relevant and recognizable frame of reference in which to anchor the communication'[15] and the conception of the 'ideal reader' who shares this frame of reference and at whom the text is aimed. We have touched on some of these matters earlier (in Chapter 5, Section 5.3.2) when we were discussing the scale of participation within the parameter of mode of discourse.

There is the text which is the semantic representation of the first text in the mind of the reader (the actual, real reader rather than the ideal reader in the mind of the writer). This is a reflection of the context of the reading, the goals and plans of the reader, the reader's knowledge – linguistic and 'real world' knowledge – and the changing nature of the reader's uptake of the original text as it grows and develops in the course of being processed.

Text-processing is, it would appear, a problematic enterprise and, hence, one which falls within general considerations of problem-solving; we shall adopt a problem-solving approach to text-processing in our subsequent discussion.

There is a particular problem; in principle, processing could go on forever; there is no definitive reading of a text nor a perfect rendering of ideas in written form (nor, therefore, a 'perfect' translation). It is for this reason that we need the notion **threshold of termination**; the point at which the writer feels that the text is adequate to achieve the goal set for it or where the reader has got enough out of the text and/or feels that, in cost-benefit terms, there is little point in continuing.

While it is essential to accept that text-processing involves two potentially very different texts, it should be realized that writers and readers do have a great deal in common; not merely linguistic knowledge and skill but, as we noted under 'norms' and 'genre', assumptions about what is normal and how to cope with the apparently abnormal.

Two principles: 'analogy (things will tend to be as they were before) and local interpretation (if there is a change, assume it is minimal) form the basis of the assumption of coherence in our experience of life in general, hence in our experience of discourse as well'.[16] Armed with these assumptions, the reader can set out confidently expecting the unexpected to be interpretable in terms of the known.

We shall demonstrate that this is the case by tackling an extremely intractable-looking 'text'; text E with its seven sentences arranged in a random order which we presented at the end of Section 6.2.3.

6.3.1 Problem-solving and text-processing

We suggested at the beginning of this chapter that text-processing might usefully be considered within the larger context of problem-solving and intend to take the point up in a moment but, first, we need to provide an initial and rather simple model of the process (Figure 6.3).

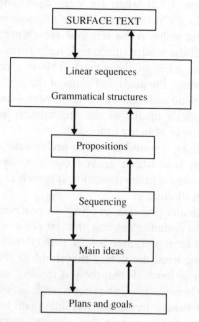

FIGURE 6.3 Text processing

The model, in its present form, suggests (1) that there are five stages involved in text-processing and (2) that these five stages are gone through, irrespective of whether the text is being received (analysed and read) or produced (synthesized and written); the difference being the direction of the processing.

A modification, difficult to show in a figure, needs to be made to the apparent unidirectional processing in each case; bottom-up for reception and top-down for production. We envisage both processes as operating in both directions – from data to concept and concept to data – in a cascaded and interactive manner which permits analysis (or synthesis) to move from stage to stage on the basis of partial completion of 'earlier' stages and for there to be constant revision of earlier decisions as processing goes on (see our earlier discussion in Chapter 2, Sections 2.1.1 and 2.1.4).

Rather than work through the model, we shall draw upon it as we go along and begin by taking up again text E, which we were attempting to process in the previous section.

The text is reproduced with each sentence numbered for ease of reference:

1. The user of English instantly recognizes it, despite the shared content, as something else: an apology.
2. This, as a speech act, is one of simple reference: the content is the burning of the toast and my attitude to that event is merely that of a reporter.
3. For example, I can refer, in a completely neutral way, to a past action of my own and say 'I burned the toast this morning'.
4. In simple terms, a speech act consists of its content + the orientation of the speaker to that content and these together give the speech act its social meaning.
5. This, clearly, is more than neutral reporting of the event.
6. Each speech act is thought of as consisting of two elements (a) the **propositional content** – what is being referred to; what it is about – and (b) the **illocutionary force**; the meaning the act is intended to convey or the emphasis given to it by the speaker.
7. However, I could take the same content and say 'I'm sorry I burned the toast this morning'.

6.3.1.1 *Processing the text*

In structural terms, the passage is curiously homogeneous; all seven sentences belong to the same grammatical, textual and discoursal categories: declarative, statement, informative. We need a more informative analysis but that can only be achieved by relating each sentence to both its co-text – the sentences around it – and its context; the speech acts surrounding it.

We can begin by noticing markers of cohesive relations (see Chapter 4, Section 4.3.3) which will allow us to decide whether a sentence could be the first in the text.

1. The user of English instantly recognizes it, despite the shared content, as something else: an apology.

In terms of bottom-up processing, we can parse the linear sequence and recognize that 'it' must refer back to some earlier nominal in the text (an example of the substitution of a proform – a pronoun – to make anaphoric reference) and infer from that that (1) is not the first sentence of the text. Equally, from the top-down point of view, even though we cannot be sure what the discourse function of the sentence is (other than crudely 'informative') until we have reorganized the text, we will already have recognized, even from this first sentence with its unqualified assertion, relatively complex syntax and abstract technical terminology having the structure

definition + example(s) + comment(s)

that this is a didactic and metalinguistic text, probably from a textbook or a paper in linguistics or a linguistically oriented sub-domain of one of the human sciences.

2. This, as a speech act, is one of simple reference: the content is the burning of the toast and my attitude to that event is merely that of a reporter.

'This' also refers back; a deictic with anaphoric reference. (2) cannot, therefore, be the first sentence either and, like (1), its speech act/functional status cannot be specified beyond the very general 'informative'. The sentence, however, provides further evidence in support of our initial assumption that the domain of this text is metalinguistic. Even in purely lexical terms the conclusion seems irresistible; 'speech act', 'reference' and (a second time) 'content'. Acting on this hunch (until there is good reason to change our minds), we recall what we know about didactic written discourse in general and about linguistics in particular and could, at this point, rush ahead and look for a definition, since we expect such texts to begin with definitions. However, we shall be cautious and continue our sentence-by-sentence reading and analysis.

3. For example, I can refer, in a completely neutral way, to a past action of my own and say 'I burned the toast this morning'.

'For example' is also anaphoric; a reference to some earlier element of the text which is to be reintroduced and exemplified. (3) cannot be the first sentence either and is marked by the phrase 'for example' as functioning as an example.

4. In simple terms, a speech act consists of its content + the orientation of the speaker to that content and these together give the speech act its social meaning.

A definition, indicated by the syntactic structure 'X consists of Y' (i.e 'has-as-parts'; see 7.3.2) and no clear indication that this is not the first sentence of *this* passage; the 'in simple terms' suggests reference to an earlier text but the evidence is not conclusive.

5. This, clearly, is more than neutral reporting of the event.

'This', as in (2) is deictic anaphoric reference and, therefore, and for the same reasons, cannot be the first sentence of the text. Equally, without knowing what the 'this' refers to, its speech act status remains as an informative.

6. Each speech act is thought of as consisting of two elements (a) the **propositional content** – what is being referred to; what it is about – and (b) the **illocutionary force**; the meaning the act is intended to convey or the emphasis given to it by the speaker.

Like (4), a definition and a possible first sentence. The definition structure 'X is thought of as consisting of Y' is clearly a variant of that used in (4), though it still has the logical structure 'X has-as-parts Y'. If we accept that texts of this kind tend to begin with definitions (and not every reader does, as we shall see at the end of this analysis in the alternative readings presented in Figure 6.5), the question here is whether we start with a 'tough' definition (6) or a 'soft' one (4); a matter of pedagogic taste.

7. However, I could take the same content and say 'I'm sorry I burned the toast this morning'.

The 'however' is concessive conceding an earlier position and moving on to a new one and therefore implicitly reference to an earlier part of the text. (7) is, therefore, not the first sentence nor can we yet decide what kind of a speech act it is other than the general 'informative'.

We have, at this point, an indication of the likely speech act being realized by four of the seven sentences (3, 4, 6, 7) and, given that we are accustomed to didactic texts (and we recognized this text as didactic rather quickly), we can suggest the function 'comment' for the remainder (1, 2, 5):

1. comment   2. comment   3. example
4. definition   5. comment   6. definition
7. example

Drawing on our expectations about the structuring of texts of this kind, we would think it likely that the text would have at least one *definition* (D) initially and that the definition(s) would be followed by *example* + *comment* sequences ($E^n + C^n$, i.e. one or more of each). All this suggests five plausible D + E + C configurations (definition + example + comment) which we can display in a branching flow-diagram (Figure 6.4).

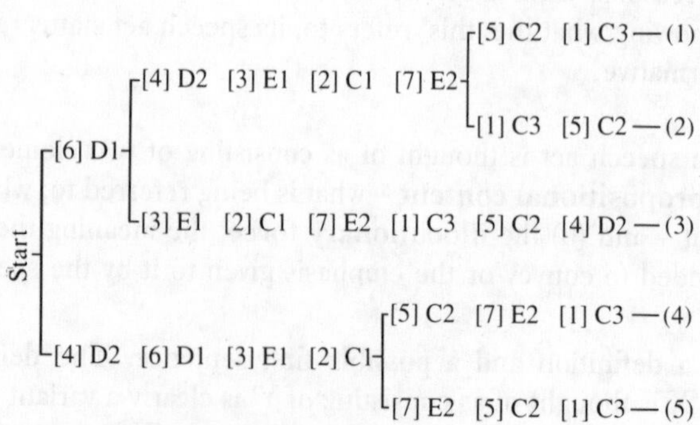

FIGURE 6.4 Readings of text E

Comment

1. Original order: D1 D2 E1 C1 E2 C2 C3 (see text F below)
2. As 1 but with C2 [5] and C3 [1] reversed.

3. Like 1 and 2 begins with D1 [6] but then follows an E1 C1 E2 C2 C3 order and elegantly rounds the text off with D2 [4]
4. Begins with D2 [4] followed by D1 [6] E1 C1 C2 E2 C3.
5. As 4 but with the last three sentences in the same order as in 1, i.e. E2 C2 C3.

Text F

Each speech act is thought of as
consisting of two elements (a) the
propositional content – what is being
referred to; what it is about – and
(b) the **illocutionary force**; the
meaning the act is intended to convey
or the emphasis given to it by the
speaker. In simple terms, a speech
act consists of its content + the
orientation of the speaker to that
content and these together give the
speech act its social meaning. For
example, I can refer, in a completely
neutral way, to a past action of my own
and say 'I burned the toast this morning'.
This, as a speech act, is one of simple
reference: the content is the burning
of the toast and my attitude to that
event is merely that of a reporter.
However, I could take the same content
and say 'I'm sorry I burned the toast
this morning'. This, clearly, is more
than neutral reporting of the event.
The user of English instantly
recognizes it, despite the shared
content, as something else: an apology.[17]

6.3.2 Synthesis: writing

At the beginning of this section (in 6.3), we proposed a model of text-processing which contained five stages and was intended to cover both reception and interpretation (reading) and production (writing). We also suggested (in Section 6.3.1) that underlying the activity of text-processing were shared assumptions – ground-rules – about the ways texts were to be created and interpreted; expectations of norms and plans for dealing with the new by analogy with the old. We shall apply these notions to the synthesis of text.

Let us remind ourselves, to begin with, that we imagine the process to be one which is

(1) both *bottom-up and top-down* in which '. . .we work out the meanings of the words and structure of the sentence. . .[and] at the same time, we are predicting, on the basis of context plus the composite meaning of the sentences already processed, what the next sentence is most likely to mean'.[18]

(2) *cascaded*, i.e. it is possible to move from one stage to the next before the 'earlier' stage has completed its work, i.e. we are able to continue to process on the basis of incomplete analysis (or synthesis, come to that) and

(3) *interactive*, i.e. constructed with *feedback loops* which allow the revision of earlier decisions on the basis of the results of later processing.

Writing, in terms of the model we presented earlier (Figure 6.4), involves the movement from plans and goals and high-level abstractions to parsing and the realization of text as a linear string of symbols.

Some have pointed out,[19] that the actual writing is preceded by a pre-writing stage dedicated to background reading, discussion, thought and general planning of *what* to write rather than *how* to do it and followed by a re-writing stage (or stages) during which revisions are made to the otherwise completed work. Naturally, the amount of time given to each stage is subject to a threshold of termination (see 6.3 on this term); the writer will stop when (s)he feels that the effort to continue outweighs the advantages to be gained. This brings us to a point which should be made; the writer has much more time to make explicit judgements of text quality, so we might take this opportunity to note the ways in which the production of texts are regulated.

We might begin by recognizing that, whereas in the previous chapter (in Section 5.1) we were engaged in setting out the defining characteristics of texts (the *constitutive rules* by which they are brought into being), we are now about to turn to the second type of rule (the *regulative*) by means of which texts are controlled and their quality judged.

Three regulative principles for texts have been suggested[19]:

(a) *efficiency*: the minimum expenditure of effort is required of the participants,

(b) *effectiveness*: success in creating the conditions for attaining a goal and

(c) *appropriateness*: providing a balance between (a) and (b), i.e. between the conventional and the unconventional.

Appropriateness is, of course, difficult to achieve. Efficiency and effectiveness tend to be in conflict; plain language and trite content are efficient but not effective since such a text is boring. Equally, creative language and bizarre content are effective, since they make a powerful impact and are memorable but they are inefficient since they take a good deal of processing. Even so, the knowledge on which the skilled reader draws – the language user's communicative competence (see Chapter 2, Section 2.1.3 on this) – suggests strategies and tactics for coping with appropriate writing, as we shall see.

We can now begin to work through the process stage-by-stage from planning to actual writing.[21]

Stage 1 – *planning* – involves the writer in goal-setting and planning to attain that goal. At this point the writer is asking *why* the text is to be written – to persuade readers of a particular view of translation theory (or, more mundanely, to increase the writer's reputation, to get a promotion, to make money. . .) – and *what form* the text should take: an article, a monograph, a book?

Stage 2 – *ideation* – concerns decisions on the main ideas which will further the plan and their mapping onto the plan; the main ideas might be that translation should be studied as process rather than product and that a model of that process should be developed which draws upon what is known in linguistics and cognitive science about human information-processing.

Stage 3 – *development* – takes the ideas, organizes them into a coherent framework (chapters and sections within chapters, for example) which shows their interrelationships with each other and carries them forward towards the attainment of the goal. It should be realized, that we are still not at the point where any of this is in language at all. We are still mulling over ideas and shifting them about in our minds. Developing the framework for this book began in 1984 and continued right up to the moment of writing when changes in overall layout and the weightings assigned to particular sections were made. The book has, in fact, a rather formal structure. There are three Parts with seven chapters divided between them (2 + 3 + 2) and each chapter consists of three sections, each of which is divided into three sub-sections. The total adds up to 63 sub-sections and the numerological effect of the threes and sevens (7 x 3 x 3) is rather striking, particularly since there is a final, single, *two* paragraph, *eight* sentence Envoi. How intentional the arrangement was initially is, of course, quite another matter.

Stage 4 – *expression* – takes the ideas and puts them into non-language-specific propositional form; Actor Process Goal, etc. (see Chapter 4: Section 4.1) which serves as the basis for the production of language-specific clauses. Some of this stage co-occurred with stage 3 and some immediately prior to stage 5; a further indication, if any were still needed, that these stages and steps are by no means linear and recursion and back-tracking to earlier stages in the course of constant revision are the norm rather than the exception.

Stage 5 – *parsing* – maps the propositional content onto the syntax through selections from the MOOD systems (see 4.2) and arranges clauses in a suitably communicative manner through selections from the THEME systems (see 4.3) and, finally, realizes them as written text; characters on a (semi)permanent medium.

Clearly, there are as many configurations of this process as there are writers and it would serve no particular purpose to try to create a set of 'typical' styles. All we are saying here is that this process seems plausible and, that being the case, we have assumed it when we built the model of translation in Chapter 2.

This brings us to the reverse of the process; the analysis of existing text (reading) rather than its creation *ab initio*, noting before we do that the whole process of revision (steps 3–5), is, actually, skilled reading.[22]

6.3.3 Analysis: reading

Reading, according to the model we are using, consists of essentially the same processing stages as writing but with the direction reversed, i.e. from surface text to plans and goals; parsing, concept recovery, simplification, idea recovery (getting the gist) and, finally, plan recovery (realizing how to take the message of the text).

We might add that, at any point, the reader may have to reinterpret earlier clauses in the light of new information. The well-known 'garden-path sentences' are a good example of this[23]:

The shooting of the Archduke infuriated his supporters.

Our initial reading of this is, very probably, that the Archduke was assassinated and that his supporters were dismayed and angered by the event. This is, indeed, a plausible interpretation on the basis of our expectations (long-term memory entries about Sarajevo 1914, etc) but the clause is, actually, ambiguous. There is an alternative to our assumption that the underlying propositions are:

> Someone shot the Archduke.
> This infuriated his supporters.

Let us suppose that, instead of continuing,

> Two days of rioting followed. . .

the next clause in the text is

> They had bet large sums that he would win the competition.

We would need to reinterpret the first clause; it was the way the Archduke shot that infuriated his supporters, not that he was shot.

Having made that point about the need for revision, we should begin our discussion with the surface text and, in particular, with the clause.

There is considerable evidence to suggest that, rather than operating a sentence at a time, processing operates a clause at a time[24] and, indeed, our own model of the translation process has been designed on this assumption. It is to be expected, for both psychological and linguistic reasons, that the clause should play such a central role since the clause:

(a) tends to be about the right length to be entered on the visuo-spatial scratch pad in the working memory (see Chapter 7, section 7.1.2. on the short-term memory and its role in information-processing) and

(b) is the focal point of all three macrofunctions of language (see Chapter 4) and 'the product of three simultaneous semantic processes; it is at one and the same time a representation of experience, an interactive exchange, and a message'[25].

Stage 1 in the process is parsing; the analysis of the linear string of symbols (the letters on the page) into clauses. It may well be, as we suggested in Chapter 2, that parsing can be by-passed if the structure of the clause is a frequent one (contained in a Frequent Structure Store) and the information passed on immediately to the next stage: concept-recovery. But, assuming that parsing needs to take place, the first question to ask is the bottom-up 'is the clause grammatical?'. If it is, the next stage is activated and, if not, the reader will attempt top-down, starting from prior knowledge and expectations to find a plausible structure in the data by adding, deleting, changing; attempting to edit the text into the form the reader assumes the writer intended; precisely the ability which has traditionally been called into play in the applied linguistic procedure of error analysis where the analyst is frequently called upon to produce a 'plausible interpretation' of a sample of idiosyncratic speech or writing.[26].

An important point here is that for readers grammaticality is a default; 'something assumed in the absence of contrary specification'.[27]

Consider texts like

They ran up a bill
They ran a bill up
They ran it up
They ran up it

where the last text is not a grammatical alternative to the one before it. The reader would assume, on the basis of the local interpretation principle, that 'it' referred to 'bill' and therefore was intended to be 'they ran it up'.

What, though, of a text like the next?

WAIT WHILE LIGHTS FLASH

Interpreted literally, this is a general instruction not to move when there are lights flashing but the reader will assume a context and insert deictics such as 'here' and 'these' to give a re-written text (the reader's text; the semantic representation) which now reads:

WAIT HERE WHILE THESE LIGHTS FLASH

When this text was met for the first time (in the mid-60s) on either side of a railway track, the reader was presented with a problem; how was the text to be interpreted? The situation makes the major contribution to 'making sense' of the text; by placing the text at a level-crossing and presenting it in a particular way, the writer makes it a sign and, by analogy with other road signs, the road-user can infer that it is an instruction to wait at the crossing while the lights are flashing.

We would suggest that the text is 'a mixture of familiar and unfamiliar content, with the bulk of it familiar'[28] and that we cope with 'new' texts by treating the unfamiliar as familiar; by analogizing. Unfortunately, this text was not as transparent in its meaning as the writer presumably intended it to be. The 'ideal' reader was, no doubt, conceived of as a speaker of southern English but the new crossings were piloted in the northwest, where 'while' means 'until'. . .

How long, we might ask at this point, is it before we know what a text is about? How much data do we need to process before we have the 'gist' of the text? This is a crucial question and, in particular, for the translator. The answer seems to be, it all depends. In many cases, the first clause is sufficient; sometimes, of course, there is a title which may be less than a clause but, nevertheless, cues the topic.

Even without a title and in the context of an unclear initial paragraph, the reader has a number of problem-solving strategies available[29]:

(1) to work steadily through the clauses in the order in which they are presented in the text, holding unresolved problems for later resolution (a breadth-first approach) or
(2) to read right through at high speed (skimming), extracting what appear to be the main points (a depth-first approach), or
(3) to combine the two and thereby avoiding the slowness of the cautious first approach and the danger of misunderstanding – getting hold of the wrong end of the wrong stick – of the second.

An indication of the skill which readers possess can be seen in the fact that, time and again, native readers of English presented with a text,[30] one word at a time and without its headline, were able by the end of the first clause (not the first sentence; some only needed the first eleven words to establish that 'credit' was being used as a metaphor rather than as a term in economics or banking and that the source was some kind of 'quality' publication) to state: 'Newspaper editorial; a "quality" English newspaper i.e. the *Times*, the *Guardian*, the *Independent*, possibly the *Telegraph*, if it is a daily, or the *Sunday Times* or the *Observer*, if it is a weekly; assessment of the achievement of the Israeli commission of enquiry into the massacres in the refugee camps in south Lebanon.' One clause was sufficient to pin down tenor, mode and domain. Here is the first sentence of the text together with the headline:

The Verdict of Kahan, and the Context

> Much credit flows to the State of Israel
> for the vigour of the Kahan commission's
> enquiry and the rigour of its conclusions.

6.3.4 Summary

In this section, we have shown the kinds of problem-solving skills the text-processor uses in coping with text and have introduced a five-stage model of text-processing which is intended to work, depending on the direction of operation, as a model of both reading (analysis; from surface text to abstract configurations of concepts) and writing (synthesis; from plans and goals, through ideas to written surface text).

These are, by virtue of the fact that the translator is a text-processor, precisely the same skills as are employed in translation and it is for that reason that we have spent time in this section spelling out what is involved.

6.4 Conclusion

This chapter has been concerned with the essential activity of text-processing which underlies human communication – monolingual or bilingual; written or spoken – and, of necessity, is at the root of the translation process.

We dealt with three topics in this chapter: (1) text-typologies, (2) the knowledge-base of the text-processor and (3) the skills the reader and writer use in processing text.

The problem of the text-types is a particularly significant one for the translator. As Hatim says (in relation to translating from English to Arabic but, clearly, of universal rather than particular relevance):

> . . .retrieving the illocutionary
> force of the entire text, as well
> as the forces of the elements making
> up the text, are basic principles
> in explicating texture in English,
> negotiating structure and ultimately
> reconstructing context, a precondition
> for efficient translating into Arabic.[31]

In order to explain the relationship between individual texts and abstract ideal 'types' of which they are thought to be 'token' realizations, we presented a hierarchical model of the relationship between (a) actual text 'samples', (b) 'text-forms' and (c) a very limited number of 'text-types' which resolves the problem by proposing a set relationship of the same kind as holds between utterance, sentence and proposition, i.e. (a) is included in (b) and (b) is included in (c).

The second topic – knowledge – brought us back to a reformulation of the three-way distinction introduced in Chapter 4: syntax, semantics and rhetoric. Since, as Halliday says, the clause is the simultaneous product of all three systems of options, and since texts are realized through clauses, it is inevitable that such knowledge should form the basis of the skilled actions which create discourse. It is equally clear, that knowledge of this kind – and in two languages – must not only form a major part of 'translator competence' (the topic of Section 2.1 in Chapter 2) but the clause itself must be the major focus of the process of translation itself.

Reading and writing have also been dealt with at some length, since they too are very obviously skilled activities which form a significant part of the process of translating. We presented reading and writing as using the same five-stage process – they are conceived of as mirror images of each other – and therefore take de Beaugrande's assertion which follows to ultimately have messages for writing as well as reading to which it explicitly refers:

> *Only if the reading process is*
> *consistently pursued to the point*
> *where the interpretation is maximally*
> *dominated by text-supplied information*
> *can a truly objective translation be*
> *produced*, that is, a translation which
> validly represents the perceptual potential of
> the original.[32]

The reference here to '*perceptual* potential' provides the justification for the final chapter of this book; human information processing. Text-processing and translating are special cases of this larger process – the manipulation and storage of information in the mind – a model of which, we believe, cannot fail to provide us with substantial insights into the 'black box' in which translating takes place.

Notes

1. de Beaugrande and Dressler, op, cit., 183.
2. Crystal and Davy, 1969.
3. Neubert, 1968.
4. Reiss, 1981; Newmark, 1988.
5. see Bühler, 1965; Hörmann, 1971.
6. Newmark, op. cit., 39–44.
7. Newmark, op. cit., 44.
8. Hatim, 1984, 147.
9. Pustejovsky, 1987.
10. See Bell, 1981, 208 for discussion.
11. Searle, 1965.
12. Hatim, op. cit., 148.
13. ibid.
14. Hymes, 1972.
15. Traugott and Pratt, 1980, 273.
16. Brown and Yule, 1983, 67.
17. Bell, 1981.
18. Brown and Yule, op. cit., 234.
19. Ellis, 1984, 61f.
20. de Beaugrande and Dressler, op. cit., 11.
21. The terminology is that of de Beaugrande and Dressler, op. cit., which clashes with Halliday's in their use of the term *ideation* in stage 2.
22. Hayes *et al.* (1987) provide a sophisticated model of the activity of revision and the cognitive processes involved.
23. Ellis, op. cit., 51.
24. Harris and Coltheart, 1986, 180–1.
25. Halliday, 1985, section 5.3.4.
26. Bell, 1981, 171–83.
27. de Beaugrande and Dressler, op. cit., 34.
28. Steinberg, 1982, 131.
29. de Beaugrande and Dressler, op. cit., 37–38.
30. Text A from Hatim, 1987.
31. Hatim, op. cit., 148.
32. de Beaugrande, 1978, 88; original emphases.

7 Information, knowledge and memory

When we built the model of the translation process (in Chapter 2), we did so on the basis of a number of assumptions which were listed at the time. Four of these assumptions which are of particular significance for this chapter are repeated here.

We assumed that the process of translating

(1) is a special case of the more general phenomenon of **human information processing**;

(2) should be modelled in a way which reflects its position within the **psychological domain** of information processing;

(3) takes place in both **short-term** and **long-term memory** through devices for decoding text in the **source language** (SL) and encoding text into the **target language** (TL), via a non-language-specific **semantic representation**

(4) proceeds in both a **bottom-up** and a **top-down** manner in processing text and integrates both approaches by means of a **cascaded** and **interactive** style of operation; analysis or synthesis at one stage need not be completed before the next stage is activated and revision is possible.

Such a model assumes links between translating and linguistic structure – 'meaning' in all its aspects – on the one hand and models of human communication on the other. Since this book has concentrated on the *linguistic* aspects of translation – 'linguistic' in a very broad sense – the balance needs to be redressed – however briefly – towards the *psychological* and the modelling of human information-processing.

Our task is easily stated. We shall make explicit in this chapter the model of human information-processing which has been implicit throughout the book and within which our model of translating is located.

In simple terms, we all agree that translation involves reading the

SLT and writing the TLT and, between the two, shifting from one code to the other. We might focus this chapter by spelling out what is involved, indicating what has already been discussed in earlier chapters and outlining what is left to be done.

Reading consists of processing text by reference to existing knowledge and applying analytic skills which permit the reader to extract information contained in the text.

Writing consists of organizing existing knowledge and applying synthetic skills to that knowledge which permit the writer to realize it as information in a text.

Translation combines the two in the way we have demonstrated in the model.

Let us consider, though, just what is implied by these definitions. Virtually all of the terms used in them are problematic: *processing, text, existing knowledge, analytic skills, extract, information, organizing, synthetic skills, realize.*

Fortunately, most of them have been the subject of considerable discussion in earlier chapters, so we can concentrate on those which have been dealt with cursorily or not at all.

What we are left with are all notions from *cognitive science*: (1) the nature of human information processing, (2) the structure of knowledge and (3) the storage of knowledge and the means of accessing it.

This is precisely what this final chapter is about; the presentation of a psychological model of human information-processing which explains how it is that we are able to take in data from the senses, convert it into meaningful information in the mind, store it in long-term memory and retrieve it, as required, for later use; all processes on which the translation process crucially depends.

7.1 Human information-processing

A model of human information processing[1] must, minimally, be able to account for the following:

1. That sensory stimuli received by the senses and transmitted to the brain for processing are chaotic rather than organized.
2. That the processing system is able to convert an input which consists of continuous stimuli into discrete units of data.
3. That even degraded or ambiguous stimuli can be (if only with partial success) processed.

4. That inherently meaningless signals can, once received, be converted into meaningful messages.
5. That enormous quantities of information can be processed, stored, retrieved and re-used with apparent ease and accuracy.

7.1.1 Three stages

Three clear stages, each associated with a specific storage system, can be distinguished in the process:

1. Reception, filtering, storage and initial processing of information by the **sensory information system** (the SIS).
2. Final analysis, short-term storage and second filtering of the data by the **short-term memory system** (the STM).
3. Accessing the **long-term memory-system** and integrating new information within the LTM database.

Within the model, attention needs first of all to be directed to an understanding of the processes of decoding or analysis (reading) and encoding or synthesis (writing), with a particular emphasis on decoding, since – as we saw in the model of the translation process – one is, in essentials, virtually the mirror image of the other. Figure 7.1 provides an outline of the process.

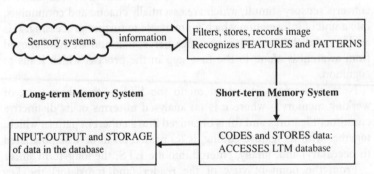

Sensory Information System

Sensory systems — information → Filters, stores, records image
Recognizes FEATURES and PATTERNS

Long-term Memory System   **Short-term Memory System**

INPUT-OUTPUT and STORAGE of data in the database ← CODES and STORES data: ACCESSES LTM database

FIGURE 7.1 Information processing; an outline model

The outline model suggests that there are three major storage systems involved in the processing of information – three distinct but interconnected systems – the sensory information store (SIS), the short-term store (STS) and the long-term store (LTS). We shall summarize the relationships between them here, provide an expansion of the model and then describe the second and third – the two main memory systems – in greater detail.

The first stage in the process is handled by the **sensory information system** which makes a record of the stimulus in the form of an *image*.

The human brain, through the **sensory systems** of the body – sight, hearing, taste, touch, smell – receives vast quantities of **information** all the time and, as studies of sensory deprivation have shown, appears to need such inputs in order to work adequately. Starved of data, the brain quickly begins to invent its own by hallucinating.[2]

However, the brain cannot cope with the incoming stimuli in their entirety. Such a vast surge of information would overload the system – probably fatally – and this means that there must be, as the first stage of the processing system, a **filter** which can reject all but the information to which the system is paying attention at any given time (a point we shall take up again in the next section).

This selected information is, according to the model as presented so far, next stored, very briefly (experimental evidence suggests about half a second; hence the half-second 'reaction time' in human beings) in a **sensory information store** – a 'sensory register'- which provides a complete and detailed record of the stimulus. This is either returned to the filter for disposal or passed on to the first of the processing systems for recording as an image rather than the aggregate it is received as from the senses. The role of this stage is crucial, since it converts sensory stimuli, which are essentially chaotic and continuous, into a unit of information which is amenable to further processing. It is at this point that sensation becomes perception and we have moved from awareness alone to the first step in the process which leads to cognition.

Next, this image is passed on to the STS – the short-term or working memory – where it is (a) analysed in terms of its distinctive constituent features and (b) is organized into a coherent pattern which, together with its feature coding, is (c) passed on to be disambiguated (if necessary) and, finally, entered into the LTS, the long-term store.

From the point of view of the reader (and translator) the key elements of the model are the second and third memory systems – the STM and the LTM – which we shall now describe.

The second storage system (STS) was, until recently, referred to as short-term memory (STM) and was envisaged as a purely passive information store, limited in capacity (7 ± 2 'chunks' of information; a 'chunk' being a unit such as a number, a letter, a word[3]), in the time information can be held (some 30 seconds, assuming no new incoming data obliterates it or that it is kept in store for a longer period by rehearsal) and likened to a leaky bucket, a pneumatic push-down plate-store or an in-tray in a busy office, constantly being filled with documents, some of which are put in the wastepaper basket (i.e 'filtered out'), others are answered immediately (passed to the encoding system) and yet others are passed on for filing (stored in the LTM).

Current thinking in cognitive science suggests that the STM is not a simple store but possesses active characteristics as well, consisting of three, or possibly four components, which allow it not only to act as a store but also as a kind of workbench – hence the term **working memory** which is now more commonly used than the earlier *short-term memory* – where data can be held, in small quantities and for a short time, while it is rehearsed and analysed in terms of both features and knowledge[4]:

(1) *articulatory loop*: a kind of 'inner voice' which can hold and repeat some two seconds' worth of syllables.
(2) *visuo-spatial scratch pad*: the visual equivalent of the articulatory loop, an 'inner eye' which can hold a small amount of non-verbal data (equivalent in amount to the syllables in the articulatory loop) for processing.
(3) *central executive*: the controller of the activity which (a) coordinates the analysis, (b) keeps attention focused on what is relevant (i.e. relates the analysis to the goal being pursued at the time and uses the filter to reject non-relevant material) and (c) handles both the retrieval of information from the LTM as required for the analysis and the input of information into the database.

The third system – the LTS – has, like the STS, both active and passive aspects which together constitute the long-term memory (LTM):

(1) an **accessing system** which allows new data to be put into the storage system and existing stored data to be accessed, and
(2) a **database** in which information is stored in a manner which facilitates access.

An analogy might be the library catalogue and shelving system. The catalogue provides a classmark for each publication and the layout of the library itself ensures that publications on related topics – with, therefore, similar classmarks – are shelved together.

We shall argue (in Section 7.3) that the library analogy is a powerful one, since it models for us not only the notion of the coding of incoming items and their storage but also the logical linkages which exist between items.

However, in two respects the LTM differs significantly from the library. First, and less importantly, the storage capacity of the database is, so far as we can tell, limitless and, second – and this makes a qualitative rather than a quantitative difference – the cataloguing system of the LTM can reorganize itself so as to maximize its efficiency in accessing and organizing data; something no library system can hope to do.

7.1.2 Three processes

This initial model presents us with a unidirectional bottom-up process; each stage having to be completed before the next can be begun and the whole activated purely by the data supplied by the sensory systems. This handy fiction must now be modified by recognizing that processing can and does operate in the opposite direction at the same time, i.e. top-down, by drawing on existing knowledge to augment data which is incomplete or resolve ambiguities, for example.[5]

7.1.2.1 Bottom-up processing

Bottom-up processing is data-driven in the sense that it begins with the input of 'raw' sensory stimuli and analyses this continuous influx of chaotic sensory stimuli into discrete meaningful units of information. These are processed, cumulatively, into progressively more sophisticated patterns which themselves build into generalizations.

7.1.2.2 Top-down processing

Top-down processing, in contrast with bottom-up, is concept-driven and begins with assumptions or hypotheses about the nature of the data and seeks regularities in it which confirm those assumptions.

There is, clearly, a need for the processing system in which we are interested to operate in both directions at once; revealing simultaneous parallel processing which is both bottom-up (data-driven and concerned with pattern recognition) and also top-down (concept-driven and concerned with the utilization of prior knowledge).

7.1.2.3 *Interactive processing*

Interactive processing combines bottom-up with top-down which permits processing to take place *simultaneously* in both directions with each process 'feeding' the other with information and, eventually, arriving at an agreed conclusion, unless the data is too degenerate to process or too ambiguous, etc. We have seen examples of interactive processing already (e.g. in the model of the translation process and also in the examples concerned with text-processing in the previous chapter).

How, though, do the processes actually operate?

7.1.3 Five demons

In keeping with the requirement for models to be memorable, we shall make use of a model in which the processes of analysis shown in Figure 7.1 are, rather charmingly, termed 'demons' – image, feature, cognitive, decision and supervisor – respectively.[6] Perhaps, too, it would be wise to reiterate the point we made about 'theories' and 'models' in the first chapter (Chapter 1, Section 1.3.3).

A theory is, as we insisted earlier, an explanation of a phenomenon, while a model is a physical embodiment of a theory. It is a tangible object which 'stands for' the theory and reveals the system inherent in the phenomenon by analogy; suggesting that it is 'as if' the phenomenon were as modelled.

There is, again, no requirement for a model to be 'real' in the sense that it is to be thought of as actually *replicating* all the features of the phenomenon itself, any more than one would expect a model of Concorde to really fly at twice the speed of sound or to carry tiny passengers; all eating caviar and drinking champagne!

Equally, we hope that no one thinks that we genuinely believe that there are little demons inside our heads. What the model does is to ask us to pretend that there are such demons (and they have a very respectable lineage, being direct descendents of Maxwell's famous early nineteenth-century demon in physics) each charged with specific information-processing tasks and we are asked to do this rather than refer to 'sub-systems' or 'mechanisms' (both, we might note, also analogies) simply because it may be an amusing and memorable way of thinking about the process; no more than that. That said, we can continue.

The model suggests that five types of demon are required to carry out the following operations: (1) to convert the sensory information into an image, (2) to analyse images in terms of their component features, (3) to gather bundles of features into coherent patterns, (4) to categorize patterns and assign them a non-ambiguous reference and (5) to co-ordinate these operations and facilitate them by drawing on information stored in the LTM.

We shall look at the role of each demon in turn, recognizing, as we did above, that the model no longer requires us to think of the process as unidirectional or bottom-up. On the contrary, by suggesting that

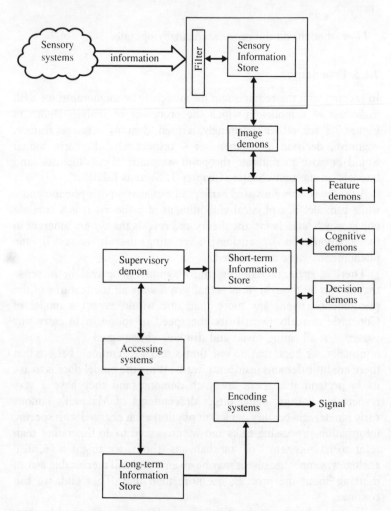

FIGURE 7.2 Human information processing

each demon writes his own analysis on some central blackboard, we can allow for cascaded processing where different stages of analysis can overlap; the gathering of features into bundles which constitute patterns, for example, can begin while the analysis into features is still taking place.

7.1.3.1 Image demon

The image demon is charged with the task of converting stimuli received from the sensory systems – sight, hearing, touch, taste, smell – into images. This demon takes the incoming aggregate and converts it into a whole; an image. It records the image and transmits it to the next group of demons for further analysis.

At this point our description is following rather closely the physical activities involved in visual perception[7]; the physical stimuli carried by the light waves to the eye are focused on the retina in the form of an image and it is this image, rather than the light waves themselves, which is passed along the optic nerve to the brain.

The image demon has a job rather like that of a very junior library assistant who unpacks books and does no more than record the title of each book in a stock-control ledger. He has, assuming that the job is limited solely to this activity, no need to understand the meaning of the title of the book, merely to record that it has arrived and has that title. Next, that information is passed on to more senior staff in accessions who will catalogue it and arrange for it to be shelved appropriately and made available to readers.

7.1.3.2 Feature demons

These receive images from the image demon, scan them in order to ascertain the features they possess and, in the event that an image contains the feature assigned to a particular demon, the presence of the feature is signalled by that demon. Each demon is thought of as being responsible for and responding to a single feature and only responding if that feature is present.

Once again, there is physiological and neurological evidence to support the notion of feature recognizing mechanisms (complex detector cells), located in the brain (in the visual cortex) which 'recognize' lines, edges, slits, curves etc., and such cells appear to exist in the visual cortex of simpler organisms than human beings; frogs, for example.[8]

At this point it becomes somewhat difficult to sustain the library analogy, unless we accept – merely to keep the analogy going – that each worker has the job of contributing a single element to the classification which the book will finally bear and that each, as it were, reports that item to a more senior librarian who has the responsibility of deciding on the correct class mark; the cognitive demons of our model.

7.1.3.3 Cognitive demons

Just as the feature demons were each responsible for the recognition of and response to a single feature, so too the cognitive demons only recognize and respond to a single pattern, i.e. a collection of features. Each cognitive demon is envisaged as receiving an image and, simultaneously, a record of the existence of features and coding parameters representing those features from the feature demons. What the cognitive demon has to do is to compare the image and its partial analysis with the pattern it already possesses. The image which fits best with an existing pattern is what will be passed on to the final processor; the decision demon.

It is clear from neurological evidence that there are specialized collections of cells in the visual cortex which have the task of pattern recognition, so there is, once again, physiological support for the model we are presenting here and it seems obvious that animals also recognize patterns; dogs recognize patterns of smells and bees recognize patterns of dance and act upon them in their search for nectar. We mention this for two reasons. First, to make the point that humanity is by no means unique in this ability and, second, to insist that patterning exists, or is perceived as existing, in all forms derived from all the senses; there are patterns other than linguistic patterns and we should not lose sight of this fact, even if our own interest is mainly in language.

If we return to the library analogy, we see the cognitive demons as fairly senior library staff who check the contributions made to the cataloguing by their juniors and come to a decision as to which classmark is appropriate for a particular title. After them, and particularly in the case of a dispute between these senior cataloguers, there is recourse to the Deputy Librarian; in our model, the decision demon.

7.1.3.4 Decision demon

The decision demon has the responsibility of arbitrating between competing claims for patterns suggested by the cognitive demons. He is a kind of very senior librarian, a deputy who would normally run the

Library but would, nevertheless, report to the chief librarian; the supervisor demon in our model.

7.1.3.5 Supervisor demon

It is the supervisor demon who has to cope with degenerate data, with images which contain too little or too much data to permit unambiguous interpretation and anything which has defeated the rest of the demons.

To take up our library analogy again; the supervisor demon is the chief librarian. He understands the cataloguing system perfectly, knows where every book should be on the shelves, can provide a classmark for a title instantly and, conversely, if given a classmark, can supply a title which would be either identical to or virtually synonymous with the actual title of a publication. His role involves the accession of new books – the addition of new information to the database – and the finding and issuing of books already in stock; the retrieval of information stored in long-term memory.

It is the supervisor who (1) controls the initial filter, ensuring that only relevant information is allowed in for processing, (2) oversees the work of the feature, cognitive and decision demons and ensures that their analyses match up with the image passed on by the image demon, (3) stands between the pattern-recognition systems and the database of long-term memory and holds incoming data in the short-term information store, while deciding, on the basis of the analysis which has been carried out and also by reference to stored knowledge, whether it is a) to be passed on into the LTM for storage or for restructuring and encoding for transmission as a message or whether it is b) to be erased from the 'blackboard' workbench of the STM and attention turned to new incoming information.

It is the supervisor who, unlike the other demons with their specific tasks, limited capabilities and unidirectional processing, constantly draws on prior knowledge and experience stored in the LTM in order to resolve problems of analysis and to speed up solutions. He is, in the terms of our earlier discussion on the components of the working memory, the central executive.

7.1.4 Summary

In this section, we have been outlining a relatively simple model of human information-processing; an integrated cascaded mechanism which operates both bottom-up and top-down to make sense of information and to prepare it for storage and recall.

Thus far we have concentrated on the description of the input systems whose task it is to 'transform "lower level" sensory representations into "higher level" conceptual representations, which are all of the same format regardless of the sensory modality from which they derive',[9] i.e. the coding supplied with the image is essentially the same even though the original stimuli may have been from different senses. This is crucially important for what follows; without this common coding, it would be impossible for the central systems to compare and integrate data from different sensory sources.

The task which remains for the rest of this chapter is to ask three key questions about the LTM: (1) What kind of knowledge is stored in it? (2) How is knowledge stored in it? (3) What mechanisms are there for gaining access to that knowledge?

In the next section we shall examine the way concepts are constructed and linkages created between them which permit the building of organized 'packages' of varying degrees of abstraction and generality. In other words, we are about to change the focus of our investigation from the input systems and data-driven bottom-up analysis to the central systems of the LTM and concept-driven top-down processing.[10]

7.2 Knowledge

We brought up earlier (in Chapter 1, Section 1.2.1) the distinction between two kinds of knowledge: (1) **factual knowledge** which we are aware of and which has come to us through our senses as against (2) **procedural knowledge** which is outside consciousness. The distinction can also be expressed in terms of (1) knowing *that* something is the case as against (2) knowing *how* to do something. Alternatively, the same distinction can be expressed in terms of (1) knowledge which we can make declarations about (hence, 'declarative knowledge'), 'that is a cat' or '"chat" is the translation of "cat" in French' as against (2) knowledge of a practical operational kind which we find hard to describe but easy to demonstrate, e.g. driving a car.

It would seem that doing a translation calls mainly upon procedural knowledge, i.e. the translator just 'translates' without being able to say how or why. The whole aim of this book is, as we have frequently stated, to provide a means of converting the translator's individual, private, procedural knowledge into general, public, factual knowledge, i.e. to externalize the internal system by modelling it.

The fundamental question we now have to face is this: How is knowledge (of either type) represented in the mind? We have to attempt to describe the 'cognitive architecture' of memory; the knowledge-store on which all else depends.

We have, then, three major tasks in front of us: (1) to consider how 'knowledge' is categorized; to show the relation between the experience we have of an entity or event and the concept(s) which represent it in the mind; (2) to investigate the nature of the conceptual entries in the database – logical, lexical and encyclopedic – and, given our particular interests, concentrate on the encyclopedic; and (3) indicate ways in which concepts can be related to form 'packages' of varying size, complexity and degree of abstraction which allow memory to cope with actual events and use stored events as cues for later understanding and action.

7.2.1 Conceptual categories and entries

The processes of perception, feature assignment, pattern recognition, coding and storage which we have been considering all depend on our ability to analyse images and to do this in a progressively abstract manner.

Although it might, in principle, be possible to store each image independently in the database, it seems far more plausible and efficient to suggest that the storage units of long-term memory are in a form which is a great deal more abstract than the individual image (the 'checking' of images and patterns against those already in store implies this), i.e. the **concept**.

However, merely providing a term like 'concept' does not, in itself, constitute a solution to the essential problem which faces anyone who attempts to explain how individual instances of experience can come to be grouped together in memory and treated as though they were the same. The paradox of the Greek philosopher who claimed that one could not step into the same river twice typifies this issue.

Let us consider an apparently simple case: cats. In an absolute sense, every cat is different from every other cat and my own experience of cats different from the experiences of anyone else. How then is it that there is substantial agreement on what is and what is not a cat? Notice that we are not asking the related but different question 'what does the word "cat" mean?'; we already considered word-meaning in Chapter 3 (in Section 3.2). Language and thought are intimately connected – the nature of the relationship is still a matter of debate – but we intend, here, to distinguish the two and concentrate on the physical entities which we experience through our senses and the abstract representation of those experiences and entities in the mind.

The centrality of this issue can hardly be overstated. Without the ability to categorize and to build concepts which act as mental representations of experience we would not only be unable to recognize entities which were, for practical purposes, the same but we would be unable to decide what to do with the entities, since our previous experience would be of no apparent value to us, and we would find it virtually impossible to communicate, since we would have no common ground for sharing our experiences with others. On what basis, though, do we carry out this categorization?

Categorization depends on the possession of shared features or attributes, some of which are essential defining properties and others additional non-essential but expected qualities. For example, to be a cat requires that the entity be a mammal, be within a particular height and weight range, have fur and retractable claws, etc., but not that it should have a particular disposition or be a particular colour; though some colours, like green, would not be included in the list of possibles. Such a listing of characteristics which can truthfully be stated of an entity – its class membership and attributes – built up by experience of actual examples of such entities has been termed a **stereotype**[11] and the process of recognizing an entity as belonging to a particular category is seen as one of matching the data available on the entity with the stored stereotype (much as we imagined the cognitive and decision demons doing in our data-processing model).

This brings us to a second issue; typicality. Given that entities can be grouped by means of stereotypes, there still remains the fact that some members of the grouping are thought of as being more typical than others. Some birds, for example, are thought of as more bird-like than others; the robin, thrush or blackbird seem closer to the 'ideal' bird than do hens, penguins or kiwis. The notion of such a typical ideal type – a **prototype**[12] – stored in memory as part of the information associated with a concept goes some way to provide an answer to the problem of classes of entity where the boundaries are fuzzy rather than clear-cut.[13]

Armed with the notion of the conceptual category with its constituent stereotypical and prototypical information, we can move on to a consideration of the way in which such categories are stored in memory.

We have already suggested the idea of each concept having a 'label' or 'address' attached to it which allows the searcher to find the place in memory at which it is stored. The issue of how this is done is the concern of the last section of this chapter (Section 7.3). What needs to be done before that is to specify what, exactly, is stored at each of these locations. What do conceptual entries contain?

Three sets of information seem essential for virtually any entry; the concept's

(1) propositional form and characteristics
(2) linguistic form and function and
(3) class membership, characteristics, etc.

The entries for most concepts would contain this kind of three-fold information but some might lack one or, possibly, two. For example, proper names would have entries under (3) and (2) but not (1); logical connectives 'and', 'but', 'implies' under (2) and (1) but not (3).

7.2.1.1 *Logical entries*
The logical forms of which the concept is a constituent[14]; the kinds of argument(s) a predicate can take and the kinds of predicate an argument can go with (cf. ANALYTIC truths, Chapter 5, Section 5.3.1).

There seems to be some neurological evidence in support of the distinction between the kinds of item which only have logical entries – items equivalent to 'closed' lexical sets; ('operators' or 'grammatical items') – and those which have all three types of entry; items equivalent to 'open' lexical sets (nouns, verbs, adjectives, adverbs). Certain kinds of aphasia – failure to handle language appropriately as a result of brain damage – can be distinguished precisely by the inability of the sufferer to cope with closed class items, while still retaining the ability with those of the open classes[15] and this seems to indicate that the two classes of item are actually kept apart from each other in some way in the neural system.

7.2.1.2 *Lexical entries*
This contains information, which is likely to be relatively stable throughout a speech community, about the natural language counterpart of the concept; the word or phrase which expresses it, syntactic category, phonological structure, graphological form but not meaning which, as we shall see, is part of the encyclopedic entry.

The address TIGER would give access to a lexical entry which would contain at least the following linguistic information:

$$\begin{bmatrix} \text{``tiger''} \\ \text{/'taɪgə/} \\ + \text{ Noun} \\ + \text{ Count} \\ + \text{ Animate} \end{bmatrix}$$

7.2.1.3 *Encyclopedic entries*

These would contain, for each concept, a series of assumptions and generalizations based on experiences of it which, though gathered in time and space, have become context-free. Each would provide information about the class of entities to which the concept belongs, the characteristics it possesses, the objects or events which exemplify it and stereotypes and assumptions about the world needed to deal with new information, e.g. that PET includes CATS, DOGS, RABBITS but *not* TIGERS, ELEPHANTS. . .

Such entries are, typically, variable across individuals and time and open-ended in that they can be added to and are never complete, related to context, concerned with synthetic truths (true by virtue of the nature of the world) and values and the representation of experience.[16] Together, they constitute our encyclopedic knowledge 'an overall model of the properties of the world'.[17]

The address TIGER would give access to an encyclopedic entry which would contain, *inter alia*, the following semantic information:

$$\begin{bmatrix} + \text{ Animal} \\ + \text{ stripes} \\ + \text{ fierce} \\ - \text{ domesticated} \\ \text{etc.} \end{bmatrix}$$

In addition, and most significantly from our point of view, the encyclopedic entry would include the knowledge we have of the linguistic systems we have acquired,[18] including our knowledge of the sound and writing systems, the rules of syntax, the meanings of words and sentences and the conventions for the appropriate use of this knowledge.

Our own interest is in the encyclopedic and lexical entries but, since Chapter 3 was specifically concerned with word-meaning (and sentence-meaning) and the particular focus of the lexical entry is on the formal characteristics of words, we shall devote the rest of this section to an examination of the encylopedic aspects of memory; initially the encyclopedic entry itself, which contains all the salient semantic features of a concept (the class or classes to which it belongs, its characteristics – defining properties and expected qualities – and instances drawn from personal experience which provide examples of it) and, finally, to the ways in which encyclopedic entries can be combined together to create complexes of meaning and representations of memory, including the linguistic knowledge required for the creation of structured texts and discourse.

7.2.2 Encyclopedic entries

So far we have been attempting to understand the nature of the individual concept but we must, of necessity, recognize that concepts are not stored isolated from each other but in ordered sets, grouped in particular ways and interconnected so that, through chains of linkages, each concept is ultimately connected to every other concept. For this organization to work, each concept must be coded and assigned its proper place by reference to three pieces of information, three coding parameters: class, characteristic and example. Hence, following fairly generally accepted views in epistemology,[19] we see that the concept has certain attributes.

(a) It belongs to a **class** of concepts, e.g. TIGER is included in the larger class of concepts, ANIMAL, i.e. there is an **isa** relationship between the two: 'A tiger **isa** animal'; the concept TIGER is included within the generic concept ANIMAL.

(b) It possesses certain **characteristics**, some shared with the larger class of which it is a member and some which distinguish it from other members of that class:

(i) **Properties** which are defining characteristics; certain properties it must possess. A tiger must have, as part of its make-up, legs, i.e. there is a **has-as-parts** relationship between the concept TIGER and the concept LEGS. We can say 'A tiger has legs' and, indeed, it is necessary for the tiger to have legs in order to be a tiger. Legs, like other properties, are inalienable and the property relationship a polar one; all-or-none; the animal either has or has not got legs. It is not a matter of degree.

(ii) **Qualities** which, in contrast with properties, are expected attributes of a concept but are not defining characteristics e.g. one of the qualities we associate with tigers is fierceness; there is **an applies-to** relationship between the concept TIGER and the concept FIERCE and we can say 'a tiger is fierce' or 'fierceness applies to the tiger'. A quality, in contrast with a property, is neither inalienable nor polar. It is alienable and variable; it is possible for a tiger to be (or to become) unfierce or more or less fierce, i.e. tigers are ranked on a fierceness scale; a continuum.

(c) It supplies **examples** of itself which can be used to reify the concept; there is a second **isa** relationship (in which the **isa** should be read as 'is an instance of') this time between the concept TIGER and an object which I perceive with my senses. I can say 'that is a tiger', i.e. the object I am indicating possesses, on the basis of my previous experience of tigers, characteristics which allow me to classify it as belonging within the class of concepts: TIGER.

We can list these relationships:

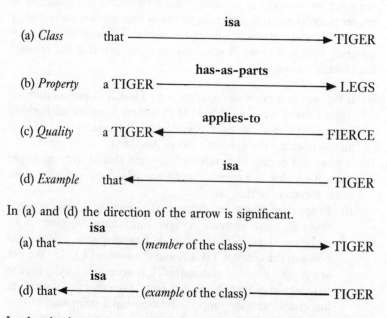

In (a) and (d) the direction of the arrow is significant.

In the database, we envisage the conceptual information as being stored in some manner analogous to the illustration below:

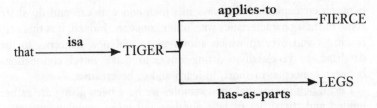

We further imagine the conceptual entries to be stored in the LTM in a way which not only provides linkages between them and their examples and characteristics but also cross-linkages not only such as those of *inclusion* (the **isa** relationship we have just exemplified with TIGER and ANIMAL) but also *overlap* or partial synonymy (particularly problematic issues which have already been discussed in Chapter 3 Section 3.1.3 in our treatment of word-meaning).

Inclusion

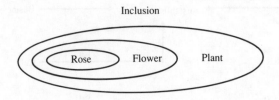

A rose is a kind of flower and a flower a kind of plant, i.e. the concept PLANT includes the concept FLOWER which itself includes the concept ROSE.

Overlap

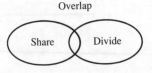

Neither SHARE nor DIVIDE subsumes the other. While we could say 'a rose is a kind of flower', we cannot say 'a flower is a kind of rose' but we can, and must, say 'to share is to divide' and 'to divide is to share'.

It may seem that there is an inherent circularity in all this; concepts are defined in terms of each other and, ultimately, in terms of themselves! Equally, there is a substantial degree of overlap between concepts and this too suggests an unfortunate vagueness in the model.

We would counter both of these criticisms by pointing to the fact that we are explicitly seeking to show this kind of interconnectedness between concepts and the ways in which concepts can and do share some of their characteristics with other concepts. Indeed, it is this very fuzziness and overlap which allows us to add new concepts to the database, to re-classify existing ones, to make novel connections between concepts; in short, to learn and to be creative.

Lest it be thought that the examples we have been giving are rather limited and trivial, let us take another and more complex concept – BEER – and begin to show in Figure 7.3 how it might be represented in memory.[20]

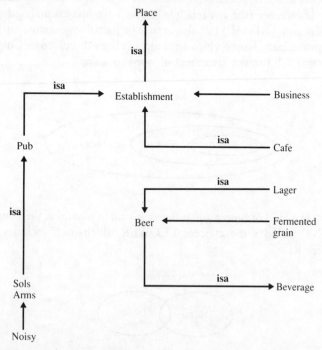

FIGURE 7.3 A schema for BEER

It is clear from this that it will take little more than the expansion of the relationship markers (shown in **bold** in the figure) to convert such a display into one which records actual events. This is precisely what we propose to do in Section 7.2.3.

7.2.3 Schemas

We made the point, as we summarized the data-processing model at the end of the previous section, that feature and pattern recognition need to be constantly enriched by reference to relevant prior knowledge and experience as the organism attempts to 'make sense' of the incoming information. The time has now come to make explicit what has, so far, only been hinted at: the nature of this prior knowledge and its structuring in memory.

To begin with, we should realize that there is ample evidence that human beings and animals possess or develop plans for coping with recurring sequences of actions (feeding, moving about, etc.) and that these plans are a response to the recognition that the actions, though 'different' in an absolute sense from any which have gone before are, for practical purposes, 'the same' and can, therefore, be treated in essentially the same way. The plans, which are the outcome of this realization, co-ordinate the information provided by the sensory systems with the appropriate motor movements and these develop into sensory motor plans or schemas. What we intend to do now is to extend this notion from the sensory-motor to other domains of activity and, in particular, to the cognitively demanding areas of coping with new experiences.

The key notions in this are *schemas*, *scripts*, *frames*, all of which constitute '. . .metaphors for the description of how knowledge of the world is organized in human memory, and also how it is activated in the process of discourse understanding'[21] and, while there is by no means universal agreement on the way the terms are to be used,[22] there is substantial agreement that all are involved in the storing of information; data structures representing stereotyped situations,[23] global patterns of knowledge[24] or generalized events stored in situational memory.[25]

They can be seen as either static data storage structures each containing information about a single stereotyped topic or as more active mechanisms which facilitate 'the processes of retrieval and inference which manipulate the stored representations',[26] but however they are interpreted they have a crucial role in 'relating new experience and knowledge to old in ways which reveal people's knowledge of recurring events' in which meanings are related to each other through dependency networks (we shall illustrate this in Figures 7.4 and 7.5); the fundamental skill of seeing similarity in diversity (we have already seen this in action when we discussed text-processing in the previous chapter).

We shall use **schema** as a generic term representing the range of organizations which consist of sets of 'mental representations. . . which incorporate all the knowledge of a given type of object or event that we have acquired from past experience'[27] and operate 'in a top-down direction to help us interpret the bottom-up flow of information from the world'.[28]

Schemas have been described as possessing five particular characteristics.[29] Schemas:

(1) represent **knowledge** of all kinds; from simple to complex motor knowledge – from blinking an eye to flying a jumbo-jet – to simple and complex visual and intellectual knowledge; from recognizing letter-shapes to translating a sonnet;

(2) are often made up of smaller, more specific, sub-schemas – **scripts** – which constitute action stereotypes and provide pre-established routines for handling particular kinds of event e.g. cashing a cheque in a bank, asking directions. . .;

(3) can be linked to form larger units – **memory organization packets**: MOPs – which bring together common features between seemingly disparate events, which themselves depend on even higher units – **thematic organization points**; TOPs – which contain abstract principles ('community ground rules' see 2.1.3) which underlie social action, including communication[30];

(4) are organized (rather as we described the MOOD systems earlier) as a chain of **slots** for which **fillers** can be chosen, some with fixed compulsory values and others with variable, optional values. In this, the schema can be compared not only with the individual encyclopedic conceptual entry – with its obligatory properties and optional qualities – but also with the syntactic structuring of the clause, which is also organized in terms of chain and choice. For example, the PICNIC schema has, as defining characteristics, slots for place, food, people, etc, the first filled, of necessity, by 'out of doors', + optional detail 'by the sea', 'in the mountains', etc., and so forth. Additionally, and the point is an important one, there are default values which suggest probable fillers if none is supplied, e.g. the 'food' slot, if not specified, has a default filler of the type 'sandwiches'.

(5) are all engaged in the **recognition** and **interpretation of new information**. For example, reading a text which begins 'The clocks were striking. . .' brings the 'normal description' schema into play but the completing of the sentence with the word 'thirteen' shifts us to the '(science) fiction' schema and prepares us for what is to follow (in Orwell's 1984).

We clearly do not normally recollect individual concepts, however full their entries, any more than we recollect individual words but whole events and series of events, much as we might recollect whole phrases, sentences or even whole texts. The unifying principle of the schema is of enormous value in helping us to bridge the gap between the processing and storage of small units of information – concepts – and the larger units and events which we commonly encounter. We have already made use of the notion of the schema on a number of occasions (particularly in Chapter 6) as we attempted to understand text and discourse structure and the problems they pose for the translator. We have not, however, made clear what a schema is and how it works. What we shall do next is to give a very simplified example of a schema for an action and follow this with a more complex one for an event.

Before we continue, we need to recognize that the examples we have given so far of conceptual entries have been, in the main, concepts which refer to objects[31] and have been displaying them along with their attributes; in linguistic terms, essentially nouns and their associated adjectives.

If we wish, as we do, to go on to consider relations between concepts such as these and the events in which they are participants and to set events within the circumstances of space and time within which they are located, we have to provide at least one example of an encyclopedic entry for a relationship between concepts; a process (again, in simplistic linguistic terms, a verb).

We propose to display the script for a particular event (Figure 7.(5) and this will require, *inter alia*, the representation of a particular action: SPILL. In preparation for this, we shall present the schema for the process SPILL in Figure 7.4.[32]

The major requirement on a schema is that it should make explicit what the user of the concept implicitly knows about the concept. In this case, the schema must provide a comprehensive answer to the question: 'What does SPILL mean?' This requires answers to at least three specific questions: (1) what **Agents** are involved in the process and what defining characteristics must they have? (must they be animate and, if so, human?), (2) what **Goals** (recipients) of the process are involved and what characteristics must they have? (animate. . .?) and (3) what temporal, spatial and manner **circumstances** are involved? Adequate answers to these questions should specify the schema for SPILL and, from our point of view, make it that much easier to present a fragment of database containing the representation of a particular event.

A further initial point needs to be made about the display. The schema has, because of the constraints put on communication by a (written) text, had to be realized by words but it is our intention that they would be read as concepts rather than words and the whole ensemble be read as a *proposition* rather than a *sentence*. The sentence is, after all, 'Someone spilled something (somewhere)', which does not tell us a great deal. But the implications are much more revealing; someone (probably human) made a liquid move from a container to a non-container unintentionally. The lack of volition is crucial, otherwise we merely have pouring.

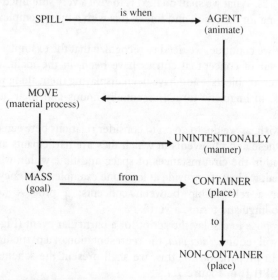

FIGURE 7.4 A schema for SPILL

This takes us beyond mere class-membership, the statement of characteristics or the indication of exemplification – signalled by the relationship markers from the **isa, has-as-part** and **applies-to** we used earlier – to statements of relationship which, by virtue of being propositional in form, give us access to the whole network of options available to us in the grammar. We can now, in principle at least, display any relationship and express that relationship by means of a huge array of natural language forms. We are close to being able to reveal the semantic representation of two brief sentences and so find ourselves on the threshold of being able to array the underlying universal structure of texts, irrespective of the language in which they are realized; a crucial goal for the translator and for our intention to describe and explain the nature of the translation process.

Let us show how an extremely trivial event might be recorded in the database of the LTM. Here is a text which describes what happened:

Roger bought Alex a pint of beer at the Sols Arms
yesterday and spilled his own whisky on the floor.

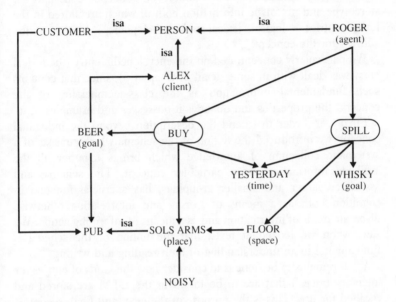

FIGURE 7.5 A schema for an event

Naturally, this could be extended to provide greater detail (BEER and WHISKY could be extended as BEER was in the previous section, etc.) or more events could be linked to this one but it is hoped that this very simple story of a minor catastrophe will make the point.

We have intentionally referred to the schema (Figure 7.5) as a 'story' and we have done that for two reasons: (1) *texts* and *events* both consist of organizations of concepts and (2) both are examples of entities which are, in an absolute sense, always unique but, in a practical sense, groupable into *types* or *genre*.

Because of this, the event and the text not only provide data for analysis but, once recognized as *tokens* or *exemplars* of a particular type, facilitate that analysis and serve as guides for future action, including – and this is extremely pertinent to our own interests – the comprehension and creation of written texts.

7.2.4 Summary

This section has been concerned with attempting to answer the questions: 'How are conceptual categories created and how are they represented in the mind?' In answer, we have pointed to the distinction between two kinds of knowledge – the factual and the procedural – and continued by building up the notion of concepts consisting of stereotype and prototype information both of which are stored in the lexical entries – logical, lexical and encyclopedic – located at the address for the concept.

We particularly concentrated on the encyclopedic entry (the lexical entry was dealt with in some detail in Chapter 3), since that contains such fundamental information as the class-membership of the concept, the properties and qualities it possesses and examples of it.

Finally, in order to extend the description beyond the individual concept, we introduced the notion of the schema which consists of a systematic collection of knowledge which brings together all the available information on a particular concept. The schema, and associated larger and smaller groupings, has a crucial function in cognition both as a means of storing and interrelating otherwise disparate items of information and as a means of informing action. We saw, when we looked at texts, that the notion of the schema is fundamental to an understanding of both reading and writing.

What remains to be done is to consider how the kinds of entries (or 'memory traces') that are to be found in the LTM are stored and recalled for use. This is the purpose of the next, and final, section.

7.3   Memory systems

In terms of our library analogy for memory, we have been describing the way new books are dealt with and now need, to continue the analogy, to describe (a) how the shelves are arranged and (b) how the books are organized on them; to distinguish two fundamental kinds of content and describe the cataloguing system (an addressing system) which permits the accession of new information and the retrieval of information stored in the database.

We make no apology for continuing with the library analogy. Where, other than from the mind itself – from the long-term memory database – would such a categorization come? We ask this to make the point that the catalogue and the library itself are both human artifacts created to handle information – the acquisition of new knowledge, its storage and the retrieval of stored information – and, as such, might be properly seen as a physical realization of a model of the mental constructs and processes we ourselves are attempting to explain.

Libraries exist to store information and their classification and cataloguing systems to provide access to encyclopedic knowledge which is located at some distance from the catalogue itself. Is this not very similar to what we have been saying about human information processing? Not only does the catalogue serve to provide access to the database (i.e. it is an *addressing system*; see 7.3.2 for this term), it also consists of a code which provides the means for classifying, representing and organizing knowledge in an orderly and consistent manner. Not that this in any way implies the existence of a single perfect cataloguing system or a universal organization of the LTM database.

We have three tasks in this section: (1) to outline the nature of two types of memory (*episodic* and *conceptual*) , (2) to provide a specification of the addressing system so as to show how data is coded for insertion into the database (the coding is, of course, crucial to the retrieval of the data at a later point) and (3) to draw the section to a close by considering the mechanisms which permit stored data to be output from the database.

7.3.1 Episodic and conceptual memory

As a preliminary to our consideration of the structure and function of the LTM, we must first distinguish two radically different types of memory[33]; **episodic** and **conceptual**[34]:

7.3.1.1 Episodic memory
This is a memory for events which contains 'the records of one's own experiences ("what happened to me")'[35]; experiences which have occurred in time and space, i.e. they are specific and context-bound.

We imagine such episodes to be stored together with addresses (see 7.3.2 on addressing systems); tags, labels or headings (in principle, smells, tastes, colours, sounds, etc.) which give access to the information stored about them and specify the situation – time, place, participants – in which they occurred (we gave a schematic representation of such an event in Section 7.2.3).

Presumably, all experiences are initially stored (if at all) in episodic memory but very few indeed seem to be recalled in their entirety. Most either fade away completely or are merged with memories of similar events – a point which, as we saw in Section 7.2, is of the greatest importance in our search to understand how memory and comprehension work – though a few do survive to provide the total recall of an event; a flash of recollection which can, it seems, be triggered by virtually any sensory stimulus ('flashbulb memories').[36]

7.3.1.2 *Conceptual memory*

This (also known as 'semantic memory' or 'reference memory') is, in contrast with episodic memory, a memory for meanings which 'reflects the inherent patterns of the organization of knowledge e.g. the structures of events and situations ("what is true about the world and how it all fits together")'.[37].

Each unit of this knowledge is stored in the form of a concept and is accessed through the same 'conceptual address'.[38] This provides the access point to the series of entries for each concept – logical, lexical and encyclopedic – which we discussed in Section 7.2.

7.3.2 Addressing systems

Whether the information stored in memory is located in the episodic or the conceptual memory, some means has to exist for accessing that information. We have hinted already at what this might be in our discussion in the previous section where we indicated that the incoming data consisted not only of an image but also of a coding; in computer terms an **addressing system**, i.e. 'a system for labelling and referring to the locations (or registers) in which information is stored'.[39]

In more commonplace terms, we can model the system on a telephone exchange which, on receipt of a number, will make the connection between the caller and the subscriber whose number has been dialled.

We might exemplify this by analysing roman numerals in terms of the possession or lack of four significant features: vertical line, horizontal line, curve, 'vee' and code accordingly:

I 1000 = one vertical
V 0010 = one 'vee'
X 0020 = two 'vees'
D 1001 = one vertical + one curve
C 0001 = one curve
L 1100 = one vertical + one horizontal
M 2010 = two verticals + one 'vee'

More complex images would merely need longer codings to access them. The problem is, in principle, not much greater than that faced when attempting to make a dialled international telephone call. For example, to call a subscriber on a particular Paris number, from Britain, requires fourteen digits:

$$010 + 33 + 1 + 4564 + 2222$$

This presents no great difficulty to us and the human brain is by no means such a simple device as even the most complex telephone exchange.

We imagine the input of information, then, to take the form (after the analysis and coding described in Section 7.1) of 'calling up' the appropriate area of the database – collections of conceptual entries – by means of the kind of coding outlined above, and the integration of the 'new' with the 'old' as part of the conceptual unit (see Section 7.2) of which it forms a part.

What we shall do next is to illustrate the way we may interrogate the database in order to recall information.

While it might appear that information retrieval is simply a mirror image of the input processes, a little thought will show that this is not the case. In our earlier discussion of feature and pattern recognition, we suggested several times that part of the role of the supervisor demon was to compare the image he had received from the earlier stages of analysis with representations of images already in store in order to discover whether the new image counted as a further example of one already in the database. If it is, it can be integrated as an additional **token** of an existing **type**.[40] If not, it must be recognized as genuinely new and integrated with what is already recorded in the 'encyclopedia' of the database in terms of its relationship with concepts already present.

Our library analogy will, once again, serve to model the retrieval of information.

The efficient user of a library, seeking information stored in it, will immediately make use of the catalogue to gain access to the data required. Three routes are very commonly available:

1. Author's name
2. Title of publication
3. Classmark of publication

Using the author's name as the **cue**, the reader will be provided with a complete listing of all the publications by that author held by the library and, conversely, the use of the title provides a listing of all the publications with that title, irrespective of the author. The use of the classmark, on the other hand, provides more global information, i.e. a listing of all publications on a particular topic.

Naturally, each display gives all three types of information – author, title and classmark – whichever is used for access. Traditionally, such information was displayed on an individual catalogue card but, increasingly today, computers are used to supply the database and to list the requested information on the screen of a VDU.

We would suggest that a computerized catalogue of this type provides us with a very convenient model for the LTM; both the database itself and the accessing systems which allow us to retrieve the information stored in it.

7.3.3 Recall from memory

We are taking up the information at the point at which it has already been passed through the SIS and the STM, broken down into its constituent features, had a pattern or patterns suggested for it and a coding attached to it and is now in the hands of the supervisor – the central executive – for further treatment.

Let us suppose that we are trying to recall a piece of information. We can imagine putting a question to ourselves, e.g. 'What is the name of the author of *War and Peace*?' or 'What is the telephone number of enquiries at Euston Station?' or 'What is the recipe for Prawn Sambal?' or 'What does "yawl" mean?' or whatever.

We shall present an algorithm of the process as we see it (Figure 7.6), listing the three stages and the steps within the stages and making a small number of comments on them.

7.3.3.1 *Stage 1: pre-processing the question*
Having, so to speak, asked ourselves the question, the next stage in the search is to probe the semantic and pragmatic status of the question; to seek, at these levels, the kind of meaningful patterning we discussed earlier.

Four steps – each enquiries about aspects of the question – constitute this first, preliminary stage and failure leads either to the abandonment of the task or, given sufficient motivation, a further

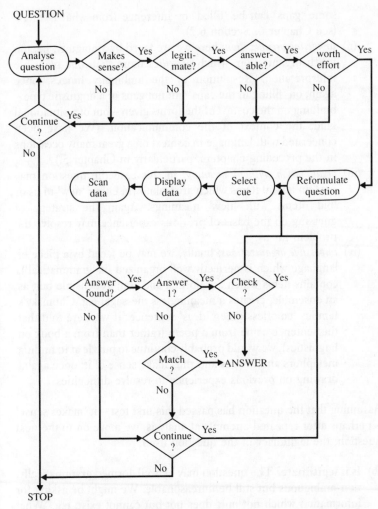

FIGURE 7.6 Recalling information

round of attempting to 'make sense' of the question. We may need to
ask:

(a) does the question make **sense**? It may be chaotic, degraded or
    ambiguous because it contains:
    (i) *insufficient organization*; the form of the question may be
        inadequate; parts of the signal may be missing and the
        message therefore difficult to decode. Just how much and
        how much of what is missing is the crucial factor here;

some 'gaps' can be 'filled' by inference from what is there (see Chapter 6, Section 6.2).

(ii) *competing organization*: here we are faced by ambiguity, i.e. too much organization, which provides more than one plausible interpretation. Resolution of the ambiguity hinges, once again, on 'filling in the gaps' but not gaps of a linguistic type – building on the co-text of the forms given – but of a situational kind; the context of the communication. (We have been concerned with language in context on a great many occasions in the preceding chapters, particularly in Chapter 5.)

(iii) *organization without meaning*: in this case the question may contain lexical items which are unknown, either 'new' to us or 'old' items with 'new' meanings. Again the strategy of guessing on the basis of previous experience may resolve the problem for us.

(iv) *impossible organizations*: finally, we may be faced by a piece of language which is perfectly well organized (is 'grammatical'), contains items which are normal and comprehensible but, as an ensemble, creates a meaningless message, e.g. Chomsky's famous 'colorless green ideas' sentence. If we were told that the sentence came from a poem (rather than from a book on linguistics), we would probably continue to puzzle at it, finding metaphors and images and thus make sense of it; once again, drawing on previous experience to resolve difficulties.

Assuming that the question has passed this first test – it 'makes sense' – perhaps after repeated attempts at analysis, we move on to the next question; the legitimacy of the question itself.

(b) Is it **legitimate**? The question may be well-formed grammatically, non-ambiguous but still be unreasonable. We might be asking for information which not only does not but cannot exist, e.g. 'What was Henry VIII's telephone number?' There is no point searching our memories for the answer to this question. It cannot be in any database and so the question is, literally, unanswerable.

(c) Is it **answerable**? If we ask the same question about H.G.Wells' telephone number, we may suspect that, unlike the earlier question, it is answerable. Telephones did exist when Wells was alive and it does not seem unreasonable to suppose that he had one and, therefore, a telephone number. The information must exist somewhere but probably not in our own database. To find the answer, we would need to read biographies of Wells and his friends; a considerable expenditure of energy on our part. This brings us to the last of this set of preliminary steps in information retrieval.

(d) Is it worth the **effort**? It all depends on why we have asked the question in the first place. Unless, for example we were contestants on Mastermind, and had decided to offer as our Specialist Subject 'The Life and Writings of H.G. Wells', we might well consider it not worth the effort. Suppose, though, that the question was 'What is the telephone number of flight enquiries at London Airport?' and we needed to confirm that the flight bringing an important visitor was on schedule. In such a case, the effort – large or small – would be worthwhile and we might begin a search of our own memories to try to locate the number. One result of this search could well be the response 'check in another database'. After all part of the encyclopedic knowledge we possess is the knowledge of the existence of other databases and the means of accessing them. In simple terms, we can answer this question by reference to the appropriate telephone directory.

Assuming that the question passes all four of these preliminary probes, we can move on to the second stage of the search; the reformulation of the question.

7.3.3.2 Stage 2: accessing the database

The question – now judged to be meaningful, legitimate, answerable and worthwhile – has next to be put to the databse but in a form which will 'unlock' the appropriate areas for our inspection.

As before, there appear to be four steps involved at this stage but, unlike those of the first stage, they appear to be best formulated as instructions rather than questions:

(a) **Reformulate the question**. The actual grammatical realization of the question is reduced to its logical form (i.e. to propositional form; see 3.3.2 on this). This is particularly important as a process for locating the key words[41] or cues which are realizations of the key concepts of the question.

(b) **Select cue**. The 'key', a word, a phrase, a mnemonic, a number, a classmark. . . (for example, 'alphabet') 'calls up' for scrutiny an area of the database.

(c) **Display data**. The cue calls up a display of the information we are seeking; rather as a combination lock will unlock a safe or an

appropriate symbol in a computerized catalogue system will display
information on the screen. We can envisage the display as taking the
form of a concept with its characteristics – properties and qualities
– and examples thus:

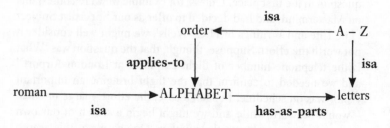

(d) **Scan data.** The displayed data is scanned to discover if it contains
the answer to the question. This brings us to the final stage of the
process; a series of up to five further questions which, it will be
seen, are recursive i.e. they can be asked again and again, until the
answer is found or the search is abandoned.

7.3.3.3 Stage 3: finding the answer

We shall work through the steps involved in this final stage by tracing
the process which results in a successful first answer to the question
and the route which has to be taken when, for some reason, the
displayed data does not provide an adequate answer.

(a) **Is the answer in the display?** if it is, the answer is accepted and
the process comes to an end passing through stages b) and c):

(b) **Is this answer 1**; is the answer the result of the first run through of
the search pattern? If so, a decision is made next on checking it.

(c) **Should the answer be checked?** if not, the process ends. If,
however, it is decided that the answer should be checked, the
question needs to be reformulated. This entails finding an
alternative cue and running through the procedure a second
time, i.e. a return to stage 2. Clearly, this loop can be activated
as many times as the questioner sees fit. Assuming that the new
cue has called up and displayed new data, the answer is no longer
'answer 1' but a subsequent answer which must be matched with
it in the next step.

(d) **Does this answer match the first?** If it does, the answer is
accepted and, as above, the process ends. If, on the other hand,
there is a mismatch or if the answer had not been found first time

round a decision must be made on whether to continue.

(e) **Continue the search?** the process can be stopped at this point or continued by reformulating the question in the way described above at step (c).

The model has important implications for understanding the questioning procedures involved in translation and would presumably (in some form) occur as part of any interactive computer-assisted translation package (see Chapter 2, Section 2.1.2 on expert systems).

7.3.4 Summary

We have now reached the end of our discussion of the LTM, i.e. we have sketched out some of the characteristics of a model of long-term memory. A major distinction has been made between *central systems* on the one hand (the subject of the previous section in which the representation of knowledge was described) – the storage of context-bound information in the *episodic memory* and the storage of context-free information in the *conceptual memory* – and *input systems* on the other; the input–output system which provides the coded data which gives us access to the database of the LTM and allows us to both add new data to the store and recall existing information from it. In addition, we have shown how we imagine accessing the database might be achieved.

7.4 Conclusion

In this chapter, we have developed a progressively more sophisticated model of human information-processing, starting in Section 7.1, where we introduced a first approximation to a model which was, at least at first, bottom-up and data-driven and focused on feature analysis; essentially, unidirectional in operation.

This was modified by bringing in and combining with it a top-down, concept-driven approach which began with assumptions and plans and applied them, as appropriate, to the analysis and comprehension of data.

The combination of the two approaches carried with it the implication that processing could not be unidirectional but must be at least parallel with all levels and both directions of processing being carried out simultaneously.

Within the model, we distinguished short- from long-term memory and indicated the importance of the working memory (within the

STM) as the locus of analysis.

The second section of the chapter continued with an investigation of aspects of the LTM; the representation and storage of knowledge. This allowed a brief development of the notion of information storage from the individual concept – with three distinguishable types of entry at each address; logical, lexical and encyclopedic – to progressively larger units, including *schemas* which consist of useable 'packets' of information made up of networks of concepts.

In the third section, we shifted our attention away from the structure of the knowledge stored in the LTM – the topic of the previous section – to the *central processing systems* of the LTM, distinguished *episodic* from *conceptual* memory, described the *addressing systems* by means of which access is gained to the database of the LTM and outlined a procedure for recalling information from memory.

It ought not, or so we hope, to be necessary to justify a chapter of this length in a book on translation. If, however, a justification is needed, the following would seem to serve well:

> The mechanisms responsible
> for our understanding of the
> printed and spoken language
> are very closely related to
> the mechanisms of perception
> and pattern recognition. . .And,
> as in perceptual processing, we
> find that language is analyzed
> by a combination of data-driven,
> bottom-up mechanisms and
> conceptually driven, top-down
> mechanisms.[42]

Notes

1. See Aitkenhead and Slack (1987); Bransford (1979), Smyth *et al.* (1987), for convenient introductions.
2. See, for example, Vernon, 1963, 117ff.
3. Miller, 1956.
4. See Cohen *et al.*, 1986, 66–75, where a 'primary acoustic store' is added to the list, and Smyth *et al.*, 1987, 134–41.
5. Slack, 1987, 10–13.

6. This is a modification of the model presented in Lindsay and Norman, 1977, 259–94. Our main modification to their model is that we have merged the function of their specialist demons with that of the supervisor.
7. Gregory, 1977, 49ff.
8. See Lindsay and Norman, op. cit., 192–5 on this.
9. Sperber and Wilson, 1986, 72.
10. Slack, op. cit., 1987., 19–23.
11. Lindsay and Norman, op. cit., 622–6.
12. Roth, op. cit., 55–61.
13. Labov, 1973.
14. Sperber and Wilson, op. cit., 89.
15. See Berndt *et al.*, 1983, 16f. and Aitchison, 1987, 104–6 for a discussion of this.
16. Sperber and Wilson, op. cit., 89.
17. Arbib, 1970, 335.
18. Some linguists (e.g Sperber and Wilson, op. cit.) would be more likely to locate this kind of knowledge in the lexical entries.
19. We are following Lindsay and Norman's conventions (1977, 381–93); see Section 2 of the Appendix.
20. We have based this on a similar display in Lindsay and Norman, op. cit., 398.
21. Brown and Yule, 1983, 238.
22. Anderson, 1977; Charniak, 1975, 42; van Dijk, 1981, 141.
23. Brown and Yule, ibid.
24. de Beaugrande and Dressler, 90f.
25. Schank, 1985, 230f.
26. Hayes, 1979.
27. Cohen *et al.*, op. cit., 26.
28. ibid.
29. Cohen, op. cit., 27.
30. Smyth, op. cit., 190–3.
31. The first of the 'primary concepts' in de Beaugrande and Dressler's list (op. cit., 95–7).
32. This is based on that given by Rumelhart and Ortony (1977) for BREAK but modified to fit the grammatical model we used in Part 2.
33. Noordman-Vonk, op. cit., 1f. Some, for example Schank (1985), would distinguish more than two.
34. Or 'semantic'; we follow de Beaugrande and Dressler, 1981, 89 in using 'conceptual'.
35. de Beaugrande and Dressler, ibid.

36. See Cohen *et al.*, op. cit., 1986, 49.
37. ibid.
38. See Sperber and Wilson, 1986, 83–93 on this.
39. Lyons, 1970, 316
40. See Hörmann, 1971, 93ff. for discussion of this distinction which can be traced back to William James in the 1890s.
41. Williams, R., 1976.
42. Lindsay and Norman *op. cit.* 488.

8 Envoi

Concluding a book on translation is probably impossible. After seven chapters, we have only managed to produce a kind of rough sketch-map of the terrain which needs to be explored and are very conscious of the way (to continue the metaphor) we have at times skirted round obstacles and settled for what seemed to be an easier route. Really dependable information on the process of translation will, in our opinion, only become available as translators themselves become more aware of how they do translating and become more skilled at explaining and sharing that experience. One way of making this happen might be, as we suggested earlier (in Chapter 2, Section 2.1.1), to build diary studies and protocol analysis into translator-training programmes and for professional translators to monitor themselves in the same way; a procedure which cannot but be of practical usefulness to the practising translator.

Linguistics too must stand to benefit from becoming seriously involved in the explanation of translation within the framework of a broad-based applied linguistics. Instead of the lack of interest and, at times, even hostility which has marked relations between linguistics and translation theory in the past, we are optimistic that the century will close with increasing numbers of insights being shared on both sides; providing translation theory with a firm intellectual base, giving the translator and translator-trainer a body of knowledge and skills on which to draw in their work and forcing linguistics to test out theory in the most challenging context imaginable. Nothing can be lost in communication and co-operation. Everything is to be gained by it.

Appendix

The purpose of this appendix is to provide outlines of the two analytical systems we use in the text which will help with the reading of the main text: (1) a very brief outline of the mechanics of analysis using a systemic model of English grammar which focuses on the examples and analyses in the main body of the text and (2) an outline of the logical relationships between concepts which is used in the specification of knowledge in the LTM and the display of schemas.

We hope, in this way, to avoid cluttering the text with information which the reader may already possess (and, perhaps, in a more sophisticated form) or may well not need.

The order of presentation follows that of the appearance of issues in the original text.

1 Systemic grammar

1.1 Assumptions

The two fundamental notions underlying the analysis of texts in terms of MOOD options are

1. *Rank scale.* A hierarchical scale of forms – running from *sentence* to *clause* to *phrase* to *word* to *morpheme* – which permits the levels of structure of the clause to be, as it were, stripped off layer by layer.
2. *Chain* and *choice* (alternatively, *function* versus *form*, *slot* versus *filler*, *syntagmatic* versus *paradigmatic*); the syntagmatic sequence of clause (Subject Predicator Object) and phrase structures (modifier head qualifier, etc.) and the paradigmatic choices which realize each place in the chain (Noun, Adjective, Adverbial, Prepositional and Verb Phrase and determiner, noun, transitive verb, etc.).

The tree for *the dog bit the man* (in Chapter 2, Section 2.2.2)

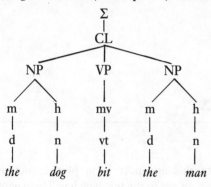

might be read:

> There is a sentence consisting of a single clause. This clause has the structure Subject Predicator Object. These 'functional slots' are 'filled' by phrases; noun phrase, verb phrase and noun phrase, respectively. Each of these has its own structure; modifier + head in the case of the noun phrases and main verb alone in the verb phrase. In the noun phrase, the modifiers are, in both cases, determiners and the heads nouns. In the verb phrase the main verb 'slot' is 'filled' by a transitive verb. Finally, these forms – determiner, noun, etc. – are realized by the words *the, dog, bit, the, man.*

1.2 Dependent clauses

Dependent clauses in English can be structured by using clauses (whether finite or non-finite) as parts of *phrase structure*. The continuation of the first line of the Valéry poem (in Chapter 2, Section 2.3) where *un mot* is repeated (making the whole of the rest of the clause in apposition) provides a good example of indirect embedding or subordination[1]; the qualifier 'slot' is 'filled' not by a word or even a phrase but by a clause:

[S P O = O (NP (m h q [S P C C C C &C &C]))]

which might be read:

> The structure of the clause is Subject, Predicator, Object.
>
> S P O
> *Je cherche un mot; un mot qui soit. . .*

The Object is a noun phrase with the structure; modifier + head + a second noun phrase (in apposition) + qualifier

The second NP has the structure

m h   q
un mot qui soit. . .

The qualifier of the noun phrase is a relative clause in which the qualifier has the structure:

Subject Predicator Complement. . . the last two Complements being linked by a coordinator *et* (shown by &)

q = S P C C C C &C &C
qui soit. . .

1.3 Finite and non-finite clauses

The final clause of the poem (Chapter 2, Section 2.2.2) – *six conditions au moins* – (in formal surface structure terms; a phrase), provides an example of dependency using a non-finite clause.

The structure indicates an unrealized *il y en a* Subject–Predicator structure before the realized Complement and Adjunct which is the clause:

(S P) C A

1.4 Mood

The MOOD system of the grammar provides a chain or structure sequence of functional positions or relations which are 'realized' or 'filled' by formal items (a) at the level of the clause by phrases and (b) at the level of the phrase by words. Just as the clause has its SPCA structure, so too phrases have their own structures; for the moment, *modifier* (m), *head* (h), *qualifier* (q).

The chain in the clause typically contains functions and forms such as:

Subject (S), *Object* (O) and *Complement* (C), typically 'realized' by formal items such as *noun phrases* (NP) 'filling' S, O and C 'slots'.

Predicator (P), realized by *verb phrases* (VP) 'filling' P 'slots'.

Adjunct (A), realized by *adverbial phrases* (AdvP) and *prepositional phrases* (PP) 'filling' A 'slots'.

For example:
The crew   tested   the atmosphere   carefully
S[NP]   P[VP]   O[NP]   A[AdvP]

Equally, phrases also contain chains and choices, e.g. in the NP, AdjP and AdvP; **modifier** (m), **head** (h), **qualifier** (q), 'filled' by formal items (normally words), as in the example below, by a determiner, an adjective, two nominals and a prepositional phrase:
The   excited   space   scientists   from Earth
NP[m (d)   m (adj)   m (n)   h (n)   q (PP)]

The suggested *modifier – head – qualifier* structures fit NP, AdjP and AdvP well enough but require re-definition for the other phrases in the case of:

(1) *verb phrases* as **auxiliary – main verb – extender** and
(2) *prepositional phrases* as **before–preposition–preposition completer** with, in principle, an unlimited number of items (including zero) 'filling' the modifier (or auxiliary) and qualifier (or extender) 'slots'.

1.4 Parataxis and hypotaxis

Logical sub-function of the TRANSITIVITY system and linkage by parataxis and hypotaxis; this organizes logical relations which link units of the same rank: phrase + phrase, clause + clause (see Section 4.2 on the MOOD systems). Two recursive systems carry these linking functions (definitions in Halliday, op. cit., 252ff.): (1) parataxis including (a) coordination and (b) apposition or (2) hypotaxis (c) subordination. Examples of these, at the rank of phrase, would be:

(a) Henry VII (and) Henry VIII (and) Edward VI (and) Mary I
(b) The first Tudor king, Henry VII, . . .
(c) The first [of the Tudor kings]. . .

2.   Logical relationships

The fundamental relationships we make use of in this book are:

isa[1]: the relationship of *entity* to *class*:
    that (cat over there) is a cat

isa[2]: the relationship of *class* to *entity*:
  a cat is (exemplified by) that

has-as-parts: the relationship of *property* to *entity*:

  a cat has (as parts) retractable claws

applies-to: the relationship of *quality* to *entity*:

  cats are affectionate i.e. affection applies to cats

We follow the convention, in the schema we display, of not showing the **applies-to** relationship.

Bibliography

Abercrombie, D. 1967. *Elements of General Phonetics*. Edinburgh University, Edinburgh.

Aitchison, J. 1987. *Words in the Mind: an introduction to the mental lexicon*. Blackwell. Oxford.

Aikenhead, A. M. and Slack J. M. (eds) 1985. *Issues in Cognitive Modeling*. Erlbaum. Hove.

Alderson, C. and Urquhart, A. (eds) 1984. *Reading in a Foreign Language*. Longman. Harlow.

Anderson, R. C. *et al.* (eds) 1977. *Schooling and the Acquisition of Knowledge*. Erlbaum. Hove.

Anderson, R. C. 1977. 'The notion of schemata and the educational enterprise' in Anderson, R. C. *et al.* (eds) 1977, 415–32.

Annett, J. *et al.* 1974. *Human Information Processing*. Open University. Milton Keynes.

Arbib, M. A. 1970. 'Cognition: a cybernetic approach' in Garvin, P. L. (ed). 1970, 331–48.

Arrowsmith, W. and Shattuck, R. 1961. *The Craft and Context of Translation*. University of Texas, Austin.

Austin, J.L. 1962. *How to do Things with Words*. Harvard University, Cambridge, Mass.

Bailey, C.J.N. and Shuy R.W. (eds) 1973. *New Ways of Analysing Variation in English*. Georgetown University. Washington DC.

Baron, N.S. 1986. *Computer Languages: a guide for the perplexed*. Penguin. Harmondsworth.

Bassnett McGuire, S. 1980. *Translation Studies*. Methuen. London.

de Beaugrande, R. 1978. *Factors in a Theory of Poetic Translating*, van Gorcum, Assen.

de Beaugrande, R. 1980a. *Text, Discourse and Process: toward a multidisciplinary science of texts*. Longman. Harlow.

de Beaugrande, R. 1980b 'Towards a semiotic theory of literary translating' in Wilss, W. (ed) 1980, 23–42.

de Beaugrande, R. and Dressler, W.U. 1981. *Introduction to Text Linguistics*. Longman. Harlow.

Bell, R.T. 1976. *Sociolinguistics: Goals, Approaches and Problems*. Batsford. London.

Bell, R.T. 1981. *An Introduction to Applied Linguistics*. Batsford. London.

Bell, R.T. 1986. 'Why translation theory is in a mess and what we can do about it', *Proceedings of GALA Congress 1985*, 280–7. Thessaloniki.

Bell, R.T. 1987. 'Translation theory; where are we going?' *META*, **31** (4), 403–15. Montreal.

Bell, R.T. 1988a. 'Modelling the translation process; a major task for translation theory' in *Proceedings of Conference on Translation Today*. Hong Kong.

Bell, R.T. 1988b. 'Specifying translator competence; a new goal for applied linguistics?' in Bickley, V. (ed), 134–47.

Benjamin, A. 1989. *Translation and the Nature of Philosophy: a new theory of words*. Routledge. London.

Berndt R.S. *et al.* 1983. *Language Functions: Syntax and Semantics* in Segalowitz, S.J. (ed.) 1983, 5–28.

Berry, M. 1977. *Introduction to Systemic Linguistics*. Batsford. London.

Bever, T.G. 1972. 'Perceptions, thought and language' in Carroll, J.B. and Freedle, R.O. (eds) 1972, 99–112.

Bickley, V.(ed.) 1988. *Proceedings of Conference on Languages in Education in a Bi-lingual or Multi-lingual Setting*. Institute of Language in Education, Hong Kong.

Bierwisch, M. 1970. 'Semantics' in Lyons, J. (ed.) 1970, 166–84.

Biguenet, J. and Schulte, R. (eds.) 1989. *The Craft of Translation*. University of Chicago. Chicago.

Blonsky, M. (ed.) 1985. *On Signs*. Blackwell. Oxford.

Bly, R. 1984. 'The eight stages of translation' in Frawley, W. (ed.) 1984, 67–89.

Bolinger, D. 1968. *Aspects of Language*. Harcourt Brace. New York.

Booth, A.D. 1958. *et al. Aspects of Translation*. Secker and Warburg. London.

Bransford, J.D. 1979. *Human Cognition: Learning, Understanding and Remembering*. Wadsworth, Belmont.

Brislin, R.W. (ed.) 1976. *Translation*. Gardner. London.

British Computer Society 1988. *A Glossary of Computing Terms: An Introduction* (5th edn). Cambridge University. Cambridge.

Brower, R.A. 1966. *On Translation*. Oxford University, Oxford.

Brown, R. 1968. 'The "Tip of the Tongue" Phenomenon' *Journal of Verbal Learning and Verbal Behaviour*, **5**.(4)., 325–37 repr. in Brown, R. 1970, 274–301.

Brown, R. 1970. *Psycholinguistics*. Collier Macmillan, New York.

Brown, G. and Yule, G. 1983. *Discourse Analysis*. Longman. Harlow.

Butler, C.S. 1985. *Systemic Linguistics: Theory and Applications*. Batsford. London.

Canale, M. and Swain, M. 1980. 'Theoretical bases of communicative approaches to second language teaching and testing', *Applied Linguistics*, **1** (1).

Carroll, J.B. and Freedle, R.O. (eds) 1972. *Language Comprehension and the Acquisition of Knowledge*. University microfilms. Ann Arbor.

Carter, R. and McCarthy, M. 1988. *Vocabulary and Language Teaching*. Longman. Harlow.

Cashdan, A. and Jordin, M. (eds) 1987. *Studies in Communication*. Blackwell. Oxford.

Catford, J.C. 1965. *A Linguistic Theory of Translation*. Oxford University, Oxford.

Chatman, S. (ed.) 1971. *Literary Style: A Symposium*. Oxford University, Oxford.

Chafe, W.L. 1977. 'The recall and verbalization of past experience' in Cole, R. (ed.) 1977, 215–46.

Chomsky, N. 1957. *Syntactic Structures*. Mouton, The Hague.

Chomsky, N. 1964. *Current Issues in Linguistic Theory*. Mouton, The Hague.

Chomsky, N. 1965. *Aspects of the Theory of Syntax*. MIT, Cambridge, Mass.

Clancy, W.J. 1988. 'The role of qualitative models in instruction' in Self, J. (ed.) 1988, 49–68.

Clark, H.H. and Clark, E.V. 1977. *Psychology and Language*. Harcourt Brace, New York.

Cluysenaar, A. 1976. *An Introduction to Literary Stylistics*. Batsford. London.

Cohen, G. *et al.* (eds) 1986. *Memory: A Cognitive Approach*. Open University. Milton Keynes.

Cole, P. and Morgan, J.L. (eds) 1975. *Syntax and Semantics*, vol. 3: *Speech Acts*. Academic Press. London.

Cole, R. (ed.) 1977. *Current Issues in Linguistic Theory*. Indiana University.

Congrat-Butlar, S. (ed.) 1979. *Translation and Translators*. Bowker, New York.

Cook, W.J. 1969. *An Introduction to Tagmemic Analysis*. Holt Rinehart. New York.

Coulthard, M. 1985. *An Introduction to Discourse Analysis* (2nd edn). Longman. Harlow.

Coulthard, M. and Montgomery, M. (eds) 1983. *Studies in Discourse Analysis*. Routledge. London.

Crystal, D. and Davy, D. 1969. *Investigating English Style*. Longman. Harlow.

Crystal, D. 1980. *A First Dictionary of Linguistics and Phonetics*. Deutsch. London.

Crystal, D. 1981. *Directions in Applied Linguistics*. Academic Press.

Crystal, D. 1987. *The Cambridge Encyclopedia of Language*. Cambridge University.

Culler, J. 1983. *On Deconstruction: Theory and Criticism after Structuralism*. Routledge and Kegan Paul. London.

Davey, D. (ed.) 1975. *Poetry in Translation*. Oxford University. Oxford.

Delisle, J. 1980. *L'analyse du discours comme méthode de traduction: initiation à la traduction française de textes pragmatiques anglais: théorie et pratique*. University of Ottawa, Ottawa.

Draskau, J. 1985. *Reflections on the Theory and Evaluation of Translation*. ARK, Copenhagen.

Dubois, J. *et al* 1973. *Dictionnaire de linguistique*. Larousse, Paris.

Duff, A. 1981. *The Third Language*. Pergamon. Oxford.

Eco, U. 1975. *Trattato di semiotica generale*. Bompiani, Milan.

Eco, U. 1985a. 'How culture conditions the colour we see' in Blonsky, M. (ed.) 1985, 157–75.

Eco, U. 1985b. 'Producing signs' in Blonsky, M. (ed.) 1985, 176–83.

Ellis. A.W. 1984. *Reading, Writing and Dyslexia*. Erlbaum. Hove.

Engel, S.M. 1984. *The Language Trap or how to defend yourself against the tyranny of words*. Prentice Hall. London.

Even-Zohar, I. and Toury, G. (eds) 1981. 'Translation theory and intercultural relations', special issue: *Poetics Today*, 2 (4).

Faerch, C. and Kasper, G. (eds) 1987. *Introspection in Second Language research*. Multilingual Matters. Clevedon.

Farmer, P.H. 1952. *Sail on! Sail on!* Better Publs, repr. in Knight, D. (ed.) 1962: *A Century of Science Fiction*. Dell, New York.

Fillmore, J.C. 1977. 'Topics in lexical semantics' in Cole, R. (ed.) 1977, 76–138.

Finlay, I.F. 1971. *Translating*. Teach Yourself Books. London.

Fodor, J.A. 1976. *The Language of Thought*. Harvester Press, Brighton.

Fodor, J.A. 1983. *The Modularity of Mind*. MIT. Cambridge, Mass.

Foucault, M. 1972. *The Archaeology of Knowledge*. Tavistock. London.

Frawley, W. (ed.) 1984. *Translation: Literary, Linguistic and Philosophical Perspectives*. University of Delaware. Newark, DE.

French, C.S. 1986. *Computer Studies: An Instructional Manual* (2nd edn). D.P. Publications. London.

Garvin, P.L. (ed.) 1970. *Cognition; A Multiple View*. Macmillan. London.

Gick, M.L. and Holyoak, K.J. 1985. 'Analogical problem solving' in Aikenhead, A.M. and Slack, J.M. (eds) 1985, 279–306.

Giglioli, P.P. (ed.) 1972. *Language and Social Context*. Penguin. Harmondsworth.

Gilling, D. and Brightwell, R. 1982. *The Human Brain*. Orbis. London.

Givón, T. 1979. *On Understanding Grammar*. Academic Press. London.

Goldman-Eisler, F. 1958. *Psycholinguistics: Experiments in Spontaneous Speech*. Academic Press. London.

Goodenough, W.H. 1956. 'Componential analysis and the study of meaning', *Language*, 32, 195–216.

Goodman, K.S. 1973. 'Psycholinguistic universals in the reading process' in Smith, F. (ed.) 1973, 21–7.

Gregory, M. 1967. 'Aspects of varieties differentiation', *Journal of Linguistics*, 3, 177–98.

Gregory, R.L. 1977. *Eye and Brain: The Psychology of Reading* (3rd rev edn). Weidenfeld and Nicolson. London.

Greene, J. 1975. *Thinking and Language*. Methuen. London.

Greene, J. 1986. *Language Understanding: A Cognitive Approach*. Open University. Milton Keynes.

Grice, H.P. 1957. 'Meaning', *Philosophical Review*, 66, 377–88.

Grice, H.P. 1975. 'Logic and conversation' in Cole, P. and Morgan, J.L. (eds) 1975, 41–58.

Gumperz, J.J. 1982. *Discourse Strategies*. Cambridge University, Cambridge.

Gurney, R. 1973. *Language, Brain and Interactive Processes*. Arnold. London.

Halliday, M.A.K. 1961a, 'Categories of the theory of grammar' *Word*, 17, 24–192.

Halliday, M.A.K. 1961b. 'General linguistics and its application to language teaching' in McIntosh, A. and Halliday, M.A.K. 1961, 1–41.

Halliday, M.A.K. 1961c. 'Linguistics and machine translation' in McIntosh, A. and Halliday, M.A.K. 1961, 145–58.

Halliday, M.A.K. 1967. 'Notes on transitivity and theme in English', *Journal of Linguistics*, **3**, 37–81, 199–244 and **4**, 179–215.

Halliday, M.A.K. 1969. 'Options and functions in the English clause', *Brno Studies in English*, **8**, 81–88; repr. in Householder, F.W. (ed.) 1972, 248–57.

Halliday, M.A.K. 1975. *Learning to Mean: Explorations in the Development of Language*. Arnold. London.

Halliday, M.A.K. and Hasan, R. 1976. *Cohesion in English*. Longman. Harlow.

Halliday, M.A.K. 1978. *Language as Social Semiotic: the social interpretation of language and meaning*. Arnold. London.

Halliday, M.A.K. 1985. *An Introduction to Functional Grammar*. Longman. Harlow.

Harman, G. and Davidson, D. (eds) 1972. *Semantics of Natural Language* (rev. edn. 1977). Reidel, Dordrecht.

Harri-Augustein, S. and Thomas, L.F. 1984. 'Conversational investigations of reading: the self-organized learner and the text' in Alderson, C. and Urquhart, A. (eds) 1984, 250–80.

Harris, B. and Sherwood, B. 1977. 'Translating as an innate skill', *NATO Symposium on Language Interpretation and Communication*, 155–70. Venice.

Harris, M. and Coultheart, M. 1986. *Language Processing in Children and Adults*. Routledge. London.

Harris, T.I. and Hodges, R. (eds) 1980. *A Reading Dictionary*. International Reading Association. Newark DE.

Hartmann, R.R.K. and Stork, F.C. 1972. *Dictionary of Language and Linguistics*. Applied Science. Amsterdam.

Hartmann, R.R.K. 1980. *Contrastive Textology: comparative discourse analysis in applied linguistics*. Groos, Heidelberg.

Hatim, B. 1983. *Discourse/text in the training of interpreters in translation theory*. Narr, Tübingen.

Hatim, B. 1984. 'A text typological approach to syllabus design in translating' *Incorporated Linguist*, **23**. (3), 146–9.

Hatim, B. 1987. 'Discourse texture in translation: towards a text-typological redefinition of theme and rheme' in Keith, H. and Mason, I. (eds) 1987, 52–62.

Hayes, J.R. 1982. *The Complete Problem-solver*. Franklin Institute, Philadelphia.

Hayes, J.R. *et al.* 1987. 'Cognitive processes in revision' in Rosenberg, S. (ed.) 1987, 176–240.

Heise, D.R. 1965. 'Semantic differential profiles for 1,000 most frequent English words', *Philosophical Monographs; General and Applied*, **79** (8) (601), 1–31.

Herriot, P. 1970. *An Introduction to the Psychology of Language*. Methuen. London.

Hill, A.A. 1958. *Introduction to Linguistic Structures*. Harcourt Brace. New York.

Hoey, M. 1983. *On the Surface of Discourse*. Allen and Unwin. London.

Hörmann, H. 1971. *Psycholinguistics*. Springer, Berlin.

Holmes, J.S. (ed.) 1970. *The Nature of Translation* Mouton, The Hague.
Holt, P. 1987. 'Communicating knowledge: an expert system prespective' in Cashdan, A. and Jordin, M. (eds) 1987, 86–96.
House, J. 1977a. 'A model for assessing translation quality' in *META* **22** (2), 103–9. Montreal.
House, J. 1977b. *A Model for Translation Quality Assessment*. Narr, Tübingen.
Householder, F.W. (ed.) 1972. *Syntactic Theory I: Structuralist*. Penguin. Harmondsworth.
Hurford, J.R. and Heasley, B. 1983. *Semantics: A Coursebook*. Cambridge University.
Hymes, D. 1972. 'On communicative competence' in Pride, J.B. and Holmes, (eds) 1972, 269–93.

Jakobson, R. 1960. 'Closing statement; linguistics and poetics' in Sebeok, T.A. (ed.) 1960, 350–77.
Jakobson, R. 1966. 'On linguistic aspects of translation' in Brower, R.A. (ed.) 1966, 232–9.
Jacobovits, L. 1970. *Foreign Language Teaching and Foreign Language Learning*. Newbury House. Rowley, Mass.
James, C. 1980. *Contrastive Analysis*. Longman. Harlow.
Johnson-Laird, P.N. 1983. *Mental Models: towards a cognitive science of language, inference, and consciousness*. Harvard Cambridge, Mass.
Joos, M. 1969. *The Five Clocks*. Harcourt Brace, New York.

Kagan, J. and Havemann, E. 1972. *Psychology; An Introduction* (2nd edn). Harcourt Brace, New York.
Kade, O. 1968. *Zufall und Gesetzmässigkeit in der Übersetzung*. VEB Verlag Enzyklopädie, Leipzig.
Katz, J.J. 1977. *Propositional Structure and Illocutionary Force: a study of the contribution of sentence meaning to speech acts*. Harvester Press, New York.
Keith, H. and Mason, I. (eds) 1987. *Translation in the Modern Languages Degree*. CILT. London.
Kelly, L.G. 1979. *The True Interpreter*. Blackwell. Oxford.
Kempson, R.M. 1977. *Semantic Theory*. Cambridge University. Cambridge.
Kipling, R. 1940. *The definitive edition of Rudyard Kipling's verse*. Hodder and Stoughton. London.
Kirk, R. 1986. *Translation Determined*. Oxford University. Oxford.
Kirk-Greene, C.W. 1981. *French False Friends*. Routledge and Kegan Paul. London.
Kuhn, T.S. 1962. *The Structure of Scientific Revolutions* (2nd rev. edn) 1970. Chicago University. Chicago.
Kuić, R. 1970. 'Translating English romantic poetry' in Holmes, J.S. (ed.) 1970, 182–91.

Labov, W. 1972. *Sociolinguistic Patterns* (rev. edn) 1978. Blackwell. Oxford.
Labov, W. 1973 'The boundaries of words and their meanings' in Bailey, C.J.N. and Shuy, R.W. (eds) 1973, 340–73.
Labov, W. and Fanshel, D. 1977. *Therapeutic Discourse*. Academic Press. London.

Lee, Y.P. *et al.* (eds) 1985. *New Directions in Language Testing*. Pergamon. Oxford.

Leech, G.N. 1965. *A Linguistic Guide to English Poetry*. Longman. Harlow.

Leech, G.N. 1971. *Meaning and the English Verb*. Longman. Harlow.

Leech, G.N. and Svartvik, J. 1975. *A Communicative Grammar of English*. Longman. Harlow.

Leech, G.N. 1981a. *Semantics* (2nd edn). Penguin. Harmondsworth.

Leech, G.N. and Short, M. 1981b. *Style in Fiction*. Longman. Harlow.

Leech, G.N. 1983. *Principles of Pragmatics*. Penguin. Harmondsworth.

Leech, G.N. *et al.* 1982. *English Grammar for Today: a new introduction*. Macmillan. London.

Lefèvre, A. 1975. *Translating Poetry: seven strategies and a blueprint*. van Gorcum, Assen.

Lindsay, P.H. and Norman, D.A. 1977. *Human Information Processing* (2nd edn). Academic Press. London.

Ljudskanov, A. 1975. 'A semiotic approach to the theory of translation', *Language Sciences*, 35, 5–8.

Lyons, J. (ed.) 1970. *New Horizons in Linguistics*. Penguin. Harmondsworth.

Lyons, J. (ed.) 1977. *Semantics* vols I and II. Cambridge University. Cambridge.

Malone, J.L. 1988. *The Science of Linguistics in the Art of Translation: some tools from linguistics for the analysis and practice of translation*. State University of New York, Albany.

McTear, M. 1987. *The Articulate Computer*. Blackwell. Oxford.

de Mauro, T. 1982. *Minisemantica*. Laterza. Bari.

McIntosh, A. and Halliday, M.A.K. 1961. *Patterns of Language: papers in general, descriptive and applied linguistics*. Longman. Harlow.

Meara, P. 1983. 'Vocabulary in a second language', *Specialized Bibiliography*, 3 CILT. London.

Meetham, A.R. and Hudson, R.A. 1969. *Encyclopaedia in Linguistics, Information and Control*. Pergamon. Oxford.

Milić, L.T. 1971. 'Rhetorical choice and stylistic option' in Chatman, S. (ed.) 1971, 77–94.

Miller, G.A. 1956. *The Psychology of Communication*. Penguin. Harmondsworth.

Miller, W.M. Jr. 1960. *A Canticle for Leibowitz*. Weidenfeld and Nicholson. London.

Morton, G. 1964. 'A preliminary functional model for language behaviour', *International Audiology* 3 216–25; repr. in Oldfield, R.C. and Marshall, J.C. (eds) 1968, 147–58.

Mounin, G. 1963. *Les problèmes théoretiques de la traduction*. Gallimard, Paris.

Mounin, G. 1972. *Clefs pour la sémantique*. Seghers, Paris.

Muir, J. 1972. *A Modern Approach to English Grammar: an introduction to systemic grammar*. Batsford. London.

Nabokov, V. 1966. 'The servile path' in Brower, R.A. (ed.) 1966, 97–110.

Nation, P. and Coady, J. 1988. 'Vocabulary and reading' in Carter, R. and McCarthy, M. (eds) 1988, 97–110.

Nestpoulous, J.L. (ed.) 1984. 'Brain, language and translation', special issue of *META*, **29**. Montreal.

Neubert, A. 1984. 'Translation studies and applied linguistics', *AILA Review* **1**, 46–64.

Newman, A. 1980. *Mapping Translation Equivalence*. ACCO. Leuven.

Newmark, P.P. 1969. 'Some notes on translation and translators', *Incorporated Linguist*, **8**(4), 79–85.

Newmark, P.P. 1973. 'Twenty-three restricted rules of translation', *Incorporated Linguist*, **12**(1), 9–15.

Newmark, P.P. 1976a. 'The theory and craft of translation', *Language Teaching and Linguistics Abstracts* **9**(1), ETIC/CILT. London.

Newmark, P.P. 976b. 'A tentative preface to translation: methods, principles, procedures', *Audio-Visual Journal*, **14**(3).

Newmark, P.P. 1982. *Approaches to Translation*. Pergamon. Oxford.

Newmark, P.P. 1988. *A Textbook of Translation*. Prentice Hall. London.

Nickel, G. (ed.) 1978. *Translation*. HochschulVerlag. Stuttgart.

Nida, E.A. 1964. *Towards a Science of Translating: with special reference to principles and procedures involved in bible translating*. Brill, Leyden.

Nida, E.A. 1966. 'Principles of translation as exemplified by Bible translating' in Brower, R.A. (ed.) 1966, 11–31.

Nida, E.A. 1978. 'Translation as communication' in Nickel, G. (ed.) 1978, 131–52.

Nida, E.A. and Taber, C. 1974. *The Theory and Practice of Translation*. Brill, Leyden.

Nirenburg, S. (ed.) 1987. *Machine Translation: Theoretical and Methodological Issues*. Cambridge University, Cambridge.

Noordman-Vonk, W. 1979. *Retrieval from Semantic Memory*. Springer. Berlin.

Norris, C. and Benjamin, A. 1988. *What is Deconstruction?* Academy Editions. London.

Nowottny, W. 1962. *The Language Poets Use*. London University. London.

Oakhill, J. and Garnham, A. 1988. *Becoming a Skilled Reader*. Blackwell. Oxford.

Ogden, C.K. and Richards, I.A. 1923. *The Meaning of Meaning*. Routledge. London.

Oldfield, R.C. and Marshall, J.C. (eds) 1968. *Language: Selected Readings* Penguin. Harmondsworth.

Osgood, C.E. *et al.* 1967. *The Measurement of Meaning* (2nd edn). University of Illinois. Urbana.

Packard, V. 1957. *The Hidden Persuaders*. Penguin. Harmondsworth.

Palmer, F.R. 1981. *Semantics*. Cambridge University, Cambridge.

Papegaaij, B. and Schubert, K. 1988. *Text Coherence in Translation* Foris, Dordrecht.

Picht, H. and Draskau, J. 1985. *Terminology: An Introduction*. University of Surrey. Guildford.

Picken, C. (ed.) 1986. *Translating and the Computer*, **7**. Aslib. London.

Popovič, A. 1976. *A Dictionary for the Analysis of Literary Translation*. University of Alberta. Edmonton.

Popovič, A. 1978. 'The concept "shift of expression" in translation analysis' in Holmes, J.S. (ed.) 1970, 78–90.

Pride, J.B. and Holmes, J. (eds) 1972. *Sociolinguistics: Selected Readings*. Penguin. Harmondsworth.

Pustejovsky, J. 1987. 'An integrated theory of discourse analysis' in Nirenburg, S. (ed.) 1987, 168–91.

Putnam, H. 1988. *Representation and Reality*. MIT. Cambridge, Mass.

Queneau, R. 1958. *Exercices de style*. Gallimard, Paris.

Quine, W.V.O. 1960. *Word and Object*. MIT. Cambridge, Mass.

Quirk, R. *et al* 1972. *A Grammar of Contemporary English*. Seminar Press. London.

Quirk, R. and Greenbaum, S. 1973. *A University Grammar of English*. Longman. Harlow.

Rabin, O. 1958. 'The linguistics of translation' in Smith, A.H. (ed.) 1958, 123–45.

Radice, W. and Reynolds, B. (eds) 1987. *The Translator's Art; essays in honour of Betty Radice*. Penguin. Harmondsworth.

Raskin, V. 1987. 'Linguistics and natural language processing' in Nirenburg, S. (ed.) 1987, 42–58.

Reber, A.S. 1985. *The Penguin Dictionary of Psychology*. Penguin. Harmonsworth.

Reiss, K. 1981. 'Type, kind and individuality of text: decision-making in translation' in Even-Zohar, I. and Toury, G. (eds) 1981, 121–32.

Richards, J. *et al*. 1985. *Longman Dictionary of Applied Linguistics*. Longman. Harlow.

Rosenberg, S. (ed.) 1987. *Advances in Applied Psycholinguistics, vol. 2: Reading, Writing, and Language Learning*. Cambridge University.

Roth, I. and Frisby, J.R. 1986. *Perception and Representation: A Cognitive Approach*. Open University. Milton Keynes.

Rumelhart, D.E. and Orthony, A. 1977. 'The representation of knowledge in memory' in Anderson, R.C. *et al*. (eds) 1977, 99–136.

de Saussure, F. 1916. *Cours de linguistique générale*. Payot, Paris.

Savory, T. 1957. *The Art of Translation*. Cape. London.

Sayers Peden, M. 1989. 'Building a translation, the reconstruction business: poem 145 of Sor Juana Iñes de la Cruz' in Biguenet and Schulte (eds) 1989. 13–27.

Schank, R.C. 1985. 'Reminding and memory organization' in Self, J. (ed.) 1985, 229–50.

Schmitz, J.R. 1984. 'Ambiguity, contrastive analysis and translation', *Tradução & Comunicaçao*, 5, 91–114. São Paulo.

Schogt, H.G. 1988. *Linguistics, Literary Analysis, and Literary Translation*. University of Toronto. Toronto.

Schubiger, M. 'English intonation and German modal particles II: a comparative study' in Waugh, L.A. and van Schoonfeld, C.H. (eds), 279–98.

Searle, J.R. 1969. *Speech Acts*. Cambridge University. Cambridge.

Searle, J.R. 1972. 'What is a speech act?' in Giglioli, P.P. (ed.) 1972, 136–54.

Searle, J.R. 1975. 'Indirect speech acts' in Cole, P. and Morgan, J.L. (eds) 1975, 59–82.

Sebeok, T.A. (ed.) 1960. *Style in Language.* MIT. Cambridge, Mass.

Segalowitz, S.J. 1983. *Language Functions and Brain Organization.* Academic Press. London.

Seleskovitch, D. and Lederer, M. 1986. *Interpreter pour traduire.* Didier. Paris.

Self, J. (ed.) 1988. *Artificial Intelligence and Human Learning.* Chapman and Hall. London.

Seuren, P.A.M. 1985. *Discourse Semantics.* Blackwell. Oxford.

Sharples, M. and O'Malley, C. 1988. 'A framework for the design of a writer's assistant' in Self, J. (ed.) 1988, 276–90.

Slack, J. 1987. *D309: Cognitive Architecture.* Open University. Milton Keynes.

Smith, F. 1971. *Understanding Reading.* Holt Rinehart. New York.

Smith, F. 1973. *Psycholinguistics and Reading.* Holt Rinehart. New York.

Smith, F. 1978. *Reading.* Cambridge University, Cambridge.

Smyth, M.M. *et al* 1987. *Cognition in Action.* Erlbaum. Hove.

Sperber, D. and Wilson, D. 1986. *Relevance: Communication and Cognition.* Blackwell. Oxford.

Spiro, R.J. *et al.* (eds) 1980. *Theoretical Issues in Reading Comprehension.* Erlbaum. Hove.

Stalnaker, R.C. 1972. 'Pragmatics' in Harman, G. and Davidson, D. (eds) 1972, 380–97.

Steinberg, D.D. 1982. *Psycholinguistics: Language, Mind and world.* Longman. Harlow.

Steiner, G. 1975. *After Babel: aspects of language and translation.* van Gorcum. Assen.

Steiner, T.R. 1975. *English Translation Theory 1650–1800.* van Gorcum. Assen.

Stevick, E. 1976. *Memory, Meaning and Method.* Newbury House.

Stubbs, M. 1981. 'Motivating analyses of exchange structure' in Coulthard, M. and Montgomery, M. (eds) 1981, 107–19.

Stubbs, M. 1983. *Discourse Analysis.* Blackwell. Oxford.

Swain, M. 1985. 'Large-scale communicative testing; a case-study' in Lee, Y.P. *et al* (eds) 1985, 35–46.

Tancock, L.W. 1958. 'Some problems of style in translation from French' in Smith, A.H. (ed.) 1958, 29–51.

Thompson, J.P. 1984. *Studies in the Theory of Ideology.* Polity Press. Oxford.

Thorndike, E.L. 1917. 'Reading as reasoning; a study of mistakes in paragraph reading', *Journal of Educational Psychology,* 8 (6), 323–32.

Traugott, E.C. and Pratt, M.L. 1980. *Linguistics for Students of Literature.* Harcourt Brace. New York.

Travis, C. (ed.) 1986. *Meaning and Interpretation.* Blackwell. Oxford.

Trier, J. 1931. *Der Deutsche Wortschatz im Sinnbezirk des Verstandes.* Winter. Heidelberg.

Trudgill, P. 1974. *Sociolinguistics.* Penguin. Harmondsworth.

Tytler, A. 1791. *Essay on the Principles of Translation.* Dent. London.

Vázquez-Ayóra, G. 1977. *Introducción a la traductología* Georgetown University. Washington. DC.

Vernon, J. 1963. *Inside the Black Room*. Penguin. Harmondsworth.

Vestergaard, T. and Schroder, K. 1985. *The Language in Advertising*. Blackwell. Oxford.

Vinay, J.P. and Darbelnet, J. 1976. *Stylistique comparée du français et de l'anglais; méthode de traduction*. Didier. Paris.

Waaub, J.M. 1983. 'Du cours de traduction consideré comme un happening. Question de méthode', *Review de Phonétique Appliquée*, 66–68, 169–202. University of Mons. Belgium.

Waldron, R. 1967. *Sense and Sense Development*. Deutsch. London.

Waugh, L.R. and van Schoonfeld, C.H. 1980. *The Melody of Language*. University Park Press. Baltimore.

Weaver, W. 1989. 'The process of translation' in Biguenet, J. and Schulte, R. (eds) 1989, 117–24.

White, G. 1789. *The Natural History of Selborne*; repr. in *The World's Classics*. Dent, London, 1937.

Widdowson, H. 1979. *Explorations in Applied Linguistics*. Oxford University. Oxford.

Widdowson, H. 1984. 'Reading and communication' in Alderson, C. and Urquhart, A. (eds) 1984, 213–26.

Williams, R. 1976. *Keywords: A Vocabulary of Culture and Society* (rev. edn 1983). Fontana. London.

Wilss, W. 1980. *Semiotik und Übersetzen*, Narr, Tübingen.

Wilss, W. 1982. *The Science of Translation*. Narr, Tübingen.

Wilss, W. 1983. 'Translation strategy, translation towards a clarification of three translational concepts', *Review de Phonétique Appliquée* 66–68, 143–52 University of Mons. Belgium.

Yebra, V.G. 1983. 'Ideas generales sobra la traducción' *Traduçao & Comunicaçao*, 2, 145–58. São Paulo.

Index